The Judge and the Proportionate Use of Discretion

The principle of proportionality plays a vital role in the judicial review of administrative decisions in most Western States. In restricting the discretionary powers of public bodies, and balancing relevant interests, proportionality promises a structured reasoning for the administration of law and the fair balancing of public and private interests.

Drawing together a selection of key experts in the field, this book analyses the principle of proportionality in the judicial review of administrative decisions. The principle of proportionality is first examined in the national contexts of Germany, France, England and the Netherlands in light of historical and recent developments in the literature and case-law. The book then moves to analyse the meaning of the proportionality principle in the specific case-law of the European Court of Justice and European Court of Human Rights, before finally examining the status of proportionality in the United States.

Taking a comparative perspective, the book asks whether judges consistently apply the same core elements of the principle of proportionality, whether case law of the European Court of Human Rights and the Court of Justice of the European Union influences national judges in the application of the proportionality test and whether it is possible to infer a global or European concept of the principle of proportionality.

As a work which takes a global view of the principle of proportionality in judicial review, this book will be of great interest to scholars of public and administrative law, comparative law and EU law.

Sofia Ranchordás is Assistant Professor of Administrative Law at Tilburg University.

Boudewijn de Waard is Professor of Administrative Law at Tilburg University.

Routledge Research in EU Law

Available titles in this series include:

Centralized Enforcement, Legitimacy and Good Governance in the EU
Melanie Smith

EU External Relations and Systems of Governance
The CFSP, Euro-Mediterranean Partnership and Migration
Paul James Cardwell

The European Constitution, Welfare States and Democracy
The Four Freedoms vs. National Administrative Discretion
Christoffer C. Eriksen

EU External Relations Law and the European Neighbourhood Policy
A Paradigm for Coherence
Bart Van Vooren

The Evolving EU Counter-Terrorism Legal Framework
Maria O'Neill

The Early Warning System for the Principle of Subsidiarity
Constitutional Theory and Empirical Reality
Philipp Kiiver

European Perspectives on Environmental Law and Governance
Suzanne Kingston

The Tangled Complexity of the EU Constitutional Process
The Frustrating Knot of Europe
Giuseppe Martinico

Criminal Law and Policy in the European Union
Samuli Miettinen

Local Government in Europe
The 'Fourth Level' in the EU Multi-Layered System of Governance
Carlo Panara and Michael R. Varney

The Legitimacy of the European Union through Legal Rationality
Free Movement of Third Country Nationals
Richard Ball

New Governance and the European Strategy for Employment
Samantha Velluti

Human Rights and Minority Rights in the European Union
Kirsten Shoraka

Turkey's Accession to the European Union
The Politics of Exclusion?
Edel Hughes

The Governance of the European Union and the Internal-External Nexus
Paul James Cardwell

Towards a System of European Criminal Justice
The Problem of Admissibility of Evidence
Andrea Ryan

The Legal Order of the European Union
The Institutional Role of the European Court of Justice
Timothy Moorhead

The Judge and the Proportionate Use of Discretion
A Comparative Administrative Law Study
Sofia Ranchordás & Boudewijn de Waard

The Greening of European Business under EU Law
Taking Article 11 TFEU Seriously
Beate Sjåfjell & Anja Wiesbrock

The Habitats Directive in its EU Environmental Context
European Nature's Best Hope?
Charles-Hubert Born, An Cliquet, Hendrik Schoukens, Delphine Misonne, and Geert Van Hoorick

Forthcoming titles in this series include:

Kadi on Trial
A Multifaceted Analysis of the Kadi Trial
Matej Avbelj, Filippo Fontanelli and Giuseppe Martinico

EU Criminal Law and Policy
Values, Principles and Methods
Joanna Beata Banach-Gutierrez and Christopher Harding

The European Union as an Area of Freedom, Security and Justice
Maria Fletcher, Ester Herlin-Karnell and Claudio Matera

European Agencies and Risk Governance in EU Financial Market Law
Paul Weismann

The Judge and the Proportionate Use of Discretion

A comparative study

Edited by Sofia Ranchordás and Boudewijn de Waard

Routledge
Taylor & Francis Group
LONDON AND NEW YORK

First published 2016
by Routledge

2 Park Square, Milton Park, Abingdon, Oxon OX14 4RN
711 Third Avenue, New York, NY 10017, USA

Routledge is an imprint of the Taylor & Francis Group, an informa business

First issued in paperback 2017

British Library Cataloguing in Publication Data
A catalogue record for this book is available from the British Library

Library of Congress Cataloging-in-Publication Data
The judge and the proportionate use of discretion : a comparative study / edited by Sofia Ranchordás and Boudewijn de Waard.
pages cm. — (Routledge research in EU law)
Includes bibliographical references and index.
1. Proportionality in law—European Union countries. I. Ranchordás, Sofia, editor. II. Waard, Boudewijn Willem Nicolaas de, 1950– editor.
KJC390.J83 2015
347.24′012—dc23
2015001803

ISBN: 978-1-138-81299-4 (hbk)
ISBN: 978-1-138-10374-0 (pbk)

Typeset in Garamond
by Apex CoVantage, LLC

Contents

Acknowledgements

The idea to edit a volume on the principle of proportionality stemmed from the organisation of the 'International Seminar on Comparative and European Public Law', the result of a longstanding cooperation between scholars and students from the universities of Freiburg, Osnabrück, Tilburg, Oxford, Strasbourg and Orléans. This initiative allows a small group of students from the universities mentioned to attend a four-day seminar at one of the host institutions. With this seminar, we have tried to fill in the educational gap on comparative administrative law that most law schools have, discuss and share new developments in case law with foreign colleagues, and, above all, stimulate legal scholarship in the field of comparative law. Since a recurrent topic of the seminar mentioned has been the judicial review of discretionary powers by administrative courts, the choice of the topic for this edited volume seemed straightforward.

With this edited volume, the editors and contributors would like to share this discussion with readers, providing new and old insights on a known – but still blurry – topic: the principle of proportionality in comparative administrative law. This volume goes, however, beyond this longstanding European cooperation, expanding the scope of the topic to the New World and to authors outside the original network. In addition, this book aims to make a contribution to the legal scholarship on comparative administrative law.

This book and the underlying cooperation between the universities mentioned would not have been possible without the efforts of a number of scholars and institutions. We would like to thank, first of all, Prof Dr J. P. Schneider (Albert-Ludwigs University of Freiburg im Breisgau), who was at the forefront of the organisation of this seminar. Second, we would like to thank all the scholars who have taught in this seminar in the past nine years and their respective law schools who were willing to make this initiative financially possible. Our gratitude is also extended to all the students who, at the end of each edition of the seminar, were able to think critically about their national legal systems, telling us how much they had learned from other jurisdictions. If this is not the main educational purpose of comparative administrative law, then we would not know what else it is.

Figures and diagrams

Abbreviations

AB	AB Rechtspraak Bestuursrecht
ABRvS	Afdeling Bestuursrechtspraak Raad van State
AC	Law Reports, Appeal Cases
AJDA	L' Actualité Juridique du Droit Administratif
AJDI	L'Actualité Juridique Droit immobilier
APA	Administrative Procedure Act
ARB	Administratief-rechterlijke beslissingen
BVerfGE	Entscheidungen des Bundesverfassungsgerichts
CBb	College van Beroep voor het Bedrijfsleven
CLJ	Cambridge Law Journal
DA	Droit Administratif
ECHR	European Convention on Human Rights
ECJ	Court of Justice of the European Union
ECR	European Court Reports
ECtHR	European Court of Human Rights
EHRR	European Human Rights Reports
EPA	Environmental Protection Act
EU	European Union
EWCA	England and Wales Court of Appeal
GAJA	Grands Arrêts de la Jurisprudence Administrative
GALA	General Administrative Law Act
HL	House of Lords
HRA	Human Rights Act (UK)
I•CON	International Journal of Constitutional Law
JR	Jurist Reports
LPA	Les Petites Affiches
MLR	Modern Law Review
OJLS	Oxford Journal of Legal Studies
RFDA	Revue Française de Droit Administratif
RSC	Revue de Science Criminelle et de Droit Pénal Comparé
RTDE	Revue Trimestrielle de Droit Européen
RTDH	Revue Trimestrielle des Droits de l' Homme
TEU	Treaty on European Union
UKPC	United Kingdom Privy Council
WLR	Weekly Law Reports (UK)

Notes on contributors

A. C. L. (Anne) Davies is a Professor of Law and Public Policy in the Law Faculty at the University of Oxford and Garrick Fellow and, Tutor in Law at Brasenose College, in the United Kingdom. Professor Davies studied at Oxford, completing the BA and the D.Phil. She was a Prize Fellow at All Souls College from 1995 to 2001. Professor Davies is the author of four books, including *The Public Law of Government Contracts* (OUP 2008), and numerous articles in the fields of public law and labour law. Professor Davies teaches in Administrative Law, Constitutional Law and Labour Law.

Catherine Haguenau-Moizard is a Professor of Public Law and Vice-Dean at the Faculty of Law, at the University of Strasbourg, in France. Her research is focused on EU law, notably on the constitutional aspects of the EU integration and the challenges to the rule of law in Europe. Professor Haguenau-Moizard is the author of several articles and books, including *États et religions en Europe* and *Les systèmes politiques européens.*

Nikolaus Marsch is a Lecturer at Albert Ludwigs University of Freiburg, in Germany. Nikolaus studied law at the Universities of Trier, HU Berlin, law and public policy at the École Nationale d´Administration (Strasbourg, France), and obtained the Diplôme international d´administration publique in 2010. In the same year, he defended his PhD dissertation on comparative administrative law at the University of Osnabrück. In 2005, he clerked at the German Constitutional Court for Professor Wolfgang Hoffmann-Riem. He is the author of numerous publications in German, English and French. He is currently preparing *Habilitation* in the field of EU data protection law.

Jud Mathews is an Assistant Professor at the Dickinson School of Law of the Pennsylvania State University, in the United States of America. Jud Mathews graduated from Yale Law School and Princeton. After law school, he clerked for Judge Guido Calabresi on the US Court of Appeals for the Second Circuit. He is currently finishing his PhD in political science at Yale University. Professor Mathews was recently a visiting assistant professor at the University of Illinois College of Law, where he taught administrative law and constitutional law. Jud Mathews is the author of a number of articles on administrative law published in major US law journals.

At Penn State, Professor Mathews teaches administrative law, civil procedure and state and government law.

Sofia Ranchordás is Assistant Professor of Constitutional and Administrative Law at the Tilburg University Law School, in the Netherlands. Sofia has a PhD in law (highest honours) from Tilburg University and University of Antwerp (Belgium). She studied law and economics at Utrecht University (the Netherlands) and law at the Catholic University of Portugal. In 2015, Sofia will be a Resident Fellow at the Information Society Project, at Yale Law School. She is the author of *Constitutional Sunsets and Experimental Legislation: A Comparative Perspective* (Edward Elgar Publishing 2014) and a number of publications in the field of public law. At Tilburg Law School, Sofia lectures in comparative administrative law and constitutional and administrative law.

Yoan Sanchez is a PhD candidate at the University of Orléans, France, where he also studied law. His PhD dissertation focuses on the role of judges in the control of administrative action in France and England. In 2013, he published a chapter on the control of proportionality in France for a comparative law book entitled *Le pouvoir discrétionnaire. Regards croisés franco-polonais* (edited by W. Jakimowicz and Pierre Serrand, published by Mare & Martin).

Vanessa Tünsmeyer is a PhD candidate at Maastricht University, in the Netherlands. She studied European law and globalisation and law at Maastricht University. Between 2012 and 2014, she worked as a researcher for the Research Network on European Administrative Law (ReNEUAL) at the *Institut für Medien- und Informationsrecht*, at the Albert Ludwigs University of Freiburg, in Germany. Her research interests are in the field of EU administrative and international law, and in particular, cultural heritage and international human rights law.

Boudewijn de Waard has been Professor of Administrative Law at the Tilburg University Law School since 1991. Boudewijn de Waard has a PhD in law (highest honours) from Utrecht University, where he also studied law. Before entering academia, Boudewijn worked as a lawyer. He is the author of numerous articles and books on Dutch administrative law, particularly in the field of administrative procedure law. At Tilburg Law School, Boudewijn lectures in administrative law (LLB Dutch Law) and administrative procedure law (LLM Dutch Law).

Jack Williams is a college lecturer at Brasenose College (University of Oxford) and a Bedingfield Scholar at Gray's Inn, London. Jack graduated from the University of Oxford (Hertford College) with a distinction in the BCL postgraduate degree in law. Before that, he graduated from the University of Cambridge (St Catharine's College) in 2012 with a First Class BA (Hons) degree in law. At Oxford, Jack teaches constitutional law and administrative law to first- and second-year students, respectively.

1 Proportionality crossing borders

Why it is still difficult to recognise sparrows and cannons

Sofia Ranchordás and Boudewijn de Waard

'The just is the proportional, the unjust is what violates the proportion'[1]

Aristotle

1.1 Introduction

In the past two decades, numerous books and articles have been written on the principle of proportionality.[2] So much has been said and done about this source of fairness, justice and hope for a better defence of human rights in a democratic society, that one could easily dismiss this topic by simply claiming that there is nothing more left to say about proportionality. Proportionality, often associated with a tripartite test composed of 'suitability', 'necessity' and 'proportionality in *stricto sensu*',[3] is indeed far from being a new phenomenon in public law.

Originally born and raised in Germany (even before the country had been baptised with this name), proportionality grew up to be 'an export hit'[4] conquering most European jurisdictions and the hearts of the judges of the Court of Justice of the European Union (ECJ) and European Court of Human Rights (ECtHR). Proportionality is an old doctrine in continental legal systems, in both public and private law. It often refers to sanctions that

1 Aristotle, *Nicomachean Ethics*, Book 5, 1131b (15) in J Barnes (ed), *The Complete Works of Aristotle. The Revised Oxford Translation*, vol 2 (Princeton University Press 1995) 1786.

2 See, for example, Grant Huscroft, Bradley W Miller, Gregoire Webber (eds), Proportionality and the Rule of Law (CUP 2014); Matthias Klatt and Mortiz Meisters, The Constitutional Structure of Proportionality (Oxford University Press 2012); Aharon Barak, Proportionality: Constitutional Rights and their Limitations (Cambridge University Press 2012); Evelyn Ellis, The Principle of Proportionality in the Laws of Europe (Hart Publishing 1999); Nicholas Emiliou, The Principle of Proportionality in European Law. A Comparative Study (Kluwer 1996).

3 Note that the classic three-step test has evolved, in some jurisdictions, into multi-step tests, see chapter 2.

4 Rainer Wahl, 'Der Grundsatz der Verhältnismäßigkeit: Ausgangslage und Gegenwartsproblematik' in D Heckmann, RP Schenke, G Sydow (eds) *Verfassungsstaatlichkeit im Wandel: Festschrift für Thomas Würtenberger zum 70. Geburtstag* (Duncker & Humblot 2013) 823. For more information on the historical background of the proportionality test see chapter 2.

are considered disproportionate because they impose excessive burdens on citizens or because they are not sufficiently burdensome considering the infringement under analysis. However, 'a clear and principled approach to the principle of proportionality is yet to emerge'.[5] Proportionality appears to be everywhere and nowhere at the same time.

First, the principle of proportionality appears to be virtually everywhere. It is included in the recent principles of global administrative law,[6] a principle to assess the lawfulness of counter-measures in international law and to 'break up escalating cycles of transnational violence',[7] and, with more or less opposition, in the context of the World Trade Organization (WTO).[8] The principle of proportionality is also very often understood as a core principle of criminal law, imposing a correlation between the punishment and the crime.[9] However, some jurisdictions still seem to avoid explicit references to and the implementation of the proportionality test.[10] This is, for example, the case in the United States, where courts assess whether agencies 'took a hard look'[11] at the available evidence. Nonetheless, recent literature has pleaded in favour of further expansion of proportionality to new jurisdictions and legal contexts as 'a supplement constitutional insights' as a reminder that 'it is not enough that an act was constitutionally authorized; the act also needs balance between the aim and the harm caused. Thus, for example, an authority's act can be disproportional if there are less harmful means to achieve the aim or if the harm the act causes exceeds the benefit it creates'.[12]

Secondly, most western jurisdictions agree that you should not use a 'sledgehammer to crack a nut' or 'shoot at sparrows with cannons':[13] 'policy solutions should be adequate for the perceived problem or risk'.[14] Proportionality seems to have spread to a number of jurisdictions and become one of the most successful legal transplants, either in virtue of a certain conceptual

5 T Hickman, Public Law after the Human Rights Act (Hart Publishing 2010) 174.

6 See Carol Harlow, 'Global Administrative Law: the Quest for Principles and Values' (2006) 17 (1) *European Journal of International Law* 187, 195.

7 Thomas M Franck, 'On Proportionality of Countermeasures in International Law' (2008) 102 *American Journal of International Law* 715.

8 See Mads Andenas, Stefan Zleptnig, 'Proportionality: WTO Law In Comparative Perspective' (2007) 42 *Texas International Law Journal* 371.

9 Bernhard Schlink, 'Proportionality' in Michal Rosenfeld, Andras Sajó (ed), Oxford Handbook of Comparative Law (OUP 2012) 719.

10 On the spread of proportionality and global constitutionalism, see Alec Stone Sweet, Jud Mathews, 'Proportionality Balancing and Global Constitutionalism' (2008) 47 *Columbia Journal of Law* 72.

11 We refer here to the 'hard look doctrine' which is thoroughly analysed in chapter 7. Jud Matthews discusses whether this doctrine can be considered as the equivalent of the principle of proportionality in the United States.

12 Michal Tamir, 'Public Law As a Whole and Normative Duality: Reclaiming Administrative Insights in Enforcement Review' (2006) 12 *Texas Journal on Civil Liberties & Civil Rights* 43, 70.

13 Fritz Fleiner, *Institutionen Des Deutschen Verwaltungsrechts* (Mohr Siebeck 1928) 404.

14 Carol Harlow, Richard Rawlings, *Law and Administration* (3rd edn, CUP 2009) 252.

necessity or because the adjudication of constitutional rights involves a certain balancing of interests.[15] Another explanation could be that the 'sense' of proportionality is intrinsically intertwined with our sense of justice and the idea that 'constitutional [or any other public decisions] are only correct if they correspond to the appropriate balancing of principles'.[16]

The proliferation of academic publications on proportionality and the spread of proportionality in case law in western jurisdictions could be explained by a shift to 'an age of balancing',[17] 'a culture of justification'[18] and indeterminacy.[19] The proportionality test requires, in a number of cases, the balancing of public and private interests, or even that a cost-benefit analysis is performed and that the benefits of a public project (e.g., a new tunnel or highway) are weighed up against its costs (e.g., costs of the project, including the need to proceed to compulsory purchases or expropriations). From a judicial review point of view, this perception of proportionality as 'balancing' means that 'the court will intervene whenever the pros and cons of a project have not yet been duly weighed against each other'.[20] The shift towards proportionality has also been regarded as the support of a culture of justification and the optimistic belief in rationality and reason. This has been visible at the level of constitutional law, where proportionality seems to have conferred an administrative dimension to this field of law.[21]

However, the critics of the principle of proportionality see this phenomenon as a road to legal indeterminacy and casuistic decision-making. Grégoire Webber remarks that the principles of proportionality and balancing 'exacerbate rather than attenuate the weak guidance offered by bill of rights to legal subjects and officials . . . [denying legal rules] the possibility of . . . more-or-less determinate test standards'.[22] While it is true that the open-endedness and vagueness of proportionality can undermine its legitimacy over time, it is important to underline that any alleged 'legitimacy deficit may be compensated by its utility as a restraint' on the sometimes unchecked arbitrariness of public authorities.[23]

15 Carlos Bernal Pulido, 'The Migration of Proportionality Across Europe' (2013) 11 *New Zealand Journal of Public and International Law* 483.

16 R Alexy, *A Theory of Constitutional Rights* (OUP 2002) 210.

17 See A Aleinikoff, 'Constitutional Law in the Age of Balancing' (1987) 96 *Yale Law Journal* 943.

18 Moshe Cohen-Eliya, Iddo Porat, 'Proportionality and the Culture of Justification' (2011) 59 *American Journal of Comparative Law* 46.

19 Grégoire Webber, 'Rights and the Rule of Law in the Balance' (2013) 129 *Law Quarterly Review* 399.

20 JF Garner, 'Reasonableness and Proportionality' (1987) *Journal of Planning & Environment Law* 836.

21 Moshe Cohen-Eliya, Iddo Porat, 'Proportionality and the Culture of Justification' (2011) 59 *American Journal of Comparative Law* 46.

22 Grégoire Webber, 'Rights and the Rule of Law in the Balance' (2013) 129 *Law Quarterly Review* 399, 400.

23 Thomas M Franck, 'On Proportionality of Countermeasures in International Law' (2008) 102 *American Journal of International Law* 715, 718.

1.2 Proportionality in administrative law

The principle of proportionality plays a vital role in the judicial review of administrative decisions in most western jurisdictions. The principle of proportionality aims to restrict the discretionary powers of public bodies, balancing the relevant interests and protecting the interested parties.[24] Proportionality promises a structured reasoning for the administration of law and the fair balancing of public and private interests. In the context of administrative law, the principle of proportionality ensures that administrators show proper respect for individuals and that relationships of powers between the state and individuals are understood as clear relationships of law.[25]

More than a mere subsidiary review ground, the proportionality test has gained its place in the judicial review context as a central safeguard of the rule of law. Although the proportionality test is not equally deep-rooted in the literature and case law of France, Germany, the Netherlands and the United Kingdom, this principle has assumed increasing importance partly due to the influence of the European Court of Justice and European Court of Human Rights. In recent decades, the winds blowing from Strasbourg and Luxembourg have been shaping the principle of proportionality both at national and European levels. The influence of the German doctrine in the judicial reviews of administrative decisions in other jurisdictions is living proof that comparative administrative law should no longer be regarded as 'the poor relation' of comparative constitutional law.[26] Instead, the local differences of administrative law enrich the research in this field and provide additional reasons to incentivise research in this area.[27] In addition, even jurisdictions that have resisted the penetration of the proportionality test – like the US – seem to have developed their own instruments to control 'arbitrary and capricious' administrative action or try to ensure that agencies 'take a hard look' at the available evidence.[28]

In administrative law, proportionality has acquired a specific meaning: public authorities are expected to 'weigh up the harm that would be caused to the public if a proposed line of action were taken, against the potential public

24 Roberto Caranta and Anna Gerbrandy, 'Introduction', in Roberto Caranta, Anna Gerbrandy (ed), *Traditions and Change in European Administrative Law* (Europa Law Publishing 2011).

25 Robert Thomas, *Legitimate Expectations and Proportionality in Administrative Law* (Hart 2000) 2, 15.

26 Some scholars have, however, made very important contributions to the field of comparative administrative law. This is, for example, the case of Susan Rose-Ackerman, Peter Lindseth (ed), *Comparative Administrative Law* (Edward Elgar 2011); Francesca Bignami, 'Comparative Administrative Law', in Mauro Bussani, Ugo Mattei (eds), *The Cambridge Companion to Comparative Law* (CUP 2012) 145; Benedikt Pirker, *Analysis and Models of Judicial Review: A Theoretical and Comparative Study* (Europa Law Publishing 2013).

27 Janina Boughey, 'Administrative Law: The Next Frontier for Comparative Law' (2013) *International & Comparative Law Quarterly* 55.

28 See chapter 7 for a critical analysis of the 'hard look' doctrine and its current meaning.

benefit; only if the latter outweighs the former should the action be allowed to proceed'.[29] There are, however, different 'proportionalities' or intensities: according to the 'original' *Wednesbury*, a disproportionate act 'is only that act which is so unreasonable that no reasonable person' could have adopted it. This highly deferential criterion of unreasonableness contrasts with the more recent intensities conferred to this test by English courts and, above all, with the proportionality test. In addition, proportionality can be symmetrical or not:[30] if only excessive and over-reaching sanctions will be annulled due to the application of this test, but too lenient sanctions will not be changed, then we shall not be in the presence of symmetrical proportionality. In fact, few jurisdictions apply the principle of proportionality to sanction public authorities who have underreached (see the cases of France, and *mutatis mutandis*, the US in chapters 3 and 7, respectively).

1.3 Proportionality: controversies and mysteries

The historical roots and the elements that compose the proportionality test, as well as its significance and practical implementation, differ in most jurisdictions. The origin of the principle might be German, but most courts seem to have reshaped it to fit their legal cultures. 'Proportionality' might have successfully spread around the western world because it is a *lingua franca* that appeals to most lawyers,[31] however, not all speak this language with the same accent and intonation. Despite the abundant literature, a multitude of enigmas seems to remain unsolved when it comes to defining that common language called 'proportionality'. In order to grasp the essence of the principle of proportionality, a number of questions regarding this principle must be analysed:

a) What does the 'proportionality test' mean exactly in the context of the judicial review of administrative decisions?
b) What is the place of the principle of proportionality in the jurisdictions under analysis?
c) Do judges always apply the same core elements or is it, rather, a flexible test that is context-dependent?
d) Has the principle of proportionality played a more significant role in particular fields of administrative law?
e) Is the case law of the European Court of Human Rights and the Court of Justice of the European Union influencing national judges in the application of the proportionality test? If so, how?

29 JF Garner, 'Reasonableness and Proportionality' (1987) *Journal of Planning & Environment Law* 836.

30 For the specific case of criminal law, see Stephen T Parr, 'Symmetric Proportionality: A New Perspective on the Cruel and Unusual Punishment Clause' (2000) 65 *Tennessee Law Review* 41.

31 Webber (n 12) 473.

In addition to sharing similarities and celebrating the differences between the jurisdictions under analysis, it is also important to question whether it is possible to infer a global – or at least, a European – concept of the principle of proportionality.

In this book, the principle of proportionality in the judicial review of administrative decisions is analysed from different perspectives: the principle of proportionality is first examined in the national contexts of Germany, France, England and the Netherlands in light of historical and more recent developments in the literature and case law, including the inevitable EU influence. Then light shall be shed on the meaning of this principle in the specific case law of the European Court of Justice and European Court of Human Rights. Finally, we look for proportionality or its equivalent where it does not seem to exist: the United States.

1.4 Comparing proportionality tests in administrative law

The principle of proportionality, as well as its application in the context of administrative law, is one of the most important subjects of academic teaching. This book makes a contribution to this field by shedding light on different dimensions of the proportionality test in different jurisdictions and by bringing the topic of the judicial review of discretionary powers to the attention of the reader. Up until now, this second element has often remained implicit in the literature on proportionality, perhaps because it was assumed to be obvious. While it is true that the principle of separation of powers prohibits judges from replacing the administration's judgment when discretionary powers have been granted, this should not mean that courts must remain at a distance when confronted with manifestly disproportionate acts. As it shall be discussed in chapter 2, individual justice is still fostered by the application of the principle of proportionality, even if the administration is entirely bound by a parliamentary statute.

1.4.1 Proportionality: a high-value product 'made in Germany'

This book starts with a historical analysis of the proportionality test. In order to understand the future destinations of proportionality, it is important to understand where this principle came from. Chapter 2 takes us to Prussian administrative law and the first steps of proportionality. Originally used to control policing measures, this instrument of judicial review would later spread to other fields and would only be temporarily stopped by the tragic period of World War II. This development is not surprising in a country with a judicial review system characterised by the idea of the protection of subjective rights of individuals and the control of discretionary powers.[32]

32 For an overview of the evolution of German Administrative Law, see Jens-Peter Schneider, 'German Traditions in Administrative Law. Obstacles to a Common Legal Framework?', in Matthias Ruffert (ed), *Administrative Law in Europe: Between Common Principles and National Traditions* (Europa Law Publishing 2013) 51.

The chapter on Germany by Marsch and Tünsmeyer provides a brief overview of the German administrative system, including an explanation on the attribution of discretionary powers and an extensive description of the development of the proportionality test. Moreover, the chapter on German administrative law explains the three- or, often, four-step test put into practice by German administrative courts. Nowadays, the principle of proportionality is well-established in Germany and does not appear to raise as many questions and controversies in this jurisdiction as in others included in this study. However, the authors highlight the gradual and worrisome expansion of the proportionality test to the judicial review of 'bound decisions', i.e., spaces with reduced or no discretionary powers.

1.4.2 Implicit-explicit proportionality: the French touch

In chapter 3, Yoan Sanchez takes us to the case law of the *Conseil d'État* with its drafting peculiarities and ambiguities, and the evolution of its approach to proportionality. The story of proportionality in France seems to start with the famous *Benjamin* case (see chapter 3), where a demonstration was prohibited in order to safeguard public order. In the early cases, the proportionality test was used implicitly by the *Conseil d'État.* However, the lack of explicit references to proportionality in the administrative jurisprudence has not impeded the expansion of the proportionality test from the adjudication of fundamental rights to different fields, notably urban planning and disciplinary sanctions. Nowadays, a three-step test appears to be alive and well in France, particularly in the more recent case law of the Constitutional Council, which is briefly mentioned in chapter 3. However, the charm of the French approach appears to reside in a certain indirect and non-systematic approach to the principle of proportionality, which might leave us wondering where this test is really going.

1.4.3 More to proportionality than Wednesbury in England?

While proportionality is an old phenomenon in Germany, proportionality seems to be a relative newcomer in English law, which is used in cases that fall under EU law, and in cases arising under the Human Rights Act of 1998. Prior to the adoption of this Act, proportionality enjoyed little – or even no visibility in UK courts and was only associated with the fulfilment of EU obligations. The Human Rights Act of 1998 seems to have opened the door to proportionality in England, a door that might actually never close.[33] Paul Craig, based on the EU implementation of proportionality, has recently

33 See on this topic, the forthcoming book Aaron Barak, *Proportionality Under the UK Human Rights Act* (Hart 2015).

argued that 'proportionality should be a general principle of judicial review that can be both used in cases concerned with rights and in non-rights cases, albeit with varying intensity'.[34] However, up until now, for any other case falling outside the realm of this act, courts will generally continue to apply a version of the well-known *Wednesbury* reasonableness test. This test is variable and has resisted the ravages of time thanks to its dynamic character. However, this reasonable variable is not the English equivalent of continental proportionality, as chapter 4 shall demonstrate.

Although this 1948 case has been criticised, there are still voices defending *Wednesbury* in the name of the principle of separation of powers.[35] Even within the scope of human rights, it has been argued in the literature that it has been rather difficult to 'develop a coherent and defensible jurisprudence of proportionality in the UK'.[36]

In chapter 4, Davies and Williams review the historical development of the highly deferential *Wednesbury* test and discuss the emergence of the proportionality review in England. More importantly, this chapter offers a compare and contrast of *Wednesbury* and proportionality tests, discussing which test would allow courts to structure better their reasoning and offer a more intense scrutiny of administrative decisions. Chapter 4 also delves into the incommensurability objection. The proportionality test requires judges to reconcile the irreconcilable: incommensurable interests must be balanced in order to reach a conclusion regarding the proportionality of an administrative measure. This should not necessarily be regarded as an objection according to some scholars. Timothy Endicott, for example, argues that the need to reconcile incommensurable interests results from the rule of law, which requires that incommensurable interests are balanced. He argues that judicial decisions:

> do not become arbitrary, in the sense that is relevant to the rule of law, merely because judges are reconciling conflicts among incommensurable values. On the contrary, the rule of law demands a system in which independent tribunals can reconcile (or 'balance' – as they call it in a misleading figure of speech) considerations that cannot be balanced.

Davies and Williams argue that the incommensurability objection is not only specific to the case of proportionality but actually a general problem that judicial review in general must be prepared to face. In chapter 4, the authors also analyse the issue of 'deference' and the varying intensity of the application of proportionality or the *Wednesbury* test to a specific case. As the scholars explain, even after having elected a specific test, more or less weight can be attributed to the administrative authority.

34 Paul Craig, 'Proportionality Rationality and Review' (2010) *New Zealand Law Review* 265.

35 James Goodwin, 'The Last Defence of Wednesbury' (2012) *Public Law* 445.

36 See Richard Clayton, 'Regaining a sense of proportion: the Human Rights Act and the proportionality principle' (2001) 5 *European Human Rights Law Review* 504.

1.4.4 Proportionality in the Netherlands: Dutch sobriety

In the Netherlands, proportionality is not a stranger to the legal system. However, this does not mean that it is often implemented by courts, in fact, it is regarded as an *ultimum remedium*. The principle of proportionality is rarely applied. The majority of examples where the principle of proportionality was used to annul an administrative decision refer to cases involving EU law. However, there are no apparent positive or normative reasons impeding Dutch courts from employing this type of control. The Dutch General Administrative Law Act actually requires public authorities to comply with the principle of proportionality. In chapter 5, De Waard provides an overview of the Dutch system of judicial review, explaining the concept of reasonableness (instead of proportionality) employed by courts, the reasoning of courts in the rare cases where proportionality was discussed, and the relevance of this test for cases involving directly human rights. This chapter also delves into the judicial review of discretionary powers and the concept of margin of appreciation, as employed by Dutch administrative courts.

1.4.5 Proportionality, human rights and the European project

In chapter 6, Haguenau-Moizard and Sanchez take us to the Court of Justice of the European Union and the European Court of Human Rights, where proportionality plays a pivotal role. The principle of proportionality is a well-established principle in the EU-law context, which can be used to challenge both EU action and Member State action. It is enshrined in Article 5(4) of the Treaty on European Union as part of subsidiarity, which reads that 'under the principle of proportionality, the content and form of Union action shall not exceed what is necessary to achieve the objectives of the Treaties'.[37] The principle of proportionality is equally present in the Charter of Fundamental Rights of the European Union, where it is stated that:

> subject to the principle of proportionality, limitations on the exercise of the rights and freedoms may be made only if they are necessary and genuinely meet objectives of general interest recognised by the Union or the need to protect the rights and freedoms of others.[38]

As chapter 6 illustrates, most cases raising issues of proportionality refer to measures pursuant to EU common policies, where one ground for challenge is that the measures mentioned infringe fundamental rights recognised by EU law.[39]

37 *Treaty on European Union, OJ C 326, 26/10/2012, p. 1–390.*

38 Article 52 (1) of the Charter of Fundamental Rights of the European Union, *OJ C 326, 26/10/2012, pp. 391–407.*

39 Paul Craig, EU Administrative Law (2nd edn, OUP 2012) 605.

The principle of proportionality is one of the most decisive elements of human rights protection since it guarantees the balance between rights and the public interest. Chapter 6 provides an overview of the most important case law of the European Court of Human Rights. This overview is complemented by a number of thoughts and considerations expressed in chapter 8, where recent case law from Strasbourg is also analysed.

1.4.6 No need for proportionality: just take a hard look

The United States has apparently resisted the proportionality test. There is no explicit proportionality principle in this jurisdiction,[40] which does not mean that the New World does not know what a proportionate or disproportionate administrative decision is, and how the latter should be sanctioned. In chapter 7, Mathews introduces us to the US administrative law system and, in particular, the system of judicial review. American judicial review is characterised by its high degree of unpredictability, particularly in the case of the review of discretionary powers. The control is still limited, thanks to 'a number of deference formulas', as Mathews calls it. Although admitting that the US is not acquainted with a European form of the proportionality test, this idea of maintaining a certain degree of reasonableness in reviewing an agency's discretion has been guaranteed by the 'arbitrary and capricious test' and, by its 'mutation' into the so-called 'hard look doctrine'. Despite the inexistence of a true proportionality test, American courts seem to apply a more 'complete' or symmetrical form of proportionality, as mentioned above. 'Proportionality' or its American equivalent means that agencies should not shoot at sparrows with cannons, but neither should they shoot at condors with peashooters. 'American proportionality' – in resemblance to that of France – imposes here a symmetrical means-ends relationship, for or against individuals.

1.5 Conclusions

In the last chapter we make concluding remarks. In that chapter, we hope to convince the reader that it was worthwhile presenting the topic of proportionality in diverse systems of administrative law, and also that the combination of chapters in that volume adds value to the thinking about proportionality. Everybody will agree that it is not sensible to shoot at sparrows with cannons. But where do we find sparrows and cannons these days? Will we all recognise them when we see them? The problem that courts have to deal with is that it is not always clear whether a case concerns a relationship that

40 See E Thomas Sullivan, Richard S Frase, *Proportionality Principles in American Law: Controlling Excessive Government Actions* (OUP 2009). Bernhard Schlink, 'Proportionality in Constitutional Law: Why Everywhere But Here?' (2012) 22 *Duke Journal of Comparative & International Law* 291.

is comparable with the relationship between sparrows and cannons. One of the purposes of this book is to show that this does not provide good reason to be afraid of the concept of proportionality.

References

Aleinikoff A, 'Constitutional Law in the Age of Balancing' (1987) 96 *Yale Law Journal* 943.

Alexy R, *A Theory of Constitutional Rights* (OUP 2002) 210.

Andenas M, Zleptnig S, 'Proportionality: WTO Law In Comparative Perspective' (2007) 42 *Texas International Law Journal* 371.

Aristotle, *Nicomachean Ethics*, Book 5, 1131b (15) in J Barnes (ed), *The Complete Works of Aristotle. The Revised Oxford Translation,* vol 2 (Princeton University Press 1995) 1786.

Baker A, *Proportionality Under the UK Human Rights Act* (Hart 2015).

Barak A, *Proportionality: Constitutional Rights and their Limitations* (Cambridge University Press 2012).

Bignami F, 'Comparative Administrative Law', in Mauro Bussani, Ugo Mattei (eds), *The Cambridge Companion to Comparative Law* (CUP 2012) 145.

Boughey J, 'Administrative Law: The Next Frontier for Comparative Law' (2013) *International & Comparative Law Quarterly* 55.

Caranta R, Gerbrandy A, 'Introduction', in Roberto Caranta, Anna Gerbrandy (ed), *Traditions and Change in European Administrative Law* (Europa Law Publishing 2011).

Clayton R, 'Regaining a Sense of Proportion: The Human Rights Act and the Proportionality Principle' (2001) 5 *European Human Rights Law Review* 504.

Cohen-Eliya M, Porat I, 'Proportionality and the Culture of Justification' (2011) 59 *American Journal of Comparative Law* 46.

Craig P, 'Proportionality Rationality and Review' (2010) *New Zealand Law Review* 265.

—— *EU Administrative Law* (2nd edn, OUP 2012).

Ellis E, *The Principle of Proportionality in the Laws of Europe* (Hart Publishing 1999).

Emiliou N, *The Principle of Proportionality in European Law. A Comparative Study* (Kluwer 1996).

Fleiner F, *Institutionen Des Deutschen Verwaltungsrechts* (Mohr Siebeck 1928) 404.

Franck TM, 'On Proportionality of Countermeasures in International Law' (2008) 102 *American Journal of International Law* 715.

Garner JF, 'Reasonableness and Proportionality' (1987) *Journal of Planning & Environment Law* 836.

Goodwin J, 'The Last Defence of Wednesbury' (2012) *Public Law* 445.

Harlow C, 'Global Administrative Law: The Quest for Principles and Values' (2006) 17 (1) *European Journal of International Law* 187.

Harlow C, Rawlings R, *Law and Administration* (3rd edn, CUP 2009) 252.

Hickman T, *Public Law after the Human Rights Act* (Hart Publishing 2010).

Huscroft G, Miller BW, Webber G (eds), *Proportionality and the Rule of Law* (CUP 2014).

Klatt M and Meisters M, *The Constitutional Structure of Proportionality* (Oxford University Press 2012).

Parr ST, 'Symmetric Proportionality: A New Perspective on the Cruel and Unusual Punishment Clause' (2000) 65 *Tennessee Law Review* 41.

Pirker B, *Analysis and Models of Judicial Review: A Theoretical and Comparative Study* (Europa Law Publishing 2013).

Pulido CB, 'The Migration of Proportionality Across Europe' (2013) 11 *New Zealand Journal of Public and International Law* 483.

Rose-Ackerman S, Lindseth P (ed), *Comparative Administrative Law* (Edward Elgar 2011).
Schlink B, 'Proportionality' in Michal Rosenfeld, Andras Sajó (ed), *Oxford Handbook of Comparative Law* (OUP 2012).
—— 'Proportionality in Constitutional Law: Why Everywhere But Here?' (2012) 22 *Duke Journal of Comparative & International Law* 291.
Schneider JP, 'German Traditions in Administrative Law. Obstacles to a Common Legal Framework?', in Matthias Ruffert (ed), *Administrative Law in Europe: Between Common Principles and National Traditions* (Europa Law Publishing 2013) 51.
Stone Sweet A, Mathews J, 'Proportionality Balancing and Global Constitutionalism' (2008) 47 *Columbia Journal of Law* 72.
Sullivan ET, Frase RS, *Proportionality Principles in American Law: Controlling Excessive Government Actions* (Oxford University Press 2009).
Tamir M, 'Public Law As a Whole and Normative Duality: Reclaiming Administrative Insights in Enforcement Review' (2006) 12 *Texas Journal on Civil Liberties & Civil Rights* 43.
Thomas R, *Legitimate Expectations and Proportionality in Administrative Law* (Hart 2000).
Wahl R., 'Der Grundsatz der Verhältnismäßigkeit Ausgangslage und Gegenwartsproblematik' in D Heckmann, RP Schenke, G Sydow (eds) *Verfassungsstaatlichkeit im Wandel: Festschrift für Thomas Würtenberger zum* 70. *Geburtstag* (Duncker & Humblot 2013) 823.
Webber W, 'Rights and the Rule of Law in the Balance' (2013) 129 *Law Quarterly Review* 399.

2 The principle of proportionality in German administrative law

Nikolaus Marsch and Vanessa Tünsmeyer

2.1 Introduction

To write on a comparative basis about the importance, function and role of proportionality in administrative law within (and even beyond) Europe would hardly be possible without considering its place in German law. Not only is proportionality a principle which has a comparatively long history within Germany and its federal states (*Länder*), but it also influenced the development of a European proportionality principle, even if the two are not congruent.[1] Indeed, few principles exist that are as firmly entrenched in German public law as the '*Verhältnismäßigkeitsprinzip*.' The German constitutional court has described it as the 'overarching principle guiding all state action',[2] German academics have similarly highlighted its importance, and Wahl[3] even described it as an 'export hit'.[4]

The principle of proportionality regulates the relationship between the purpose or aim of an (administrative) action and the means used to realise that aim. This relationship must satisfy a specific standard developed by the German Constitutional Court.[5] This standard consists of a four-stage

1 Christoph Knill, Florian Becker, 'Divergenz trotz Diffusion?: rechtsvergleichende Aspekte des Verhältnismäßigkeitsprinzip in Deutschland, Großbritannien und der Europäischen Union' (2003) 36 *Die Verwaltung* 447, 449–450.

2 BVerfGE 23, 127, para 19 'übergreifende Leitregel allen staatlichen Handelns' (own translation); the decisions of the Federal Constitutional Court are available under http://www.servat.unibe.ch/dfr/ accessed 14 October 2014.

3 Rainer Wahl, 'Der Grundsatz der Verhältnismäßigkeit: Ausgangslage und Gegenwartsproblematik' in D Heckmann, RP Schenke, G Sydow (eds) *Verfassungsstaatlichkeit im Wandel: Festschrift für Thomas Würtenberger zum 70. Geburtstag* (Duncker & Humblot 2013) 823.

4 Critically on the (in his view) excessive contemporary application of the principle, Detlef Merten, 'Zur verfassungsrechtlichen Herleitung des Verhältnismäßigkeitsprinzips' in J Hengstschläger, HF Köck, K Korinek, K Stern, A Truyol y Serra (eds), *Für Staat und Recht – Festschrift für Herbert Schambeck* (Duncker & Humblot 1994) 350 'Early warnings about the immoderate use of the principle of moderation remained unconsidered and thus proportionality became the mass's measure.' (translation by the authors, originally: '*Frühe Warnungen vor Maßlosigkeit mit dem Mäßigungsgrundsatz und Verformungen der Form blieben unbeachtet, und so wurde Verhältnismäßigkeit der Masse Maß.*').

5 For the development of the principle after 1945 see also section 2.5 of this chapter.

test[6] and is employed by the Court to control the legislature as well as by the administrative courts to control administrative action.

To satisfy the proportionality standard, an action must first pursue a legitimate aim, that is to say the objective of a measure must be permissible under German law. Second, the means taken to achieve the aim chosen must, in fact, be suitable to foster – if not achieve – the said aim (*Geeignetheit*). This criterion is often referred to as the suitability criterion in its English translation, which is more of a literal translation of the term. Nolte has rightly pointed out, however, that this term might be misleading in the sense that a measure is considered to fulfil the '*Geeignetheit*' criterion even if the administrative measure is theoretically capable of contributing to achieving the statutory aim.[7] However, even though the translation proposed by Nolte, 'capacity of furthering an aim', might be more precise, the term suitability seems well-established today.[8] Moreover, it is useful for comparative purposes.[9]

Third, the means chosen must be necessary (*Erforderlichkeit*). This condition is fulfilled if the aim cannot be pursued by another means, which is as suitable to achieve the aim chosen by the authority, but less restrictive with regard to the rights of the citizen (the less restrictive but equally suitable means). Fourth, the action taken must satisfy the proportionality *stricto sensu* or adequacy (*Angemessenheit*) test. In other words, the means must be adequate for the pursued aim. German courts also employ the German equivalent of the term reasonableness at this fourth stage. While the definition is always the same, the application of the test differs with regard to the legal instrument (statute or administrative act) and the field of law (see below).

As the principle of proportionality is considered to be *the* German contribution to European Law, the definition and content of the principle within Germany is barely influenced by EU or ECHR definitions. In the eyes of the Constitutional Court, the principle is rooted in the rule of law (or in the German notion of the *Rechtsstaat*) and the nature of fundamental rights, which are themselves located in the Basic Law.[10] It is for this reason that the principle has the status of unwritten constitutional law, binding all public bodies.

Although its precise theoretical foundation is debated, the prevalent opinion in German doctrine accepts the importance of the principle in the

6 While the courts nowadays mostly apply the four-stage-test, the academic literature has also structured the test in 2, 3 or 5 stages without changing the fundamental elements of the principle, see Philipp Reimer, 'Verhältnismäßigkeit im Verfassungsrecht, ein heterogenes Konzept' in O Lepsius/M Jestaedt (eds), *Verhältnismäßigkeit – Struktur und Funktion eines rechtlichen Schlüsselkonzepts* (forthcoming) sect. II.

7 See Georg Nolte, 'General Principles of German and European Administrative Law: A Comparison in Historical Perspective' (1994) 57 *The Modern Law Review* 191, 193.

8 See for instance Mahendra P Singh, *German Administrative Law in Common Law Perspective* (Springer 2001) 163–164.

9 See for the question with regard to the ECJ case law Johanna Wolff, *Ausländische Staatsfonds und Staatliche Sonderrechte – Zum Phänomen 'Sovereign Wealth Funds' und zur Vereinbarkeit der Beschränkung von Unternehmensbeteiligungen mit Europarecht* (Berliner Wiss.-Verl. 2009) 196–197.

10 BVerfGE 30, 1 (20) *Abhörurteil*.

protection of fundamental rights and its relation to the rule of law.[11] Therefore, the present contribution will not consider at length whether such a principle exists in the German context – since it does, unequivocally – or whether its existence is highly disputed in academia or case law – since that is not the case.[12] Rather, the authors wish to show how the position of the principle of proportionality has been safely secured in both case law and the academic literature (see subsection 2.3.) and how it is applied in contemporary practice (see subsection 2.4.). Moreover, while its existence and function cannot be disputed, open questions remain and challenges arise due to its application in recent cases to decisions that do not give the administration discretion (*'gebundene Entscheidung'*) and which should therefore not fall under the principle in the eyes of some academics. These issues are explored in Section V. However, before we can proceed to the principle of proportionality itself, a brief introduction to the German system of judicial review is necessary to set the foundation for discussion of the principle as such.[13]

2.2 Judicial review of administrative action in Germany

2.2.1 Effective judicial review of administrative action as a constitutional obligation

Administrative courts have been established in several German states since the nineteenth century.[14] The current system of judicial review is divided into three layers featuring administrative courts and developed after the Second World War.[15] It consists of fifty-two administrative courts (*Verwaltungsgerichte*) acting as the courts of first instance, fifteen appellate administrative courts (*Oberverwaltungsgerichte* or *Verwaltungsgerichtshöfe*),[16] and the Federal Administrative Court (*Bundesverwaltungsgericht*) in Leipzig.[17]

11 See Section 2.4. and 2.5. below.

12 Andreas von Arnauld observes in his article 'Theorie und Methode des Grundrechtsschutzes in Europa – am Beispiels des Grundsatzes der Verhältnismäßigkeit' (2008) 1 *Europarecht-Beiheft* 2008 41, 44 'Little needs to be said about the rank of the principle of proportionality in the German legal order' (translation by the authors, originally 'Für die deutsche Rechtsordnung muss über den Stellenwert des Grundsatzes der Verhältnismäßigkeit nicht viel gesagt werden').

13 For an introduction to German administrative law see also Martina Künnecke, *Tradition and Change in Administrative Law – An Anglo-German Comparison* (Springer 2007); Meinhard Schröder, 'Administrative Law in Germany' in R Seerden (ed), *Administrative Law in the European Union, its Member States and the United States – A Comparative Analysis* (3rd edn, Intersentia 2012) and Singh (n 8).

14 For an overview on the historic development of the Administrative Court system, see Eberhard Schmidt-Aßmann, Wolfgang Schenk, 'Einleitung' in F Schoch, J-P Schneider, W Bier (eds), *Verwaltungsgerichtsordnung* (CH Beck 2014) para 76–88.

15 In addition to the general administrative courts, specialised courts exist in the field of social law and tax law.

16 Every federal state has one Appellate Administrative Court, only Berlin and Brandenburg have one conjoint court.

17 See Section 2 of the Code of Administrative Court Procedure.

According to Section 40(1) of the Code of Administrative Court Procedure,[18] 'recourse to the administrative courts shall be available in all public-law disputes of a non-constitutional nature insofar as the disputes are not explicitly allocated to another court by a federal statute.' In contrast to other countries, such as France, all types of administrative action can be challenged before the administrative courts. Thus, administrative decisions, as well as factual or informal administrative acts, may be subject to judicial review.[19] This is a direct effect of the constitutional guarantee of an effective judicial remedy in Art. 19(4) of the Basic Law,[20] which states that every person whose rights have been violated by a public authority may have recourse to the courts.[21]

Apart from the above, Art. 19(4) Basic Law also provides the foundation for the subjective conception of judicial review. In contrast to systems of objective judicial control, such as France,[22] German courts in general do not assess the legality of administrative actions *in extenso*. Instead, they examine whether the administration has violated a subjective right.[23] Such a subjective right can derive from the Constitution (meaning, inter alia, the fundamental rights in Arts. 1 to 19), as well as from every (objective) norm that aims, among others, to protect individual interests.[24] In consequence, only a person who can demonstrate a possible violation of a so-called *Schutznorm* (protective norm) has standing (see Section 42(2) Code of Administrative Court Procedure). Indeed, the courts will only assess whether a *Schutznorm* has been violated. This aims namely to protect the plaintiff's individual interests (Section 113(1) Code of Administrative Court Procedure).[25]

However, the conceptual difference between the subjective system in Germany and objective systems in other countries has been 'softened'.[26] In virtue of an early judgment of the Federal Constitutional Court, Art. 2(1)

18 See (also for the following citations) the English translation of the Code of Administrative Court Procedure under http://www.gesetze-im-internet.de/englisch_vwgo/englisch_vwgo.html) accessed 14 October 2014.

19 Statutory instruments can be subject either to judicial control by the administrative courts or by the Federal Constitutional Court, if the former constitute infringements of subjective rights of the claimant, see Marcel Krumm, 'Verwaltungsrechtsschutz gegen materielle Rechtsnormen' (2011) *Deutsches Verwaltungsblatt* (DVBl) 1008–1015.

20 An English translation of the Basic Law is available under http://www.gesetze-im-internet.de/englisch_gg/englisch_gg.html#p0101 accessed 18 October 2014.

21 Friedhelm Hufen, *Verwaltungsprozessrecht* (9th edn 2013) § 13 para 1ff.

22 See chapter 3 in this book.

23 For a comparison of the (subjective) German system and the (objective) French system see Nikolaus Marsch, *Subjektivierung der gerichtlichen Verwaltungskontrolle in Frankreich – Eilverfahren und Urteilsimplementation im objektiv-rechtlich geprägten Kontrollsystem* (Nomos 2011) 33–123.

24 The notion of subjective public right (*subjektives Öffentliches Recht*) is a key term of German public law, see only Bernhard W Wegener, 'Subjective Public Rights – Historical Roots versus European and Democratic Challenges' in H Pünder, C Waldhoff (eds), *Debates in German Public Law* (Hart 2014).

25 The question, whether a norm aims to protect individual interests or not, gave reason to a broad and complex casuistic, see only Rainer Wahl, Peter Schütz, '§ 42 Abs. 2' in Schoch/Schneider/Bier (n 14).

26 See Marsch (n 23) 33–123, esp. 90–91.

of the Basic Law (general right of freedom of action) is interpreted very broadly, protecting every person from any unlawful burden.[27] Therefore, the addressee of an administrative decision, which puts a burden on the former, will always have standing to challenge that decision.[28] Furthermore, in such cases the courts undertake a full objective control of the lawfulness of the decision. As a result, the violation of any norm – not only of a *Schutznorm* – can be brought forward by the addressee of an administrative decision. Nevertheless, the *Schutznorm* concept remains essential because it structures the entirety of German public law. It is, for example, important to differentiate private interests, which have to be balanced as individual rights and on which the claimant can base a complaint, from those based on the public interest, as the latter cannot be relied upon by the claimant.

2.2.2 Proportionality as a boundary to legislative and administrative discretion

Having considered the structure of the judiciary as well as the constitutional background of judicial review in the Basic Law, it is now time to consider the role that the principle of proportionality plays within the system of judicial review. The principle of proportionality acts as a means of control in two different stages: first, as regards the legal act upon which an administrative action may be based, and second, the administrative action itself.[29]

2.2.2.1 The constitutional requirement of a proportionate legal basis for all burdensome administrative action

First, all administrative action that puts an obligation or a burden on a person needs a legal basis (principle of legality). This legal basis itself has to be lawful and has to conform to the Constitution. As the legal basis enables the administration to put an obligation or a burden on a person, it restricts the general right of freedom of action enshrined in Art. 2(1) Basic Law (see above). As is the case with all limitations of fundamental rights, the restriction has to be proportionate, so that any burdensome administrative action can only be based on a proportionate legal basis. For this reason, the administrative courts have to assess the legality and proportionality of the legal basis upon which the administration has based its action.

27 BVerfGE 6, 32 (Elfes); see for the substantive and procedural importance of the judgment by Wolfram Cremer, 'The Basic Right to "Free Development of the Personality" – Mere Protection of Personality Development versus General Right of Freedom of Action' in Pünder, Waldhoff (n 24).

28 See (also for the following) Hufen (n 21) § 14 para 60.

29 Merten (n 4), points out, that a 'double-control of proportionality' can be necessary. See also Lothar Michael, 'Grundfälle zur Verhältnismäßigkeit' (2001) 41 *Juristische Schulung* 764. For an introduction to the German conception of discretion and its judicial control, see Friedrich Schoch, 'Das verwaltungsbehördliche Ermessen' (2004) 26 *Juristische Ausbildung* 462ff.

However, if the legal basis is anchored in a parliamentary statute, the administrative courts will not be competent to leave the statute unapplied simply because it is violating the Constitution.[30] In this case, the court has to refer the question of unconstitutionality to the Federal Constitutional Court,[31] which is competent to declare the invalidity of a parliamentary statute. By contrast, the violation of international treaties by a parliamentary statute generally does not justify a referral to the Federal Constitutional Court, because international treaties do not have a higher rank in the German hierarchy of norms than parliamentary statutes.[32] Recent case law from the Federal Constitutional Court suggests the possibility that a violation of a conventional right of the ECHR by a statute could also constitute a violation of the rule of law (enshrined in Art. 20(3) Basic Law), which would open an indirect possibility to refer the question to the Constitutional Court.[33]

2.2.2.2 *The principle of proportionality as a boundary for administrative discretionary powers*

2.2.2.2.1 (I) THE APPLICABILITY OF THE PRINCIPLE OF PROPORTIONALITY ON ADMINISTRATIVE ACTION

In a second step, the administrative action itself has to respect the principle of proportionality. At this stage, it is of fundamental importance to ask whether the applicable law leaves discretion to the administration. If the administration is entirely bound by the law (*gebundene Entscheidung*), and is only competent to execute what is already ordered by the law, there is (generally) no need for an application of the principle of proportionality to the administrative action itself.[34] In the case of bound decisions, the administrative action is proportionate as long as its legal basis respects the principle of proportionality. Only if the legal basis foresees any discretion does the administration have to assess whether its intended measures are proportionate.

30 Of course, all administrative courts are competent (and obliged) not to apply a statute that is contrary to EU law.

31 Art. 100(1) Basic Law: 'If a court concludes that a law on whose validity its decision depends is unconstitutional, the proceedings shall be stayed, and a decision shall be obtained from the Land court with jurisdiction over constitutional disputes where the constitution of a Land is held to be violated, or from the Federal Constitutional Court where this Basic Law is held to be violated.'

32 Art. 59(2) Basic Law.

33 See Eckart Klein, 'Konkretes Normenkontrollverfahren' in: E Benda, E Klein, O Klein (eds), *Verfassungsprozessrecht* (3rd edn, CF Müller 2012) para 880.

34 Mike Wienbracke, 'Der Verhältnismäßigkeitsgrundsatz' (2013) *Zeitschrift für das Juristische Studium* 148, 155. However, this is now questioned by several recent judgments, s. below Sect. V. 3.

2.2.2.2.2 (II) THE GERMAN CONCEPT OF ADMINISTRATIVE DISCRETIONARY POWERS

The legal norms of German administrative law are traditionally structured in a conditional way.[35] In a simplified way, norms consists of an 'if-side' – enumerating the preconditions for an administrative action; *Tatbestand* – and a 'then-side' – detailing what kind of administrative measures can be taken; *Rechtsfolge*). This is also demonstrated in the diagram below.

The administration generally has no discretion over the concretisation of the legal terms on the if-side. Even the application of very indefinite legal terms (*e.g.*, the assessment of whether a businessperson is unreliable, Sect. 35 of the *Gewerbeordnung*) will be subject to full control by German courts. This very rigid control of the assessment of the facts and the interpretation of such indefinite legal terms follows from the constitutional guarantee of an effective judicial remedy in Art. 19 (4) Basic Law.[36]

In some fields of law, and only for specific types of measures, the administration nevertheless has a margin of appreciation (*Beurteilungsspielraum*), which only undergoes restricted control by the courts. These cases differ from others in the type of decision-maker or the type of decision. Generally, such a margin of appreciation is left to the administration implicitly and has to be detected by the courts by identifying the functional limits of judicial review.[37] This is the case when subjective assessments are required (*e.g.*, school or university exams, staff reports about civil servants), if decisions are taken by multi-member bodies or expert commissions (*e.g.*, a commission deciding whether

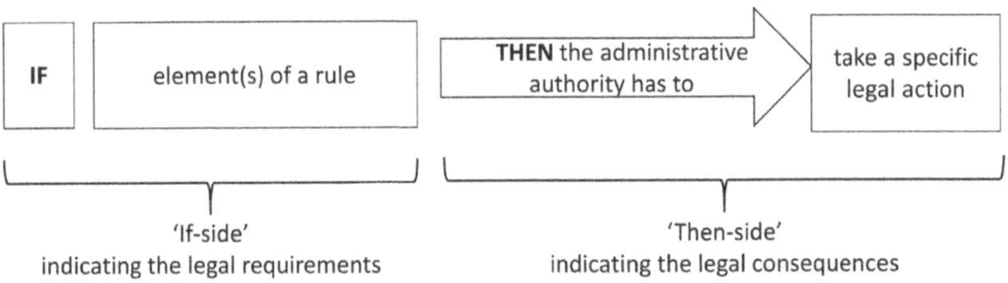

Figure 2.1 The conditional structure of norms in German administrative law

35 See Hartmut Maurer, *Allgemeines Verwaltungsrecht* (18th edn, CH Beck 2011), § 7 para 1ff. For the historic development see Christian F Fonk, 'Die konditionale Rechtsetzung in der Tradition Otto Mayers – ein antiquiertes Normstruktur- und Gesetzgebungsmodell?' (2010) *Deutsches Verwaltungsblatt* 626.

36 Schmidt-Aßmann and Schenk (n 14), para 183. This point of view is criticised by Matthias Jestaedt, 'Maßstäbe des Verwaltungshandelns' in U Erichsen, D Ehlers (eds), *Allgemeines Verwaltungsrecht* (14th edn, De Gruyter 2010) § 11 para 38–39.

37 Schmidt-Aßmann and Schenk (n 14), para 188. As an example for an explicitly given margin of appreciation see Sect. 10(2) of the Telecommunications Act, which foresees a margin of appreciation of the regulatory agency in defining particular markets (http://www.gesetze-im-internet.de/tkg_2004/__10.html accessed 14 October 2014).

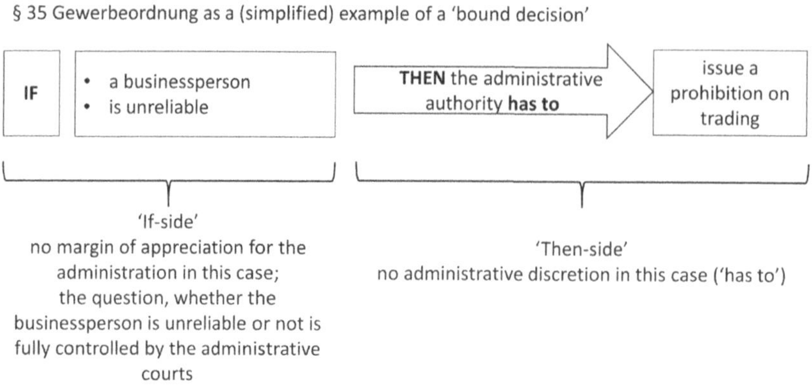

Figure 2.2 Simplified example of a 'bound decision' in German administrative law

a book or a film could be inappropriate for children below a certain age), if decisions are based on complex forecasts (*e.g.*, in regulatory or in environmental law) or if the administrative action consists of a balancing planning decision.[38] In these cases, courts merely examine whether procedural rules have been respected, whether the facts have been established correctly by the administration, whether the administration has correctly identified its room to manoeuvre and whether it has used its discretion in an illegitimate way (misuse of powers). Compared to other legal systems, such margins of appreciation (*Beurteilungsspielräume*) on the if-side are rather rare and terminologically they are distinguished from the administrative discretionary powers on the then-side (*Ermessen*).

These discretionary powers on the then-side can concern (a) the decision of the administration to act or not to act (*Entschließungsermessen*)[39] and (b) the question as to which (of at least two possible) measures the authority should take (*Auswahlermessen*). Furthermore, it is possible that the legislator combines the two types of discretion in a norm. It is here, in the way in which the administration exercises its discretion to act or not to act and its discretion as to which measure should be taken, where the principle of proportionality comes into play. As mentioned above, the proportionality test (in general) only applies to the administrative action. If the administration has no such discretion on the then-side, but is entirely bound by a statutory legal basis, the court will only control whether the legal basis complies with the principle of proportionality.

38 See (also for the following) Maurer (n 35), § 7 para 26ff; Schröder (n 13), 66–67.

39 An *Entschließungsermessen* regularly is left to the administration by the legislator by using verbs like 'may' or 'can'.

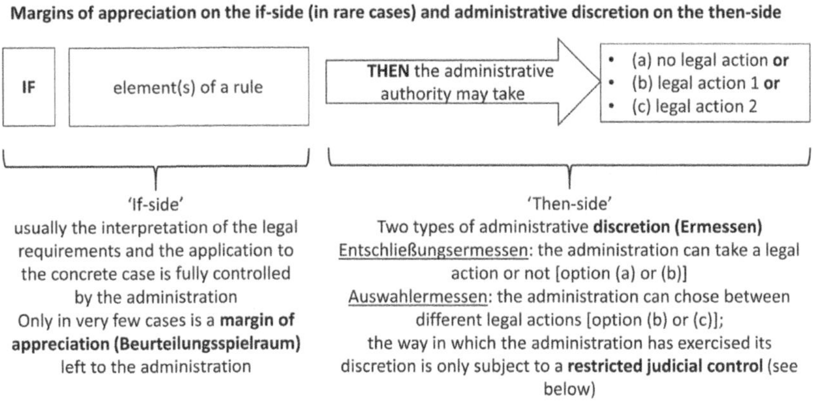

Figure 2.3 Margin of appreciation on the if-side and administrative discretion on the then-side

2.2.2.2.3 (III) THE JUDICIAL REVIEW OF ADMINISTRATIVE ACTION AND THE PRINCIPLE OF PROPORTIONALITY

If the legislator has left some discretion to the administration, the latter has to exercise its discretionary powers in accordance with Section 40 of the Administrative Procedure Act (APA), which provides that '(w)here an authority is empowered to act at its discretion, it shall do so in accordance with the purpose of such empowerment and shall respect the legal limits to such discretionary powers'.[40] These boundaries for the use of administrative discretion are reflected in Section 114 of the Code of Administrative Court Procedure restricting the court's control to an examination of 'whether the administrative act or the refusal or omission of the administrative act is unlawful because the statutory limits of discretion have been overstepped or discretion has been used in a manner not corresponding to the purpose of the empowerment.'

In accordance with the mentioned provision, German courts do not fully control the exercise of administrative discretion. Instead, they assess whether (a) the administration was aware of its discretion and has exercised it (no lack of discretion, *Ermessensausfall* or *Ermessensnichtgebrauch*), whether (b) the administration did not use its discretion for a purpose other than the statutory one (*Ermessensfehlgebrauch* or *Ermessensmissbrauch*); or (c) whether the administration exceeded its discretion by adopting a measure, which was not foreseen by the legal basis (*Ermessensüberschreitung*).[41]

40 Based on the unofficial translation of the APA, published some years ago by the Federal Ministry of the Interior. This translation is no longer available online.

41 The terminology in German doctrine is not uniform, see Wilfried Erbguth, *Allgemeines Verwaltungsrecht – mit Verwaltungsprozess- und Staatshaftungsrecht* (6th edn, Nomos 2014) § 14 para 43–46; Wolfgang Hoffmann-Riem, 'Eigenständigkeit der Verwaltung' in W Hoffmann-Riem, E Schmidt-Aßmann, A Voßkuhle (eds), *Grundlagen des Verwaltungsrechts – Band I: Methoden, Maßstäbe, Aufgaben, Organisation* (2nd edn, CH Beck 2012), § 10 para 88; Maurer (n 35) § 7 para 20ff; Franz-Joseph Peine, *Allgemeines Verwaltungsrecht* (10th edn, CF Müller 2011) para 216ff; Schröder (n 13) 76–77.

In addition to the mentioned limits, the administration must also respect the so-called objective limits of discretion any time it exercises discretionary powers. Any administrative measure has, therefore, to be in line with both fundamental rights and with the principle of proportionality.[42] If the administration has not exercised its discretion in conformity with Section 40 of the Administrative Procedure Act, the fundamental rights and the principle of proportionality, an administrative act (a single case decision) is illegal and will be annulled by the courts (Sect. 113(1) Code of Administrative Court Procedure). Thus, as illustrated by the enshrinement in the Administrative Procedure Act *and* the Administrative Court Procedure Act, the principle of proportionality is at the same time a standard of action for the administration and a standard of control for the administrative courts.

Finally, courts are only competent to control the legal limits of the exercise of discretionary powers, but not to advise on the utility of the administrative measure. It should be emphasised that while administrative courts do control the proportionality of the administrative use of discretion, this does not mean that the courts take the position of the administration and that there is no discretion at all left for the administration. This is illustrated by Section 113(5) of the Administrative Court Procedure Act, which provides that:

> insofar as the rejection or omission of the administrative act is unlawful and the plaintiff's rights are violated thereby, the court shall announce the obligation incumbent on the administrative authority to effect the requested official act *if the case is mature for adjudication*. Otherwise, it shall hand down the obligation to notify the plaintiff, taking the legal view of the court into consideration.

This means that the courts can only oblige the administration to issue a specific administrative act if the administration has no discretion or if only one concrete decision could legally be taken ('if the case is ripe for adjudication'). If this is not the case, the courts can only compel the administration to exercise its discretion again, by issuing a new decision that takes into account the courts' view on the legality of the first rejection.

2.3 Historical background and evolution

2.3.1 Overview

Having gained a better understanding of the German system of judicial review, it is now time to examine the historic evolution of the proportionality

42 Erbguth (n 41) § 14 para 47; Maurer (n 35), § 7 para 23; Peine (n 41) para 222.

principle. Together, these two sections provide the necessary background to fully grasp the position of the principle in current German administrative law and the challenges it faces.

For a considerable time, 'Germany' in the sense of a unified territory did not exist. Instead, it was fragmented into numerous territories, each with their own executive power(s) and laws. As a result, the history of German administrative law is a convoluted one, following the process of unification of the different territories into one federal state.[43] As a consequence, this chapter can only trace the general trends that contributed to the creation and further development of the principle of proportionality. We thus leave out of the scope of this article the route and historic background of this principle in the different territories.

While the notion of proportionality in justice can be traced back to antiquity and the ideas of Hesiod, Euripides and others,[44] for its German background it suffices to start with the eighteenth century. It was during this century that the *raison d'être* of the state changed and German administrative law took a more defined shape with the emergence of the *Allgemeine Landrecht für die Preußischen Staaten* (a General Code of Law for the Prussian territory, hereinafter 'ALR'). This code provided the foundation for the development of the principle of proportionality in the nineteenth century. In fact, the 'suitability' and 'necessity' criteria that still exist today were developed back then.

2.3.2 The eighteenth century

Before discussing the limitation of state power, a number of conditions had to be met first. Most importantly, it was necessary to realise that state (or at the time, monarchical) power was not limitless and pre-given.[45] State structures in Germany in the Middle Ages and up to the seventeenth century had not fostered an understanding of state power that could be limited by independent organs – let alone one that would necessitate a principle of proportionality.[46]

Over time, the perception of the boundaries of state power changed and the state's legitimation to govern its citizens was seen in the citizen's consent to be governed. The citizen was seen to give this consent in return for the state caring for his or her safety, as well as happiness, which was to occur by

43 Jens-Peter Schneider, 'German Traditions' in M Ruffert (ed), *Administrative Law in Europe: Between Common Principles and National Traditions* (Europa Law Publishing 2013) 52.

44 Merten (n 4) 352.

45 Compare Stephanie Heinsohn, *Der öffentlichrechtliche Grundsatz der Verhältnismäßigkeit* (Inaugural Dissertation Westfälische Wilhelms-Universität zu Münster 1997) 5ff.

46 See Michael Stolleis, *Öffentliches Rechts in Deutschland: Eine Einführung in seine Geschichte – 16.-21. Jahrhundert* (CH Beck 2014), 21–26. Cf. Michael Stolleis, *Geschichte des öffentlichen Rechts in Deutschland – Reichspublizistik und Policeywissenschaft 1600–1800* (CH Beck 1988) in more detail focusing on the academic discussion at the time.

the state furthering the public's welfare.[47] This contractual angle on the relationship between the monarch and the citizens constituted one of the central elements in the natural law theory of the state, which was highly influential in eighteenth-century academic discussions.[48] Such a definition of state purposes entailed that, theoretically, the executive could act outside of the limits of the contract with its citizens, if its actions did not secure the citizen's safety or were not geared towards their welfare. It was, in effect, an eighteenth-century interpretation of the Aristotelian conception of the purposes of a state.[49] This limitation of state power remained a theoretical one since this eudemonistic understanding of the state's existence opened the door to a very wide scope of governmental action. It could not only limit but also justify state action.[50] For example, a specific administrative action might interfere with the property rights of one individual but be in the interest of 'greater' public good, and as such be justified. Furthermore, not only was the possible scope of action a very wide one, but an independent organ, which could examine the administrative action, was missing.[51] Instead, a citizen could file a complaint against a specific action but the dispute was ultimately decided by the administration itself.[52]

At the end of the eighteenth century, a regional code was enacted. This code, while still eudemonistic in its construction of the state, would be decisive for the application of the principle of proportionality by the first administrative courts approximately one hundred years later. In addition, this code influenced the academic discussion and gradual development of the criteria of suitability and necessity during the nineteenth century.

In 1794, the General Law for the Prussian States (ALR) was adopted.[53] Provision §10 II 17 ALR deserves particular attention in the context of this article. This provision, sees the start of the gradual evolution of the police as a specific part of the administration.[54] It describes the function of the police,[55] 'Die noethigen Anstalten zur Erhaltung der oeffentlichen Ruhe, Sicherheit und Ordnung, und zur Abwendung der dem Publico, oder

47 Barbara Remmert, *Verfassungs- und verwaltungsrechtsgeschichtliche Grundlagen des Übermaßverbotes* (CF Müller Juristischer Verlag 1995) 14.

48 Heinsohn (n 45) 7–8. Heinsohn mentions important textbooks of natural law inter alia being written by Samuel Pufendorf (1632–1694) and Christian Wolff (1679–1754) whose theories influenced the drafters of the ALR.

49 Heinsohn (n 45) 6.

50 Ibid (n 45), 10.

51 Administrative Courts only came into being in the late nineteenth century, see section III.3 below.

52 Michael Stolleis, *Public Law in Germany 1800–1914* (Berghahn Books 2001) 216.

53 See Heinsohn (n 45) 22–26.

54 The old German term '*Policey*' in the eighteenth century was used to describe the entire body of administrative action (Heinsohn (n 45), 14) and covered many actions which are nowadays considered to be part of the administration, the corresponding academic sciences would later develop into the academic examination and development of administrative law. In Michael Stolleis, *Public Law in Germany* (n 52) it is in effect translated with policy rather than police, see especially 222–224.

55 Ibid (n 45) 22–23.

einzelnen Mitgliedern desselben, bevorstehenden Gefahr zu treffen, ist das Amt der Polizei.'[56] (To take the measures necessary to retain public peace, safety and order, and to deflect danger to the public or a member thereof, is the office of the police.)[57]

This provision already featured a restriction of permissible measures to those that were necessary (at least in theory), and the theoretic possibility for restricting the functions of the police to the safety of the public was created. Yet, this literal interpretation of the provision was only taken up by administrative courts roughly one hundred years later, shortly after they were created in the late nineteenth century.[58] This can be explained, namely, by the prevailing welfare function of the state, an understanding shared by one of the ALR's drafters, the academic Carl Gottlieb Svarez.[59] Svarez still remarked on the limits of state power, clearly recognising the limiting dimension of the contract between the monarch and the citizens. In one of his speeches to the crown prince he observed, 'He [the regent/monarch] may limit the natural freedom of his subjects only in so far as is necessary to protect and uphold the safety and freedom of all.'[60]

2.3.3 The nineteenth century

2.3.3.1 (i) Overview

The nineteenth-century political and legal landscape in Germany was one of upheavals. Academically speaking, under the influence of Kant, a number of academics started to critically examine the natural law teachings, and defended a more extensive protection of the freedoms of the individual as one of the state's functions.[61] Politically speaking, the demands of the liberal movement were met and led to a separation of state and society and an effective limitation on the exercise of state power.[62]

Between 1848 and 1914, the individual states gradually became based on the law.[63] Yet, this separation of state and society did not bring with it a democratisation of state institutions. This democratisation had failed in 1848,[64] and the administration still remained dependent on the monarch and lacked

56 *Allgemeines Landrecht für die Preußischen Staaten* (Volume 4, 3rd edn, Berlin 1796).

57 Translation by the authors.

58 Merten (n 4) 355 seems to interpret the ALR as clearly limiting the police's function to security, thereby deleting the previous dual function of caring both for the security as well as the welfare of citizens.

59 Heinsohn (n 45) 24–26.

60 Hermann Conrad, Gerd Kleinheyer (eds), *Carl Gottlieb Svarez – Vorträge über Recht und Staat 1791/92* (Westdt Verlag 1960) 9 (translation by the authors).

61 Heinsohn (n 45) 27.

62 Ibid (n 45) 29.

63 Remmert (n 47) 100, 164. However, the constitutions did not yet have a status equal to that of the Basic Law; they were not primary to other pieces of legislation.

64 See Stolleis, *Public Law in Germany* (n 52) 248–254.

parliamentary oversight. Still, the monarch no longer had all-encompassing power either, leading the balance of power between reformists and monarchy to a decisive compromise. While the monarchy remained in power, the freedoms of the individual were protected against state intervention by creating legal limits. The 'Rechtsstaat' emerged in this context as something that both liberalists and conservatives could agree upon.[65]

This new understanding of the state's functions facilitated, in turn, the recognition of *a* principle of proportionality as a legal principle. This principle was, however, not congruent with *the* principle of proportionality we know today. Despite regional differences in the respective police laws, this was facilitated by the notion that public administration should be bound by law.[66] While the police undoubtedly had a wide margin of discretion to interfere with an individual's freedom, the executive at least theoretically needed legitimation in the law.[67] This was an important precondition for the applicability of a test limiting administrative discretion.

The individual sphere of freedom that needed safeguarding covered both personal and economic aspects, and was protected by the recognition that the administration could not act without being permitted to do so in a given law. In general, a specific law permitted the administration to take a given action and limit an individual's freedom, which meant that the legislature had already balanced the public good against the personal freedoms at risk.[68] Thus only when the legislature had left the executive with the freedom to decide, could it exercise administrative discretion.[69] Courts then applied a form of the principle of proportionality at the end of nineteenth and early twentieth century, relatively soon after they were created. The establishment of independent administrative courts had long been advocated by liberalists and resisted by the states.[70] In 1863, the first independent administrative court was established in Baden; Prussia followed in 1872/75, with Hamburg and Bremen being the latecomers with the first independent administrative courts being established only during the Weimar Republic.[71]

This slow evolution of judicial control prior to 1933 is of course restricted to the application of the principle to administrative action by administrative courts. The second application of the principle of proportionality that we know today, the check of legislation for possible violation of fundamental rights granted in the Basic law by the Constitutional Court, did not exist at the time. In the nineteenth century, by contrast, the system of constitutional monarchy implied a limited degree of political control given that, in the legislative process, the

65 Knill, Becker (n 1), 455; Stolleis, *Public Law in Germany* (n 52) 257.
66 Remmert (n 47) 164.
67 Ibid (n 47) 140, 165.
68 Ibid (n 47) 164–165.
69 Ibid (n 47) 164–165.
70 Schneider (n 43) 52; Nolte (n 7) 198–199.
71 Ibid (n 43) 52.

monarch had to reach an agreement with the parliament of the federal state in question.[72] However, this institutional protection was dependent on the composition of the respective parliament and this inherently political process cannot be equated with the contemporary legalised control by the judiciary.[73]

2.3.4 Academic discussion and development of the specific criteria

When discussing the historic dimension of the principle of proportionality, its different criteria and roots in the nineteenth century, caution is advised in one important regard. The contemporary usage of a specific term is not necessarily congruent with its historic one. This is especially the case for the principle of proportionality. This term already existed in the nineteenth century and was used by different academics, but what was being discussed was, in effect, whether or not a measure was *necessary*. Thus, academic discussion at the time seems to have restricted itself to requiring an action to be suitable and necessary.

The suitability criterion was clearly accepted by a number of academics in the nineteenth century. This was visible, for example, in the writings on police law by Robert von Mohl,[74] who also established the term *Rechtsstaat*.[75] Otto Mayer, who taught in Strasbourg, wrote a highly influential textbook on German administrative law, which not only structured German administrative law, but because of its wide distribution also aided the wide acceptance of the necessity criterion (then called the principle of proportionality).[76] Mayer expressly recognised the principle of proportionality as a legal principle, that is to say as a legal limit on police action, even where police laws only provided for it in an inadequate manner.[77] It is for this reason, that Otto Mayer has been called the 'father of the principle of proportionality' by many German authors.[78]

2.3.5 Case law

The principle of proportionality was expressly formulated by German courts for the first time at the end of the nineteenth century. In an important first step, the Prussian Appellate Administrative Court limited the function of the police in its 1882 Kreuzberg judgment to cover only those included in the previously mentioned §10 II 17 ALR, meaning for the prevention of a concrete danger to the public.[79] However, this did not yet equal an immediate

72 Wahl (n 3) 825.

73 Ibid (n 3) 826.

74 Robert von Mohl, *Encyklopädie der Staatswissenschaften* (Tübingen 1859) 134, as cited in Remmert (n 47), 82.

75 Robert von Mohl, *Die Polizeiwissenschaft nach den Grundsätzen des Rechtsstaats* (Tübingen 1832/33), see Stolleis, *Public Law in Germany* (n 52) 229.

76 Heinsohn (n 45) 49.

77 Klaus Stern, 'Zur Entstehung und Ableitung des Übermaßverbots' in P. Badura, R. Scholz (eds), *Wege und Verfahren des Verfassungslebens – Festschrift für Peter Lerche zum 65. Geburtstag* (CH Beck 1993) 168.

78 For example by Lothar Hirschberg, *Der Grundsatz der Verhältnismäßigkeit* (Otto Schwartz & Co 1981) 4.

79 Schneider (n 43) 52.

recognition of the two criteria. Instead, during the late nineteenth and early twentieth century, the Prussian Administrative Appellate Court applied two theories to check police action in parallel.[80]

In the first theory, the court maintained that judicial control was limited and that the court would not check an administrative decision if it was based on a valid act or order.[81] In these cases, it refrained from examining suitability and necessity. In the second string of cases, the court did, in fact, decide that an action went far beyond the pursued aim and did examine the suitability and necessity of the measure (necessity theory).[82] Thus, 1903 was the last year in which the court applied the first, more restrictive theory, paving the way for regular application of a suitability and necessity test in the 1920s.[83]

As a last step, it is worthwhile considering not only whether administrative courts did check the 'proportionality' of police action, but also in how far individuals generally had access to a review of a specific administrative action. Again, this was regulated very differently in the respective German states. That said, options for redress covered, first of all, the filing of a complaint in front of the administrative authority that was the immediate superior of the one accused of the violation.[84] Second, the citizen could apply for remedies in front of the civil law courts.[85] Third, and most important for present purposes, the individual could file a complaint in front of administrative courts, albeit their competence varied.[86] Thus, in the case of a police order (*polizeiliche Verfügung*), the competence of the administrative courts depended on whether or not the individual could demonstrate that his or her rights had been violated and on the specific standard that the court applied.[87] The outcome of the case then depended, not only on the facts of the case[88] and on the state in which the court was located, but also, in the case of Prussia, on whether the court applied different standards.

2.3.6 The first half of the twentieth century

2.3.6.1 The proportionality principle between a floundering republic, a dictatorship and the Second World War

After the end of the First World War, and with the end of constitutional monarchy in Germany, the parliament became sovereign.[89] This wide-ranging

80 Heinsohn (n 45) 42–43.
81 Ibid (n 45) 43–44.
82 Ibid (n 45) 44–46, 52.
83 Ibid (n 45) 52.
84 Remmert (n 47) 158.
85 Remmert (n 47) 158.
86 Remmert (n 47) 158.
87 Ibid (n 47), 159–163.
88 For a long time, courts were reluctant in reviewing discretionary decisions, arguing that the discretion of administrative authorities where it was not bound by the law could not be subject to control. On this see the academic, Fleiner, *Institutionen des Deutschen Verwaltungsrechts* (Tübingen 1911) 214 as quoted by Remmert (n 47) 160.
89 Wahl (n 3) 827.

legislative power during the Weimar Republic, without a strong constitution, would be one of the main weaknesses of the system leading to its fall in the 1930s. In the meantime, however, the criteria of necessity and suitability were widely accepted in academic literature on administrative law, and constituted settled case law in the 1920s.[90] One example for relevant literature in the early twentieth century is a famous expression by the academic, Fleiner, who observed '[t]he police should not use cannons to shoot at sparrows . . . The relevant measure must be suitable to the respective circumstances, it must be proportionate'.[91] His legacy is such that even today frequent reference is made to 'not shooting at sparrows with cannons'.

It is not surprising that the evolution of the principle of proportionality and its application by the courts stopped in the years of the Third Reich.[92] The application of Nazi ideology in legal interpretation, as well as its methodology, would have rendered independent judicial review of state action impossible. In fact, judicial review of state action was completely abolished, and the application of the principle of proportionality by courts was both dogmatically and factually suppressed.[93]

2.3.7 *Since 1949: proportionality and the constitutionalisation of administrative law*

After the Second World War and the end of the Nazi dictatorship, proportionality became one of the most important principles of German public law. Since the 1950s, the Federal Constitutional Court elevated the principle of proportionality to a constitutional principle deriving from the principle of *Rechtsstaat*[94] and/or fundamental rights.[95] While its concrete constitutional basis remains controversial until the present,[96] German doctrine is unanimous in the existence of a constitutionally based principle of proportionality.[97] It was this constitutionalisation[98] of the principle of proportionality that

90 Heinsohn (n 45) 52–54.

91 Heinsohn (n 45) 58 citing Fleiner.

92 For a more detailed account of German administrative sciences during the Third Reich, Stolleis, *A History of Public Law in Germany 1914–1945* (OUP 2004) 335–372.

93 Schneider (n 43) 54.

94 For a comparative approach to the German concept of *Rechtsstaat* see Rainer Grote, 'Rule of Law, *Rechtsstaat* and "État de droit"' in C Starck (ed), *Constitutionalism, Universalism and Democracy – A Comparative Analysis* (Nomos 1999) 269–306; Luc Heuschling, *État de droit, Rechtsstaat, Rule of Law* (Dalloz 2002).

95 For the development of the jurisprudence see Wahl (n 3) 828ff.

96 See, inter alia, Karl-Peter Sommermann, 'Article 20' in H v Mangoldt, F Klein, C Starck (eds), *Grundgesetz – Kommentar* (6th edn, Vahlen 2010) para 308 (proportionality is anchored in the concept of *Rechtsstaat* and in the fundamental rights); Detlef Merten, 'Verhältnismäßigkeitsgrundsatz' in D Merten, H-J Papier, *Handbuch der Grundrechte III – Allgemeine Lehren II* (CF Müller 2009) para 24ff, 35ff; Reimer (n 6), sect I (both pleading for fundamental rights as the only basis); Stern (n 77) para 172 (Rechtsstaat as the only basis).

97 Stern (n 77) 171.

98 See Johannes Saurer, *Die Globalisierung des Verhältnismäßigkeitsgrundsatzes* (2012) 51 *Der Staat* 3, 6.

resulted in its proliferation. While historically, the scope of the principle was restricted to the German laws of police and public safety, the case law of the Federal Constitutional Court entailed that the entire realm of German public law came under the influence of the principle of proportionality.[99] Yet, the proliferation of the principle of proportionality is only one facet of the general constitutionalisation of the German administrative law since 1949, which is often described as 'concretised constitutional law'.[100]

The principle of proportionality was often associated with the designation '*Übermaßverbot*' or 'interdiction of over-reach'. As a mirror image to this concept, the Federal Constitutional Court and the German doctrine developed the concept of *Untermaßverbot* (or approximately, 'interdiction of under-reach'). This *Untermaßverbot* is closely linked to a duty to protect, which has been recognised since the 1970s as being an objective dimension of fundamental rights.[101] Generally speaking, it provides that the public authorities have to guarantee at least a minimal standard of protection with regard to the fundamental rights of citizens.[102] However, it is rare that the administration or even the legislator can be obliged by the courts to take a specific and concrete measure, because there is usually more than one possibility to comply with a duty to protect.

2.4 The proportionality test – actual meaning and practice

2.4.1 The four-step test and the varying intensity of control

Since the constitutionalisation of the principle of proportionality dominates the entire sphere of German public law, all branches of administrative law[103] fall into the scope of the constitutional principle of proportionality.[104] Even in fields of law where the administration is not infringing

99 Fritz Ossenbühl, 'Maßhalten mit dem Übermaßverbot' in P Badura, R Scholz (n 77) 153.

100 See the well-known title of an article by the former President of the Federal Administrative Court Fritz Werner, 'Verwaltungsrecht als konkretisiertes Verfassungsrecht' (1959) *Deutsches Verwaltungsblatt* 527–533.

101 The duty to protect and the *Untermaßverbot* were mainly developed with regard to the right to life and physical integrity (Art 2(2) Basic Law) in two judgments of the Federal Constitutional Court, BVerfGE 39, 1 (Abortion), BVerfGE 46, 160 (Schleyer). For this reason (and contrary to the principle of proportionality) the *Untermaßverbot* is regarded as following from the fundamental rights and the constitutionally anchored principle of the welfare state, but not as a consequence of the rule of law, see Sommermann (n 96) para 320.

102 See (also for the following) Michael (n 29) 765–767.

103 In contrast to other legal orders like the French (see chapter 2) or the Dutch (see chapter 4), the law of administrative sanctions in Germany is mostly governed by criminal law. Nevertheless, the principle of proportionality also applies in this field of law.

104 See only BVerfGE 76, 256 (359); Ossenbühl, 'Maßhalten mit dem Übermaßverbot' (n 99), 153; Fritz Ossenbühl, 'Der Grundsatz der Verhältnismäßigkeit (Übermaßverbot) in der Rechtsprechung der Verwaltungsgerichte' (1997) 19 *Juristische Ausbildung* 617; Andreas Voßkuhle, 'Der Grundsatz der Verhältnismäßigkeit' (2007) 47 *Juristische Schulung* 429, 430.

individual rights, the principle is still applied.[105] The same is true for those private law cases that are influenced by fundamental rights. In these cases, the fundamental rights affected must be balanced in order to allow both individuals to exercise their fundamental rights.[106] However, the principle of proportionality does not apply when the delimitation of the competences of two public bodies is at stake, for example in the relationship between the federal states and the municipalities.[107]

For the administrative courts, the principle of proportionality is an indispensable instrument of control[108] and its application is routine work for administrative judges.[109] Scope and meaning of the proportionality principle seem so obvious, that many German textbooks on general administrative law only spend a few pages on it.[110] Besides the question of whether this attitude is justified, and before having a closer look at the four steps of proportionality, a general remark with regard to the intensity of control has to be made. While the identical four steps apply to both administrative and constitutional law, their control by the administrative courts – when examining a concrete administrative measure – is much more intense than the control undertaken by the Federal Constitutional Court with regard to a parliamentary statute. The legislator has a wider margin of appreciation as to the suitability and the necessity criteria, whereas there is generally no margin of appreciation left to the administration with regard to the different steps.[111] It must be said, however, that the intensity of the control conducted by the Federal Constitutional Court varies, depending on the specific fundamental right that is infringed by the legislator.[112]

Finally, German courts often explain their reasoning in decisions rather exhaustively,[113] especially in comparison to court decisions in other legal orders. Furthermore, the administrative courts give one single motivated judgement, upon which at least the majority of judges in the chamber has agreed

105 Ossenbühl, 'Der Grundsatz der Verhältnismäßigkeit' (n 104), 617.

106 For instance, the Constitutional Court judged that in regard to the question of whether a lodger from a foreign country has the right to install a parabolic antenna in order to receive TV programmes from his domestic country, the fundamental rights of the landlord (property) and the lodger (freedom of information) has to be balanced, see BVerfGE 90, 27.

107 See Voßkuhle (n 104), 430. This may be seen as strengthening the position that the principle of proportionality is based on fundamental rights, not on the rule of law, Merten (n 96) para 33. Consequently, Sommermann (n 96), in whose opinion the principle is rooted in the rule of law, is in favour of an application also on the conflicts of competences between public bodies.

108 Ossenbühl, 'Der Grundsatz der Verhältnismäßigkeit' (n 104) 617.

109 Stern (n 77) 167.

110 See as examples only, Erbguth (n 41) § 14 para 53 (one page in a textbook of 500 pages); Maurer (n 35) § 10 para 17 (one page out of over 800).

111 Merten (n 96) para 45ff; Thomas von Danwitz, *Europäisches Verwaltungsrecht* (Springer 2008) 23; Voßkuhle (n 104) 430.

112 Merten (n 96), para 45.

113 This is not the case with other administrative courts in Europe, see chapter 3 for criticism of the opacity and concision of the decisions of the French Council of State.

upon. In the German system, the possibility of dissenting opinions only exists for constitutional judges, but even the judges of the Federal Constitutional Court regularly attempt to reach a consensus.[114] All this has possibly facilitated the development of a uniform structure of control of the principle of proportionality by the courts and its uniform application.

2.4.1.1 (i) Legitimate aim

In constitutional law, the first step of proportionality is that the legislator must pursue a legitimate aim. Due to its strong and direct democratic legitimation, the legislator is relatively free to define the aims of a statute and is only bound by constitutional interdictions.[115] In the end, the legitimacy of the aim in constitutional law simply means that a statute and its aim have to be legal. In this sense, this stage of control could be considered unnecessary and even superfluous.[116] Still, the judicial control is structured by a separate stage, which determines the aim of the measure itself.[117]

However, in administrative law, the identification of the aim is more than a didactic effort, because the administration – in applying a statute – has to pursue the aim that the legislator wanted to achieve by adopting the statute. While in some (especially newer) statutes, this statutory aim is explicitly concretised in one of the first sections, other statutes remain silent in this regard, so that the statutory aim has to be identified through interpretation.[118] Only within the statutory framework has the administration the discretion to pursue one statutory aim with an administrative measure, while neglecting another statutory aim.[119]

2.4.1.2 (ii) Suitability (Geeignetheit)

Suitability does not mean that the administrative measure has to be optimal. It means, rather, that there is the probability that the aim is achieved or at least its achievement is fostered.[120] Therefore, this stage of the proportionality test is rarely problematic.[121] For instance, an administrative measure in

114 See Wolfgang Hoffmann-Riem, 'Die Klugheit der Entscheidung ruht in ihrer Herstellung – selbst bei der Anwendung von Recht' in A Scherzberg (ed), *Kluges Entscheiden – Disziplinäre Grundlagen und interdisziplinäre Verknüpfungen* (Mohr Siebeck 2006) 13.

115 Voßkuhle (n 104) 430.

116 See Reimer (n 6) sect II 1, who also points out that there a few restrictions in this regard.

117 The value of a structuration of control is also recognised by Reimer (n 6), sect II 8 with regard to the stage of suitability which he also considers (with good argument) as being superfluous.

118 Ingo Kraft, 'Der Grundsatz der Verhältnismäßigkeit im deutschen Rechtsverständnis' (2007) 1 *BDVR-Rundschreiben* 11, 14; Ossenbühl, 'Der Grundsatz der Verhältnismäßigkeit' (n 104) 618.

119 Compare Jestaedt (n 36) § 11 para 63.

120 See – for suitability in constitutional law, but also applicable in administrative law – Horst Dreier, 'Vorbemerkungen' in H Dreier, *Grundgesetz – Kommentar: Band I* (3rd edn, Mohr Siebeck 2013) para 146.

121 See – also for the following examples – Ossenbühl, 'Der Grundsatz der Verhältnismäßigkeit' (n 104) 618.

police law is not suitable if the addressee of an administrative order is not able to follow the order for factual or for judicial reasons. For this reason, a demolition order can only be addressed to the owner of a building, while the eviction of a rented building must be addressed to the tenant. Contrary to the control of the necessity, the assessment of the suitability of a measure is an empirical-technical question, which is free from subjective assessments.[122]

2.4.1.3 (iii) Necessity (Erforderlichkeit)

As described above, necessity is the historical nucleus of the principle of proportionality and it has remained the centre of its gravity until today.[123] Necessity means that, among several measures that are comparably effective, the administration has to choose the one measure that is the least burdensome for the addressee.[124] In other words, necessity is not established if the administration could have chosen another measure, which would have been (at least) just as suitable as the challenged measure, while infringing to a lesser degree the rights of the addressees. Moreover, the alternative measure itself has to be legal, meaning that only those alternative measures may be considered, which could have legally been taken by the administration.[125]

A historically important example for a statutory concretisation of the necessity is the so-called right to a substitution of means (*Mittelaustausch*). In many of the police laws of the federal states, the principle of proportionality is concretised as in Sect. 3(2) of the police law of North Rhine-Westphalia. Here it is stated that, upon request, the addressee has to be allowed by the administration to use a means other than the one ordered in order to achieve the aim pursued by the administration. This will be allowed, provided that the alternative means is just as effective and if it is not more burdensome for the general public than the measure ordered.[126] In this way, the subjective preferences of the addressee are also protected.[127]

2.4.1.4 (iv) Adequacy (Angemessenheit) *or proportionality stricto sensu*

The adequacy or proportionality *stricto sensu* of the last stage of the proportionality test seems to be a German particularity, which has not been adopted by a number of countries.[128] 'Adequacy' means that in an overall balance of all relevant factors, the infringement of the rights of the

122 See – for suitability in constitutional law, but also applicable in administrative law – Dreier (n 120) para 146.

123 Kraft (n 118) 14; Ossenbühl, 'Der Grundsatz der Verhältnismäßigkeit' (n 104) 618.

124 See – also for the following – Ossenbühl, 'Der Grundsatz der Verhältnismäßigkeit' (n 104) 618–619.

125 Michael (n 29) 764–765.

126 See Bodo Pieroth, Bernhard Schlink, Michael Kniesel, *Polizei- und Ordnungsrecht, mit Versammlungsrecht* (7th edn, CH Beck 2012) § 10 para 28–29.

127 Ossenbühl, 'Der Grundsatz der Verhältnismäßigkeit' (n 104) 619.

128 Saurer (n 98), 30ff; Wahl (n 3), 833ff.

addressee of the administrative measure has to be proportionate in relation to the advantages for the general public. In addition, the execution of the administrative order by the addressee must be such that it can reasonably be expected.[129]

The adequacy test differs fundamentally from the control of necessity. While the assessment of the necessity criterion requires the comparison of two or more administrative measures with regard to their effectivity and their impact on the addressee and the general public, the adequacy test consists of asking whether the pursued objective justifies the infringement of the addressee's subjective rights. In other words, the question is whether the objective is worth the infringement.[130] For example, a demolition order for a building is not adequate if the distance allowed to the neighbour's site of three metres has been exceeded unintentionally by 3–6 centimetres and the overstepping does not lead to any relevant disadvantages for the neighbour.[131] In another very famous case, the Federal Constitutional Court held that it is not adequate to order a cerebrospinal fluid puncture (a painful medical test with potential health risks) in order to clarify the criminal responsibility of a person, if the matter of the criminal proceedings is a minor offence.[132] The same has been held for a search of a lawyer's office, when only a minor traffic offence was at stake, which could only have resulted in the application of an administrative fine of fifteen euros.[133]

Beyond the outcome in such obvious cases, the application of the adequacy test is not free from subjective assessments and clear criteria for the control are hard to find.[134] However, many German judges seem to be aware of this and they exercise a rather reluctant control of the adequacy of administrative measures,[135] limiting themselves to a legal control of adequacy that does not interfere in questions of utility or advisability.

2.4.2 The German 'export hit' and the European influence on German law

2.4.2.1 *(i) The principle of proportionality as a German 'export hit'*

Contrary to the legal orders of some other EU Member States, the (ubiquitous) application of the principle of proportionality in Germany is deeply rooted in the German (national) law and has generally remained unaffected

129 Dreier (n 120), para 149. The assessment on whether the execution by the addressee can reasonably be expected is often seen as a fifth stage of the proportionality test called *Zumutbarkeit*.

130 Reimer (n 6), sect II 5.

131 Ossenbühl, 'Der Grundsatz der Verhältnismäßigkeit' (n 104) 619.

132 BVerfGE 16, 194.

133 BVerfG *NJW* 2006, 3411, 3412.

134 Reimer (n 6) sect II. 5.

135 See, for example, Kraft (judge at the Federal Administrative Court) (n 118) 14.

by European influences. In fact, the German doctrine considers the triumphant advance of proportionality in Europe as being strongly influenced by German legal thinking.[136]

One reason for the importance of the proportionality test in German administrative law has to be stressed in the following. As the violation of procedural rules in many cases does not lead to the illegality of the administrative measure, the German administrative courts cannot focus on the procedural aspects (as the ECJ often does). Rather, they have to undertake a control on the merits by assessing whether the measure is proportionate.[137] By and large, it can be concluded that the German administrative courts, when dealing with most cases with a European law dimension, can easily follow the application of the proportionality principle by the ECJ and the ECtHR. This could be possible even if their own case law has to be modified with regard to the outcome of the application. However, the general application of the principle has not been influenced by the jurisprudence of the European courts.

2.4.2.2 (ii) The (outdated) distinction between margin of appreciation on the if-side (Beurteilungsspielraum) *and discretion on the then-side* (Ermessen) *of norms*

Conversely, the traditional sharp distinction between the if-side and the then-side of norms (see subsection 2.2), and the ensuing distinction between the rather rare margins of appreciation and the numerous discretionary powers of the administration, is increasingly criticised in Germany. From a theoretical perspective, the binary distinction is considered to be excessive[138] especially as the exact formulation of a norm is often random with regard to the question of which elements are anchored on the if-side and the then-side.[139] For some authors, the intensity of control applied by the courts should follow functional arguments and should not be the result of the assignment of parts of the norm to the if-side or to the then-side.[140] At this point of the debate, references are often made to the jurisprudence of the ECJ and to comparative law studies in order to illustrate that the traditional distinctions are widely unknown in Europe. However, as these distinctions are very

136 Von Arnauld (n 12) 62–63.

137 In constitutional law, a rather new (and intensively discussed) development in the case law of the Constitutional Court is to focus more on a control of the coherence and the legal certainty of statutes in order to give the legislator a wider margin of appreciation in regard to the proportionality of the statute (see, for instance, the decision on the statute implementing the Data Retention Directive, BVerfGE 125, 260).

138 Jestaedt (n 36) § 11 para 14 and following.

139 However, Michael Gerhardt, '§ 114' in Schoch/Schneider/Bier (n 14) para 55 considers the separation of the if-side and the then-side as an important factor of rationalisation.

140 Hoffmann-Riem (n 41) § 10 para 102–105.

deeply and firmly rooted in German law, it seems rather improbable that they could be abandoned in the future in favour of the comprehensive European approach to discretionary powers of the administration.

2.5 The status quo and recent developments in the literature and case law

2.5.1 A core element of German public law

In the German literature, the promotion of proportionality to constitutional principle and the implementation in the judicial practice have been estimated as being two of the most relevant innovations of German public law and its outstanding performance.[141] In the words of *Rainer Wahl* 'balancing became a cypher for the adequate way of judicial thinking and arguing'.[142] As an element of justice, the principle as such is not disputed any more, only the application of the principle by the courts is subject to some discussion.[143]

2.5.1.1 (i) The eternal question of the intensity of control

The adequacy test has been subject to criticism, particularly in constitutional law.[144] One concern is that the balancing exercise threatens to blur the boundaries between law and politics,[145] especially as the adequacy test is lacking objective criteria.[146] Even if it might be necessary to discuss this question unrelentingly in order to remind judges of the legal limits of their control, it is unlikely that a solution for the problem of how to identify the appropriate intensity of control will be found. Moreover, the fact that the principle of proportionality *and its application* is one of the most important subjects of academic teaching[147] leads to a certain consensus on how to apply the principle and what kind of arguments are allowed in applying it.

Although dogmatically different, a more disputable topic is the most recent case law of the Federal Constitutional Court, stating that the legislator has to pursue its aims in a consequent and consistent way.[148] This perception is

141 Wahl (n 3).
142 Ibid (n 3) 837.
143 Ossenbühl, 'Maßhalten mit dem Übermaßverbot' (n 99) 156.
144 See for different criticism Wahl (n 3) 838ff.
145 See, for example, Bernhard Schlink, 'Der Grundsatz der Verhältnismäßigkeit' in P Badura, H Dreier (eds), *Festschrift 50 Jahre Bundesverfassungsgericht* (Mohr Siebeck 2001) 460–462, who explicitly differentiates between the adequacy test in constitutional and in administrative law.
146 Ossenbühl, 'Der Grundsatz der Verhältnismäßigkeit' (n 104) 620–621.
147 Matthias Klatt, Moritz Meister, 'Der Grundsatz der Verhältnismäßigkeit – Ein Strukturelement des globalen Konstitutionalismus' (2014) 54 *Juristische Schulung* 193.
148 See, for instance, BVerfGE 121, 317, 359ff. For the wide doctrinal critic, see only Philipp Dann, 'Verfassungsgerichtliche Kontrolle gesetzgeberischer Rationalität' (2010), 49 *Der Staat* 630–646.

reminiscent of the ECJ jurisprudence on gambling monopolies, by which the Court introduced the new criteria of coherence.[149] In both cases, it is the sincerity of the legislator that is assessed, in what could be seen as part of the suitability test.[150] While this case law seems to be very convincing at first glance, its problematic aspect resides on a certain blindness with regard to the parliamentary process, which does not always lead to coherent and consistent results, but to acceptable compromises.[151]

2.5.1.2 (ii) The value of administrative discretionary powers

After the Second World War, a strong judicial control of all administrative action quickly became a kind of ideal to be achieved. As seen above, the Federal Constitutional Court has strengthened the judicial control of administrative acts by activating the fundamental right for a judicial remedy. However, nowadays, several German authors question whether the judicial control of administrative acts goes too far into the domain of administrative discretion. The hypertrophy of the German judicial review is deplored and the question of the autonomy of the administration is raised[152] within the more general question of the adequate separation of powers. In that vein, the administrative courts are often criticised for searching for the 'only correct' measure the administration should have taken, instead of respecting the will of the legislator to endow the administration with the power to take a discretionary decision.[153]

2.5.2 'Bound decisions' and the principle of proportionality

Finally, a recent development in the case law of the Federal Administrative Court and some Appellate Administrative Courts has to be mentioned, as it fundamentally affects the relationships between the administration, legislators and the administrative courts.[154] As mentioned above (subsection 2.2.), the principle of proportionality can apply in two different stages. First, the legal basis of any burdensome administrative act has to comply with the

149 Case C-243/01 Gambelli and others (2001) ECR I-13031.

150 Reimer (n 6) sect II 7.

151 See the dissenting opinion of Judge Bryde, BVerfGE 121, 317, 378.

152 See Hoffmann-Riem (n 41).

153 Rainer Pitschas, 'Maßstäbe des Verwaltungshandelns' in: W Hoffmann-Riem, E Schmidt-Aßmann, A Voßkuhle (eds), *Grundlagen des Verwaltungsrechts – Band II: Informationsordnung, Verwaltungsverfahren, Handlungsformen* (2nd edn, CH Beck 2012) § 42 para 109; in the same sense Jestaedt (n 36), § 11 para 63 footnote 264.

154 See for this recent development in the jurisprudence first Kolja Naumann, 'Die Prüfung der Verhältnismäßigkeit im Rahmen gebundener Entscheidungen' (2011)64 *Die Öffentliche Verwaltung* 96–104 as well as Tristan Barczak, 'Der gebundene Verwaltungsakt unter Verhältnismäßigkeitsvorbehalt' (2014) 105 *Verwaltungsarchiv* 142–181 and Veit Mehde, 'Die Prüfung der Verhältnismäßigkeit bei gebundenen Entscheidungen' (2014) 67 *Die Öffentliche Verwaltung* 541–548.

principle of proportionality. Second, the administrative act itself has to be proportionate *if the legislator has left discretion to the administration.*

According to the traditional literature, if the administration has no discretion at all, but is entirely bound by the legal basis (so called *gebundene Entscheidung* – bound decision), the principle of proportionality only applies to the legal basis, but not to the administrative act. This means that a bound administrative decision cannot be disproportionate if the legal basis complies with the principle of proportionality.[155]

However, in several recent judgments, the Federal Administrative Court and several Appellate Administrative Courts controlled the proportionality of administrative decisions, even though the legal basis adopted by parliament did not foresee any discretionary powers of the administration.[156] In some of these cases, the judgments can be seen as an interpretation of the parliamentary statutes in conformity with the Basic Law.[157] But in other cases, an interpretation in conformity with the Basic Law was not possible, as the wording of the parliamentary statute was clear and did not leave any room for interpretation. This is particularly true in several cases related to the expulsion of foreign nationals. Although there was no doubt in the interpretation of the parliamentary statute that the will of the legislator was that, in specific cases, foreigners *have* to be expulsed, the administrative courts – instructed by the Federal Constitutional Court – controlled whether the expulsion was proportionate in the concrete case.[158] For the criteria of this application of the principle of proportionality, the Federal Constitutional Court explicitly referred to the case law of the ECtHR on Art. 8 of the ECHR.[159]

In support of this recent jurisprudence, one can be of the opinion that individual justice is fostered by the application of the principle of proportionality even if the administration is entirely bound by a parliamentary statute. Nevertheless, this development in the German jurisprudence gives cause for serious concerns. First, the legislative decision to opt for a bound administrative decision aims at strengthening the legal certainty.[160] The recent case law not only makes it more difficult for the legislator to bind the administration in the desired way, but also makes it more difficult for the administration to apply the law. Second – and this is highly problematic – the separation of powers is challenged by this case law.[161] By interpreting the legal basis contrary to its clear wording, the administrative courts impose their own assessment on the legislator. Instead of referring the case to the Federal Constitutional

155 Compare Naumann (n 154) 97.

156 BVerwG NJW 2009, 2905. For further examples, see the contributions cited in footnote 154.

157 See also for the following Naumann (n 154) 98.

158 See also Barczak (n 154), 165–166; Mehde (n 154) 543.

159 BVerfG NVwZ 2007, 1300.

160 See also for the following, Naumann (n 154) 99–100.

161 See also for the following, the critical comments of Naumann (n 154) 100, 103–104; Barczak (n 154) 170–181; Mehde (n 154) 545–548.

Court in order to achieve an annulment of the parliamentary statute, the courts, to some extent, rephrase the statute. This also means that the administration gathers discretionary powers in cases in which the legislator wanted the administration to act in a specific and concrete way. If this recent jurisprudence will not be restricted to very specific cases, but will be generalised to a broader field of application, the fear expressed by *Ernst Forsthoff* in the early 1970s could become true, that all 'shall'-rules in administrative law could turn into 'can'-rules one day.[162]

2.6 Conclusion

This chapter aimed to demonstrate the solid position held by the principle of proportionality within German case law and academic literature, while giving due consideration to the recent turn in case law, which leaves room for critical discussion. It did so by introducing the reader to the German system of judicial review and providing a historical overview of German administrative law. This may help the reader to understand better both past and present developments of the principle of proportionality.

The historical account has shown that the principle first evolved through the interplay of academics, such as Svarez and Otto Mayer, and administrative courts, notably the Prussian Appellate Administrative Court. However, while the Nazi regime was in power, the evolution of the principle was temporarily stopped, interrupting an evolution that had taken over one hundred years. With the entry into force of the Basic Law, a new basis strengthening the notion of the *Rechtsstaat* had come into being. It is not surprising that it only took the Federal Constitutional Court around ten years to (re)invent the principle of proportionality. Since then, its application in both constitutional and administrative law terms has been widespread.

The wide application by the judiciary and general acceptance of the core of the principle in academic literature should, however, not be mistaken to imply that there is no room (or need) for change. On the contrary, the recent application of the principle to bound decisions, which by their nature put the administration in an ambiguous situation, is a worrisome turn. It has yet to be seen whether this will develop into a more general trend or whether the instances in which courts applied the principle to such decisions remain isolated. If indeed it were to become a more general trend, it would be a worrisome one. So far, the strict application of the principle of proportionality to decisions in which the administrator has not been fully bound by the legislator, has kept the courts on the right side of the divide between activism and a necessary independent control of the administration. To undermine the principle of proportionality by its broader application to bound decisions could tip this scale, which would be ill-advised.

162 Ernst Forsthoff, *Der Staat der Industriegesellschaft* (CH Beck 1971) 139.

References

Arnauld A von, 'Theorie und Methode des Grundrechtsschutzes in Europa – am Beispiels des Grundsatzes der Verhältnismäßigkeit' (2008) 1 *Europarecht-Beiheft* 41–64.

Barczak T, 'Der gebundene Verwaltungsakt unter Verhältnismäßigkeitsvorbehalt' (2014) 105 *Verwaltungsarchiv* 142–181.

Conrad H, Kleinheyer G (eds), *Carl Gottlieb Svarez – Vorträge über Recht und Staat 1791/92* (Westdt. Verlag 1960).

Dann P, 'Verfassungsgerichtliche Kontrolle gesetzgeberischer Rationalität' (2010) 49 *Der Staat* 630–646.

Danwitz T von, *Europäisches Verwaltungsrecht* (Springer 2008).

Dreier H, *Grundgesetz – Kommentar: Band I* (3rd edn, Mohr Siebeck 2013).

Erbguth W, *Allgemeines Verwaltungsrecht – mit Verwaltungsprozess – und Staatshaftungsrecht* (6th edn, Nomos 2014).

Fonk CF, 'Die konditionale Rechtsetzung in der Tradition Otto Mayers – ein antiquiertes Normstruktur- und Gesetzgebungsmodell?' (2010) *Deutsches Verwaltungsblatt* 626–633.

Forsthoff E, *Der Staat der Industriegesellschaft* (CH Beck 1971).

Grote R, 'Rule of Law, Rechtsstaat and "État de droit"' in C Starck (ed), *Constitutionalism, Universalism and Democracy – A Comparative Analysis* (Nomos 1999) 269–306.

Heinsohn S, *Der öffentlichrechtliche Grundsatz der Verhältnismäßigkeit* (Doctoral Dissertation Westfälische Wilhelms-Universität zu Münster 1997).

Heuschling L, *État de droit, Rechtsstaat, Rule of Law* (Dalloz 2002).

Hirschberg L, *Der Grundsatz der Verhältnismäßigkeit* (Otto Schwartz & Co 1981).

Hoffmann-Riem W, 'Die Klugheit der Entscheidung ruht in ihrer Herstellung – selbst bei der Anwendung von Recht' in A Scherzberg (ed), *Kluges Entscheiden – Disziplinäre Grundlagen und interdisziplinäre Verknüpfungen* (Mohr Siebeck 2006) 3–24.

—— 'Eigenständigkeit der Verwaltung' in Hoffmann-Riem W, Schmidt-Aßmann E, Voßkuhle A (eds), *Grundlagen des Verwaltungsrechts – Band I: Methoden, Maßstäbe, Aufgaben, Organisation* (2nd edn, CH Beck 2012) 677–776.

Hufen F, *Verwaltungsprozessrecht* (9th edn 2013).

Jestaedt M, 'Maßstäbe des Verwaltungshandelns' in U Erichsen, D Ehlers (eds), *Allgemeines Verwaltungsrecht* (14th edn, De Gruyter 2010) 329–378.

Klatt M, Meister M, 'Der Grundsatz der Verhältnismäßigkeit – Ein Strukturelement des globalen Konstitutionalismus' (2014), 54 *Juristische Schulung* 193–199.

Klein E, 'Konkretes Normenkontrollverfahren' in: E Benda, E Klein, O Klein (eds), *Verfassungsprozessrecht* (3rd edn, C.F. Müller 2012), 310–362.

Knill C, Becker F, 'Divergenz trotz Diffusion?: rechtsvergleichende Aspekte des Verhältnismäßigkeitsprinzip in Deutschland, Großbritannien und der Europäischen Union' (2003) 36 *Die Verwaltung* 447–481.

Kraft I, 'Der Grundsatz der Verhältnismäßigkeit im deutschen Rechtsverständnis' (2007) 1 *BDVR-Rundschreiben* 11–16.

Krumm M, 'Verwaltungsrechtsschutz gegen materielle Rechtsnormen' (2011) *Deutsches Verwaltungsblatt* 1008–1015.

Künnecke M, *Tradition and Change in Administrative Law – An Anglo-German Comparison* (Springer 2007).

Marsch N, *Subjektivierung der gerichtlichen Verwaltungskontrolle in Frankreich – Eilverfahren und Urteilsimplementation im objektiv-rechtlich geprägten Kontrollsystem* (Nomos 2011).

Maurer H, *Allgemeines Verwaltungsrecht* (18th edn, CH Beck 2011).

Mehde V, 'Die Prüfung der Verhältnismäßigkeit bei gebundenen Entscheidungen' (2014), 67 *Die Öffentliche Verwaltung* 541–548.

Merten D, 'Zur verfassungsrechtlichen Herleitung des Verhältnismäßigkeitsprinzips' in Hengstschläger J, Köck H F, Korinek K, Stern K, Truyol y Serra A (eds), *Für Staat und Recht – Festschrift für Herbert Schambeck* (Duncker & Humblot 1994) 349–379.

—— 'Verhältnismäßigkeitsgrundsatz' in D Merten, H-J Papier, *Handbuch der Grundrechte III – Allgemeine Lehren II* (C. F. Müller 2009), 517– 567.

Michael L, 'Grundfälle zur Verhältnismäßigkeit' (2001) 41 *Juristische Schulung* 764–767 and 866– 870.

Naumann K, 'Die Prüfung der Verhältnismäßigkeit im Rahmen gebundener Entscheidungen' (2011) 64 *Die Öffentliche Verwaltung* 96–104.

Nolte G, 'General Principles of German and European Administrative Law: A Historical Perspective' (1994) 57 *The Modern Law Review* 191–212.

Ossenbühl F, 'Der Grundsatz der Verhältnismäßigkeit (Übermaßverbot) in der Rechtsprechung der Verwaltungsgerichte' (1997) 19 *Juristische Ausbildung* 617– 621.

Peine FJ, *Allgemeines Verwaltungsrecht* (10th edn, CF Müller 2011).

Pieroth B, Schlink B, Kniesel M, *Polizei- und Ordnungsrecht, mit Versammlungsrecht* (7th edn, CH Beck 2012).

Pitschas R, 'Maßstäbe des Verwaltungshandelns' in: Hoffmann-Riem W, Schmidt-Aßmann E, Voßkuhle A (eds), *Grundlagen des Verwaltungsrechts – Band II: Informationsordnung, Verwaltungsverfahren, Handlungsformen* (2nd edn, CH Beck 2012) 1689–1811.

Remmert B, *Verfassungs- und verwaltungsrechtsgeschichtliche Grundlagen des Übermaßverbotes* (CF Müller Juristischer Verlag 1995).

Saurer J, *Die Globalisierung des Verhältnismäßigkeitsgrundsatzes* (2012) 51 Der Staat 3–33.

Schlink B, 'Der Grundsatz der Verhältnismäßigkeit' in Badura P, Dreier H (eds), *Festschrift 50 Jahre Bundesverfassungsgericht* (Mohr Siebeck 2001) 445–465.

Schmidt-Aßmann E; Schenk, W, 'Einleitung' in F Schoch, J-P Schneider, W Bier (eds), *Verwaltungsgerichtsordnung* (CH Beck 2014).

Schneider J-P, 'German Traditions' in M Ruffert (ed), *Administrative Law in Europe: Between Common Principles and National Traditions* (Europa Law Publishing 2013) 49–65.

Schoch F, 'Das verwaltungsbehördliche Ermessen' (2004) 26 *Juristische Ausbildung* 462–469.

Schröder M, 'Administrative Law in Germany' in Seerden R (ed), *Administrative Law in the European Union, its Member States and the United states—A Comparative Analysis* (3rd edn Intersentia 2012) 39–100.

Singh MP, *German Administrative Law in Common Law Perspective* (Springer 2001).

Stern K, 'Zur Entstehung und Ableitung des Übermaßverbots' in Badura P, Scholz R (eds), *Wege und Verfahren des Verfassungslebens – Festschrift für Peter Lerche zum 65. Geburtstag* (CH Beck 1993) 165–175.

Stolleis M, *Geschichte des offtlichen Rechts in Deutschland – Band 1: Reichspublizistik und Policeywissenschaft 1600–1800* (CH Beck 1988).

—— *Public Law in Germany 1800–1914* (Berghahn Books 2001).

—— A *History of Public Law in Germany 1914–1945* (OUP 2004).

—— *Öffentliches Recht in Deutschland: Eine Einführung in seine Geschichte – 16–21. Jahrhundert* (CH Beck 2014).

Voßkuhle A, 'Der Grundsatz der Verhältnismäßigkeit' (2007) 47 *Juristische Schulung* 429–431.

Wahl R, 'Der Grundsatz der Verhältnismäßigkeit: Ausgangslage und Gegenwartsproblematik' in Heckmann D, Schenke R P, Sydow G (eds) *Verfassungsstaatlichkeit im Wandel: Festschrift für Thomas Würtenberger zum 70. Geburtstag* (Duncker & Humblot 2013) 823–854.

Wegener BW, 'Subjective Public Rights – Historical Roots versus European and Democratic Challenges' in Pünder H, Waldhoff C (eds.), *Debates in German Public Law* (Hart 2014).

Werner F, 'Verwaltungsrecht als konkretisiertes Verfassungsrecht' (1959) *Deutsches Verwaltungsblatt* 527–533.

Wienbracke M, 'Der Verhältnismäßigkeitsgrundsatz' (2013) *Zeitschrift für das Juristische Studium* 148–155.

Wolff J, *Ausländische Staatsfonds und Staatliche Sonderrechte – Zum Phänomen 'Sovereign Wealth Funds' und zur Vereinbarkeit der Beschränkung von Unternehmensbeteiligungen mit Europarecht* (Berliner Wiss.-Verl. 2009).

3 Proportionality in French administrative law

*Yoan Sanchez**

3.1 Introduction

In France, administrative law is predominantly judge-made, evolving with solutions developed by its highest court: the Council of State (*Conseil d'État*). As such, the proportionality test is no exception to the rule. There is no legal provision providing for this general principle. While some laws refer to the idea of proportionality,[1] the principle only applies to specific areas, and the 'principle of proportionality' or the 'proportionality test' are never mentioned explicitly.[2] Consequently, case law has been the main source of development in terms of the principle of proportionality. For a long time the Council of State used this control implicitly. Times seem to be changing, however, and more recently, this court entered a new phase, embracing a new role as a true guardian of proportionality.

Although this study on proportionality will focus mainly on the case law of administrative courts, I start by making a brief reference to the case law of the Constitutional Council (*Conseil Constitutionnel*).[3] Since the decision on the 2008 *Loi relative à la rétention de sûreté*,[4] the Constitutional Council has started to perform an explicit control of proportionality. Resorting to a systematic and structured control, the judge performs the three classical

* PhD Candidate, University of Orléans. I would like to thank Catherine Haguenau-Moizard for her assistance.

1 The Charter of Environment is constitutional by nature and is applicable to all public authorities (see *Loi relative aux organismes génétiquement modifiés* (2008) rec. 313 (*Conseil Constitutionnel*) and for the Council of State (*Commune d'Annecy* 2008) rec. 322 (*Conseil d'État*). It stipulates in its article 5 that the precautionary principle requires that a public authority has to take 'proportionate and provisional measures to deal with the occurrence of the damage'.

2 It is possible to contrast the French situation with the Dutch one, particularly since the introduction of the GALA in the Dutch system (see chapter 5).

3 The Constitutional Council was created by the Constitution of the Fifth Republic (1958). Its role is to control the constitutionality of parliamentary statutes (*loi*) This control of constitutionality refers not only to the constitutional text of 1958 but also the preambles of the Constitution of 1958 and 1946, the Charter of Environment and the Déclaration des droits de l'Homme et du citoyen (1789).

4 (2008) rec. 89 (*Conseil Constitutionnel*).

checks: adequacy, necessity and proportionality.[5] Before this decision, the Constitutional Court performed merely an implicit control of proportionality.[6] For example, in 1979, the Constitutional Court had referred to the 'idea of proportionality', by stating that parliament may limit the right to strike, if it damages the continuity of public services.[7] Parliament must, however, make conciliation between these two elements, ensuring that the limitations imposed on the right to strike are not disproportionate. This evolution is important since, as I shall explain later, the Council of State and the Constitutional Council do not perform identical forms of control of proportionality.

The recent case law of the Constitutional Council demonstrates that the explicit use of a full control of proportionality is perfectly feasible in France. It is nonetheless worth noting that the formulation of the aforementioned decision of 2008 seems to be an isolated example of the use of a systematic and structured control of proportionality. In more recent cases, the Constitutional Council has used the three-step proportionality terminology (adequacy, necessity and proportionality *stricto sensu*) in the same sentence, without including it in the context of a systematic control of proportionality. To wit, in a decision of 2012, the constitutional judge stated that limitations on freedom of expression have to be 'necessary, adequate and proportionate'.[8] In this case, the Constitutional Council did not use the three-step test to control the constitutionality of the statute under analysis.[9] It is difficult to understand why the Constitutional Court has not adopted a uniform formulation of the control of proportionality. Up until now, its decisions on this matter have been unclear, and this gap has not been solved by the academic literature.[10]

Having said this, the control of proportionality suffers in France from a certain degree of ambiguity. Although the principle of proportionality is far from being an unknown instrument to the Council of State, it has been handicapped by the lack of a systematic approach. This is particularly unfortunate at a time when judges are increasingly using the control of proportionality, revealing a pragmatic approach to this control and its utility.

5 Ibid (11)–(23).

6 *Loi de modernisation sociale* (2002) rec. 49 (*Conseil Constitutionnel*) (85–86).

7 *Loi modifiant les dispositions de la loi n° 74–696 du 7 août 1974 relatives à la continuité du service public de la radio et de la télévision en cas de cessation concertée du travail* (1979) rec. 33 (*Conseil Constitutionnel*).

8 *Loi visant à réprimer la contestation de l'existence des génocides reconnus par la loi (2012)* rec. 139 (*Conseil Constitutionnel*).

9 See also *M. Laurent A et autres* (2013) n° 2013–302 QPC [4–6) JORF 6186. The 'question prioritaire de constitutionnalité' ('QPC') or, literally, question with constitutional priority, was introduced in 2008, allowing claimants to ask a preliminary constitutional question to the Constitutional Council.

10 G Chetard, 'La proportionnalité de la répression dans la jurisprudence du Conseil constitutionnel' (2013) *Révue de Science Criminelle et de Droit Pénal* 51.

3.2 History and overview of the use of the proportionality review by the Council of State

3.2.1 An unacknowledged control

Proportionality review in French administrative law is often traced back to the *Benjamin* case.[11] In *Benjamin*, the mayor of the city of Nevers had banned a conference organised by René Benjamin, a journalist and a public speaker with extreme-right sympathies whose writings were highly controversial. As a response to the conference organized by Benjamin, a number of trade unions and left-wing parties called for demonstrations against his presence in town. In view of the imminent conflict, it was argued at the time that the presence of the aforementioned journalist in the town of Nevers could have threatened public order. In an attempt to avoid further trouble, the mayor decided to use his public order powers to ban the planned conference. René Benjamin decided to challenge this decision.

In the abovementioned case, the Council of State considered that the mayor had to reconcile the requirements of public order with freedom of assembly. To this end, he could have taken other measures to allow the conference to take place, while ensuring public order. This type of 'liberal' reasoning was, however, not really widespread at the time. Rather, the desire to reconcile apparently opposed requirements had already been expressed in earlier case law. In the decision *Abbé Olivier* of 1909, the mayor of the town of Sens took a decision banning all religious events on the town's streets, notably during religious funerals.[12] The Council of State specified that the statute authorising the mayor to impose such restrictions for the protection of public order requires that 'local habits and traditions be respected as much as possible and to restrict them *only when required by the need to maintain public order*'. As the decision was finally annulled on the grounds of abuse of power, the highest administrative court stated clearly the obligation to adapt administrative measures to the risk level for public order. In a word, public bodies should ensure that the measures are proportionate. The exact same reasoning is followed in the *Benjamin* decision. The public authority is required to reconcile public order with freedom.[13]

The judicial source of the proportionality test cannot be ignored when studying its development, use and formulation. Indeed, one of the key

11 *Benjamin*, (1933) rec. 541. This link is made by a lot of authors. See, P Serrand, 'Le contrôle juridictionnel de l'administration à travers la jurisprudence récente', (2012) 4 *Révue de Droit Public* 901, 916; J Petit, 'Les ordonnances *Dieudonné*: séparer le bon grain de l'ivraie', (2014) *L'Actualité Juridique: Droit Administratif* 866; J-P Costa 'Le principe de proportionnalité dans la jurisprudence du Conseil d'État' (1988) *L'Actualité Juridique: Droit Administratif* 434. For a general survey of the development of the proportionality test, see chapter 2.

12 *Abbé Olivier* (1909) rec. 181 (*Conseil d'État*).

13 In *Abbé Olivier*, the case was about the freedom of conscience and religion.

characteristics of the proportionality test in France is that it is not explicitly applied by the judge. The judge never explains the steps followed to decide why a measure is proportional or not. In addition, French administrative courts do not explain in detail their concrete use of the proportionality test. There is, for example, no distinction between the control of the adequacy – capacity of the measure to fulfil the purpose assigned to it, of the necessity, i.e., to ensure that the public authority could not achieve the aim by resorting to less restrictive means for the rights and freedoms of individuals, and proportionality *stricto sensu*, whether an administrative action or decision is excessive in relation to the purpose.[14]

The lack of explanation is common in French judicial reasoning and decisions are often concise. In both *Abbé Olivier* and *Benjamin*, there is no reference whatsoever to 'proportionality' or to the need for the measure to be 'proportionate'. Such a control results from the method adopted by the administrative courts, which has been described as being conciliatory.[15] Since the court must ensure that such measures are conciliatory and not excessive, the court will verify whether the administrative action was proportionate. This has been formulated 'in a negative way' since several judgments show that courts are rather willing to verify whether the measure was not 'disproportionate.'[16] Until recently, this was the only clear reference to the idea of proportionality.

3.2.2 Acknowledging the control

Often criticised for its laconic brevity, the Council of State has made some changes in its case law in the last few years. In the past, the decisions of the Council of State were meant to be brief, and consequently contained little explanation. This drafting peculiarity explains in part (but not fully) why the administrative courts did not resort explicitly to the proportionality test. This hesitation can also be explained by the desire to keep the court's reasoning secret so as to avoid criticism or the need to justify some decisions fully. However, more recently, the reasoning in the judgments of the administrative courts has tended to be clearer and more educational.[17] This trend has also influenced the formulation of the proportionality test.

14 This three-step definition was first used in Germany. See H Maurer, *Droit administratif Allemand* (LGDJ 1995), 248–249; P Moor, 'Systématique et illustration du principe de proportionnalité', *Mélanges Michel Fromont* (Presses Universitaires de Strasbourg 2001) 318–341 (on Swiss law).

15 C Eisenmann, *Cours de droit administratif* (vol I, LGDJ 1982) 121–122; C Debbasch and F Colin, *Droit administratif*, (10e éd, Economica 2011) 26.

16 For an example, see *Mme Duvignères* (2002) rec. 463 (*Conseil d'État*).

17 D Baranger 'Retour sur Dieudonné' (2014) *Revue Française de Droit Administratif* 525, in which the author states that, under the influence of the Martin report (April 2012) on the possible reforms on the writing of decisions by administrative judges, 'the Council of State nowadays tries to draft longer and much more articulated decisions'. See also B Stirn 'Panorama: le mouvement de réforme de la justice administrative' (2012) *L'Actualité Juridique: Droit Administratif* 1193.

Jacques Petit remarks that since 2011, 'the triple test . . . has entered the case law of the Council of State.'[18] In the case *Association for promoting image and others* concerning biometric passports, the court noted that 'measures prescribed by the order are not *suitable, necessary and proportionate*.'[19] Since then, the administrative courts have repeated the tri-partite reasoning of adequacy, necessity and proportionality *stricto sensu* in the formulation of the control of proportionality.

In the recent interim decision *Dieudonné n 1* of 9 January 2014, the Council of State has restated that 'limitations to the exercise of fundamental freedoms for the protection of public order must be *necessary, adapted and proportionate*.'[20] But while this formulation is gaining ground, it has so far not been included in all decisions where the proportionality of administrative measures was explicitly or implicitly assessed. In another interim decision, *Mr C* of 26 July 2014, the Council of State specified that:

> the respect for the freedom of expression, that has the character of a fundamental freedom, must be reconciled with the protection of public order and it is up to the relevant police authority . . . under the control of the administrative court to take measures to prevent such disorders including, where appropriate, the prohibition of the event, if such a measure is the only one likely to maintain public order.[21]

While the idea of proportionality is found in the requirement of conciliation, the relevant terminology and the three-step approach appear to be missing from the reasoning of the court.

The mentioned semantic evolution has not meant there was a revolution in the use of the proportionality test. The Council of State still refuses to articulate its control around the three proportionality steps that are used in other jurisdictions. In most cases, the court requires the administration to apply the principle of proportionality formulated in three distinct *stages*, but without controlling the decision as a whole on its proportionality.[22] Even when the Council of State applies EU law or the ECHR, French administrative courts do not follow explicitly the reasoning of the relevant courts.[23]

Up until now, the explicit use of the proportionality test by the administrative court is more a matter of communication than a methodological revolution. This is evidenced by a number of points. First, the fact that the court does not

18 J Petit (No 10) 870.

19 (2011) rec. 505 (*Conseil d'État*). See M Guyomar et X Domino, 'Le passeport biométrique au contrôle: empreintes et clichés' (2012) *L'Actualité Juridique: Droit Administratif* 35 (emphasis added by the author).

20 (2014) *L'Actualité Juridique: Droit Administratif* 866 (*Conseil d'État*) (4) (emphasis added by the author).

21 (2014) req. n° 383091 (*Conseil d'État*) 4.

22 See M Guyomar et X Domino, 'Le passeport biométrique au contrôle: empreintes et clichés', (2012) *L'Actualité Juridique: Droit Administratif* 35. Guyomar and Domino highlight the influence of European and comparative law on the administrative courts to explain the semantic evolution of the proportionality test.

23 See *Section française de l'observatoire international des prisons* (2014) req. n° 369692 (*Conseil d'État*) (on art 8 of the ECHR); *Mme B* (2011) req. n° 329439 (*Conseil d'État*) (freedom of movement of persons).

systematically use this expression each time it resorts to a control of proportionality, reveals that this concept does not frame its control. Second, the fact that the court avoids referring to the standard three-step test, as opposed to the Constitutional Council,[24] is evidence that the administrative court seems to use the three stages of proportionality merely on an indicative basis. Finally, the reference to this sentence shows the rather limited impact that both European law and comparative law have on the case law of the administrative court.[25] Although the reference to proportionality reveals the importance of these two areas of law for French administrative law, the foreign origin of the control still triggers a certain degree of reticence in the Council of State. Therefore, this court seems to employ the expression because of 'an obligation' (EU law) or of 'a legal trend' (comparative law), without actually including a systematic control of proportionality in its judicial practice.

Urban planning has been, however, the exception to this implicit control of proportionality. Since the *Commune de Levallois-Perret* case,[26] the Council of State formulates the control of public utility of an urban development project in three stages. It then relies on each step to exercise its control. When controlling the public utility of an urban project, the court must ensure that:

> '[the project] serves a purpose of general interest, that the public authority would not have been able to complete the transaction in the same way without resorting to compulsory purchase . . . and, finally, that the damage to private property rights, the financial costs and, where applicable, the disadvantages of a social or economic nature, caused by the project are not excessive in view of the interest of the project.'[27]

While the first step that emerges from this case is control over the general interest of the project, and thus refers to the ground of abuse of power,[28] the other two are similar to a review of necessity and proportionality *stricto sensu*.

The control of necessity in the case of compulsory purchases and urban planning can be explained by the need to verify whether 'the public authority had been able to complete the transaction in the same way without resorting

24 See introduction.

25 See M Guyomar et X Domino, 'Le passeport biométrique au contrôle: empreintes et clichés' (2012) *L'Actualité Juridique: Droit Administratif* 35.

26 (2012) *RDI* 2012.617 (*Conseil d'État*).

27 For an earlier but perhaps less clear example, see *Fédération Alto et a.* (2009) req. n° 311831 (*Conseil d'État*). For an example with all steps clearly stated but not included in the main considerations, see *Collectif contre les nuisances du TGV de Chasseneuil, du Poitou et de Migne-Auxances* (2011) req n° 330256 (*Conseil d'État*).

This three-step control had already been resorted to by the *Commissaire du Gouvernement* Dondoux in the *Malardel* (1979) rec. 294 (*Conseil d'État*) 296–297, 299.

28 See R Houstiou, 'Expropriation: précisions sur la mise en oeuvre de la théorie du bilan' (2012) *RDI* 617. However, the question of the link between the control of misuse of power and control of the fit/match can be applied. For example, see P Moor (n 14) 332. See also the *Dame Veuve Borderie* (1964) rec. 157 (*Conseil d'État*) where the lack of 'a match' between the decision and the aim was an argument used by the court to conclude that there was abuse of power.

to compulsory purchase'. This means that the court must look for alternatives that will have a smaller impact on the rights of individuals. Here, three aspects must be identified. First, the necessity control exists only to protect the right to property and *not* other rights or freedoms. In addition, the alternative measure can be chosen only if would avoid the use of compulsory purchase entirely, i.e., if it does not have any impact on property rights. This means *a contrario* that it does not concern a project that would simply reduce the number of properties to be compulsorily purchased. The choice of alternative measures is therefore reduced. It was possible to have some hesitance about this solution while reading, for example, the reasoning of the Council of State in the case *Féderation Alto et autres* of 2009. When deciding on the legality of an order of 26 October 2007, which recognised the public utility of a planned high-speed rail link, the court specified that it was not clear from the (available) evidence that the use of Pendolino trains on the existing railways, rather than the planned new rail connection, would produce *similar results without requiring a higher number of compulsory purchases.*[29] This statement makes us wonder whether the alternative project – by allowing a reduction in the number of compulsory purchase orders, while carried out under the same conditions – would have triggered the decision that the original project lacked public utility.

Finally, the third point concerns the control of necessity in *Commune de Levallois-Perret*, where the Council of State stated that it would favour an alternative scheme if it avoided all compulsory purchases while delivering 'similar results'. This rather vague requirement seems to refer back to the advantages of the scheme. In the *Fédération Alto* case, the 'similar results' of the scheme were clearly mentioned. This formulation expresses the same idea contained in the expression 'similar conditions', even though the latter appears wider and seems to include, if necessary, the actual means necessary to complete the project. In any event, the combined reading of the *Commune de Levallois-Perret* and *Fédération Alto* cases seems to show that the court controls the 'fit' of the alternative project, i.e., its efficiency and even effectiveness, through a control of similar conditions. The court may not perform a direct control of the fit of the original scheme, but it reviews instead the fit of the alternative scheme.[30]

With regard to the control of proportionality *stricto sensu*, this is carried out using cost-benefit analysis. For the court, the aim is to annul the schemes whose disadvantages are manifestly excessive in comparison with their advantages.

Still, one should not overstate the significance of the aforementioned cases. The review of the necessity and proportionality *stricto sensu* of the projects submitted to the court has not expanded since then, as we shall see later.

29 *Fédération Alto et al.* (n° 27). Emphasis added by the author.

30 Based on this, it is possible to argue that the similarities with the German system are gradually increasing: the first step of the control on *Commune de Levallois-Perret* is close to the control of the legitimacy of the aim in the German proportionality test.

3.3 Scope of the proportionality test

The proportionality test is usually viewed as a liberal method of review of administrative decisions. It is often stated that it was developed in the area of freedoms, and police measures that may affect them (3.3.1.). However, the Council of State has extended the proportionality test to other areas, despite the absence of explicit mention (3.3.2.).

3.3.1 The traditional field: the protection of rights and freedoms

As mentioned above, the proportionality test has been originally applied to the field of police measures so as to protect rights and freedoms as seen in the *Abbé Olivier*, *Benjamin* and *Dieudonné* cases.[31] As police powers interfere with the exercise of civil liberties, the proportionality test allows, in principle, upholding the maxim dear to the *Commissaire du Gouvernement*[32] Corneille: 'Freedom is the principle, police limitation is the exception.'[33] In the *Benjamin* case, the judge quashes the mayor's decision because banning the conference was not the only option. Public order could have been protected with less coercive means. The necessity of the decision is the main question for the court. The police authority forgot freedom in the name of law and order, when it should have remembered to reconcile both of them.

The necessity of the measure has been analysed in the *Dieudonné* judgment of 9 January 2014.[34] The facts are quite similar to those of *Benjamin*. In the *Dieudonné* case, there were question as to whether it was lawful for a mayor to cancel the show of a comedian whose jokes could be considered an incitement to hatred and discrimination. In contrast to *Benjamin*, the court concluded in this case, that the police authority could cancel the show in view of 'the risks that the show could create for the public order.'[35] On this matter, the court seemed ready to accept the justification of the public authority to cancel the show on the basis that it could lead to 'serious risks of disturbances to the public order that would be very difficult for the police to control.'[36] The *Dieudonné* decision is, however, questionable with regard to this

31 *Abbé Olivier* (n 12); *Benjamin* (n 11); *Dieudonné* (n 20).

32 The *commissaire du gouvernement*, now *rapporteur public* (since 2009), is an administrative judge who helps the court to reach a decision in a case, by proposing a solution in what it is called '*conclusions*' or 'opinions'. However, the *rapporteur public* takes no part in the final judgment. Considering the concision of the judgment of administrative courts, the mentioned *conclusions* are very helpful to understand the reasoning of the court as they are often followed by judges giving the final judgment.

33 *Conclusions* on *Baldy* (1917) rec. p 637 (*Conseil d'État*).

34 *Dieudonné* (n 1).

35 Ibid (6).

36 Ibid (5).

very same point.[37] In this case, the Council of State made a very limited use of the proportionality test and its requirements. The aim of the proportionality test is to reconcile the protection of freedom and the maintenance of public order. The fact that it might be 'very difficult' for the public authority to safeguard public order may be taken into consideration when it comes to the selection of a police measure but it cannot justify a prohibition.[38] Moreover, the court itself seems to have realised the weaknesses of its reasoning. In its subsequent decisions of 10 and 11 January 2014, the court allowed a comparable ban on the grounds that 'the establishment of police forces is not sufficient to prevent harm *of this nature* to the public order such as . . . incitement to hatred and racial discrimination.'[39] When the breaches of public order consist of verbal expressions of prejudice, the use of police force might not be able to guarantee public order. In this context, the show might have to be cancelled on the grounds that no further action was appropriate, that is to say, effective. The difference with *Benjamin* resides, here, in the fact that in the first case the threat to public order would not be caused by 'mere words' but mainly by public demonstration around the conference.

The Council of State has been able to apply the proportionality test to protect a number of rights and freedoms, such as the freedom of assembly,[40] freedom of trade and commerce,[41] freedom of religion and belief,[42] and labour rights.[43] The judge has progressively extended the application of the proportionality test to ensure that the deportation of aliens does not infringe their right to a normal family life.[44] We can also include in this list the principle of equality that allows administrative authorities to treat differently persons who are in different situations.[45] However, it should be noted that the principle of proportionality can only be applied if the right or freedom in question is not absolute. By contrast, when a right or freedom is absolute, such conciliation is not possible since any measure must yield to that right or freedom.[46]

37 For other analyses of this case, see B Seiller, 'La Censure a toujours tort', (2014) *L'Actualité Juridique: Droit Administratif* 129; C Broyelle, 'Retour sur l'affaire Dieudonné', (2014) *L'Actualité Juridique: Droit Administratif* 473, C Broyelle, 'Retour sur Dieudonné' (2014) *Revue Française de Droit Administratif* 521; D Baranger 'Retour sur Dieudonné' (2014) *Revue Française de Droit Administratif* 525.

38 See J Petit Ibid.

39 *Dieudonné* (n 20) (2014) *L'Actualité Juridique: Droit Administratif* 2014 866 (*Conseil d'État*) 9.

40 *Maugendre* (1997) rec. 826 (*Conseil d'État*).

41 *Daudignac* (1951) rec. 362 (*Conseil d'État*).

42 *Abbé Olivier* (n 12).

43 *Ministre du travail, de l'emploi et de la santé c Comité d'entreprise de la société Caterpillar* (2012) *L'Actualité Juridique: Droit Administratif* 385 (*Conseil d'État*). *Dehaene* (1950) rec. 426 (*Conseil d'État*).

44 *Belgacem* (1991) rec. 152 (*Conseil d'État*).

45 *Villemain* (2002) rec. 229 (*Conseil d'État*).

46 For example, when human dignity is at stake, see *Commune de Morsang-sur-Orge* (1995) rec. 372 (*Conseil d'État*).

The application of the proportionality test has not been limited to police powers. Another relevant field is the limitation of the right to strike. While the French executive was granted the right to limit the right to strike of civil servants, this limitation must be justified by the maintenance of public order.[47] Therefore, if the exercise of the right to strike may cause a serious public order disturbance, the government may prohibit its exercise altogether. This possibility has recently been extended to civil servants employed in public service that meets 'the basic needs of the country.'[48] In other situations, the public authority is allowed to impose preconditions for the exercise of the right to strike but it may not prohibit its exercise.[49] The Council of State has decided, for example, in two cases in 1981 and 2003, that a general and absolute prohibition of the right to strike, regarding public servants that had little contact with the public, was illegal.[50]

From the above-described evolution in the protection of rights and freedoms, it can be concluded that the proportionality test originated primarily from a spirit of conciliation between public order and the exercise of freedom. However, when a public authority is required to protect both requirements, this does not prevent the court from allowing decisions based entirely on the respect of law and order. Even the most radical limitation of freedoms and rights may be permitted in certain cases. It is, nonetheless, not uncommon to see an administrative court overturn a decision considered to be excessive. This has gradually occurred in new areas, revealing a gradual expansion of the application of the proportionality test.

3.3.2 New areas: urban planning and disciplinary sanctions

More recently, the proportionality test has been applied in fields beyond the traditional conciliation of public order and freedom. Administrative courts have extended it to the areas of urban planning and administrative sanctions against civil servants.

3.3.2.1 Urban planning

The first area in which the proportionality test was extended is planning, including control of the utility of a project. Since its 1971 *Ville nouvelle Est* decision, the Council of State controls the content of the proposed scheme, and weighs up the costs against the benefits of a project in order to determine

47 *Dehaene* (1950) rec. 426 (*Conseil d'État*).

48 *Fédération Force Ouvrière Énergie et Mines et autres* (2013) rec. 94 (*Conseil d'État*) 96.

49 *Fédération des syndicats chrétiens de cheminots* (1964) rec. 484 (*Conseil d'État*).

50 *Fédération CFTC des personnels de l'environnement, de l'équipement et du logement, des transports et du tourisme* (1981) rec. 45 (*Conseil d'État*). See also *Mme Aguillon*, (2003) rec. 497 (*Conseil d'État*): quashing of a requisition order of an entire health service while the mayor should have limited these orders to some persons of the service.

its utility.[51] If the economic, social or environmental costs are clearly excessive in relation to the benefits of the project, then the order stating the public interest of the project will be annulled on the grounds of illegality.

In the 1970s, those decisions were innovative for two reasons: first, due to the implementation of the so-called cost-benefit analysis, which allowed the Council of State to introduce a control over the merits of the project; second, due to the balance of the elements of a specific case. This technique allowed the court to innovate by explicitly weighing all the pros and cons. In 'disclosing' its reasoning, the court made an educational move for the benefit of the decision-maker. While this is an encouraging development, few declarations of public utility have been quashed as a result of this apparent innovation. In fact, although the technique has allowed the court to delve into administrative decision-making, the court has remained cautious. This position has been regretted by a number of scholars.[52] The more extensive a project is, the less likely it is that it will be quashed on the grounds of the aforementioned cost-benefit analysis. In recent years, only small projects were prohibited through the use of this test.[53]

The idea of implementing a cost-benefit analysis was to identify, first of all, the advantages of public projects, not only for the public interest, but also for private interests. In the case *Ville Nouvelle-Est,* the *Commissaire du Gouvernement* Braibant stated in his opinion that 'private interests that benefit from the project carry more weight in the decision-making process than the public interests that may be compromised by it'.[54] This is particularly the case when the project leads to the appreciation of surrounding lands that are the property of private owners.

After having identified the benefits of a public project, the court continues by weighing the components that might be impacted adversely by the administrative decision, such as environmental data, financial costs for the public body, private property rights and social costs. The concept of 'social

51 *Ministre de l'équipement et du logement c. Fédération de défense des personnes concernées par le projet actuellement dénommé 'Ville Nouvelle Est'* (1971) rec. 409 (*Conseil d'État*). We will just refer to that field with regard to the cost-benefit analysis. For a study of the use of this control in planning decisions, see *Grands Arrêts de la Jurisprudence Administrative* (hereinafter 'GAJA') (Dalloz, 19e ed, 2013) 599.

52 See B Seiller, 'Pour un contrôle de la légalité extrinsèque des déclarations d'utilité publique', (2003) *Revue Française de Droit Administratif* 1472; P Janin, 'La jurisprudence du bilan est-elle toujours utile?' (2011) 195 *Droit de l'environnement* 318; Wachsmann, 'Un bilan du bilan en matière d'expropriation. La jurisprudence Ville Nouvelle Est, trente ans après', in *Gouverner, administrer, juger. Liber amicorum Jean Waline* (Dalloz 2002, 733–748). See also the observations in the GAJA (n 51) 596–599.

53 See observations in *Ville Nouvelle Est* (see above) 419. For administrative decisions that were quashed because they were too costly: the decision to build an airfield in a very little town (*Grassin* 1973) rec. 598 (*Conseil d'État*). Sometimes, the decision quashed has great importance: see *Association interdépartementale et intercommunale pour la protection du lac de Sainte-Croix, des lacs et sites du Verdon*, (2006) rec. 332 (*Conseil d'État*) (quashing of a decision to build a high-voltage power line because of the excessive impact on the environment). On this case, see M-F Delhoste, 'La théorie du bilan et la protection de l'environnement' (2006) *Revue Française de Droit Administratif* 990.

54 *Ville Nouvelle-Est* (n° 53) (419).

costs' has been broadly interpreted and can include, for instance, the adverse impact on a monument.[55] The court can add to the list of disadvantages the adverse impact on 'other public interests'. This was the case in *Société civile Sainte Marie de l'Assomption*, where the court was asked to check the legality of a project concerning a new highway, the building of which would compromise the functioning of the only psychiatric hospital in the area, even though it was privately owned.[56]

Once this double weighing is completed, the judge shall weigh advantages against disadvantages. Should the latter be manifestly 'heavier', the court will annul the declaration of public utility. This methodology explains why courts tend to annul smaller projects more easily. In large projects, the interests embodied in these projects are smaller and the costs for the public administration, notably financial, are larger, especially when compared with the local character of the public authority that initiates the process. This is clearly evidenced by the case *Association contre l'autoroute Transchablaisienne*, in which the Council of State reviewed the legality of 35 km of a new motorway to meet the needs of estimated daily traffic of 10,000 vehicles a day for a cost of 2.6 billion francs. There, the court stated that 'in light of the estimated traffic, the financial cost must be regarded to have exceeded the interest of the project and to have subtracted it from public interest.'[57] In this case, the court did not even analyse whether the environmental costs of the project would be excessive since the financial costs of the project were themselves disproportionate in relation to the potential benefits for the traffic in the area.

We should, however, distinguish between the proportionality test over the control of public utility and cost-benefit analysis. As mentioned above, the court controls the proportionality of the interference with rights before turning to the balance of interests. Thus, in a case of compulsory purchase, the court will control the requirement of necessity by checking whether the public authority that owned the land would carry out the project under the same conditions. This type of control ensures that the administration runs a project effectively, without interfering with property rights.[58] However, if avoiding a compulsory purchase does not ensure that the project under analysis is executed under equivalent conditions, then the court will maintain the declaration of public utility. Controlling the cost-benefit analysis reveals a proportionality test *stricto sensu*. The court, acknowledging that the administration does not have any other options, evaluates the project to assert whether it is

55 Ibid. In his conclusions, the *Commissaire du Gouvernement* Guy Braibant included in the social costs the impact on the environment. More recently, with the development of new instruments to protect the environment, this consideration is no longer analysed together with social costs, but is treated separately.

56 (1972) rec. 657 (*Conseil d'État*).

57 Association contre le projet de l'autoroute Transchablaisienne (1997) rec. 121 (*Conseil d'État*).

58 *Consorts Metayer* (1987) rec. 121 (*Conseil d'État*), *Fédération Alto* (n 27); *Collectif contre les nuisances du TGV de Chasseneuil, du Poitou et de Migne-Auxances* (n 27).

not too costly, in the broad sense, that is to say, excessive in relation to its usefulness. This line of reasoning is obvious in the *Commune de Levallois-Perret* decision discussed above.[59]

More recently, the control of the necessity of a declaration of public utility has acquired a new facet: the precautionary principle. The Council of State relies on the new constitutional status given to that principle by the Charter of the Environment.[60] It reviews urban planning projects as regards the precautionary principle independently from the aforementioned balance of interests. The precautionary principle was not previously ignored by the judge but it was included in the cost-benefit analysis.[61] Conversely, in the decision *Association la coordination interrégionale Stop THT et autres* of 12 April 2013, the Council of State controlled the respect of the precautionary principle autonomously.[62] If the principle is not respected, the declaration of public utility is annulled. The court proceeds in three stages: first, the court checks for the existence of a risk of serious and irreversible damage to the environment, then it ensures that all the formal requirements have been complied with, and finally that 'considering, on the one hand, the plausibility and severity of the risk and on the other hand, the interest of the scheme, the safety precautions responsible for avoiding the occurrence of such damage, are neither insufficient nor excessive'.[63]

Urban planning projects respect the precautionary principle when they fulfil two requirements: first, the administrative measures contained must be adequate in the sense of 'sufficient'. The *rapporteur public* in the case *Association coordination interrégionale Stop THT et autres* explained that this does not mean that the project has no risks, but that the administrative measures are meant to 'help reduce the risk' and bring it to a collectively acceptable level.[64] In addition, the measures must be adequate in the sense of effective. The second requirement is that the measures are not 'excessive'. This means that the steps taken to ensure compliance with the precautionary principle are not too financially costly when compared with the importance of the project.

59 *Commune de Levallois-Perret* (n 23).

60 See the growing impact of the precautionary principle in the case *Association du Quartier les Hauts de Choiseul* (2010) rec. 333 (*Conseil d'État*). See C Denizeau 'Principe de précaution et droit de l'urbanisme' (2012) *Revue Française de Droit Administratif* 864; S Gilbert 'Principe de précaution et déclaration d'utilité publique' (2013) *AJDI* 531. Before that, the principle was referred to in a statute of 2 February 1995. This statute imposed the proportionality of precautionary measures with regard to their economic cost.

61 *Association intercommunale 'Morbihan sous très haute tension'* (1999) req. n° 184268 (*Conseil d'État*). See also the *conclusions* of Alexandre Lallet in the case *Association coordination interrégionale Stop THT et autres* (2013) rec. 61 (*Conseil d'État*).

62 *Association coordination interrégionale Stop THT et autres* (*ibid*); X Domino et A Bretonneau, 'Principe de précaution et théorie du bilan: mille plateaux' (2013) *L'Actualité Juridique: Droit Administratif* 1046; A Van Lang 'L'application du principe de précaution à la déclaration d'utilité publique' (2013) *Revue de Droit Immobilier* 305.

63 *Ibid* (67).

64 *Ibid* (83).

The choice of the measure by the public authority must be made after a cost-benefit analysis of each decision, so as to 'retain the precautionary measures that offer the best cost-benefit analysis or for incorrigible pessimists, the least bad balance.'[65] Therefore, the court controls the alternative measures that ensure compliance with the precautionary principle.[66]

It is too early to say whether, in the context of the precautionary principle, the court will engage in a review of the proportionality of the measures in the strict sense, that is to say, whether the court shall check that, while the alternative measures are not better, those selected do not impact the project adversely, in terms of their interest for the environment.[67] Once the project is found to respect the precautionary principle, the court reviews the cost-benefit of the whole scheme, incorporating the data resulting from the review of the precautionary principle. These are not considered as a benefit for the project: the precautionary measures appear in the balance of interests as a cost because they impose a financial burden on the project. Hence, it is possible to conclude from the *Stop THT* decision that the precautionary principle may not be on the side of the benefits but it will be regarded as an element that can 'reduce the environmental disadvantages of the project which are listed as costs for the project.'[68]

The Council of State has extended the proportionality test to a complex area and has had to resort to a slightly different method. In the area of urban planning, the Council of State has managed to adapt the binary logic of public order versus freedom and to transform it into a 'polycentric' logic. However, this logic has not 'contaminated' other new centres of proportionality in France, such as disciplinary proceedings, where the logic remains mainly binary.

3.3.3 Disciplinary sanctions

The control of the proportionality of disciplinary sanctions in the civil service was inaugurated in 1978 by the *Lebon* case.[69] However, it is difficult to identify this control just by reading the judgment. The terms 'disproportionate' or 'excessive measures' do not appear in the decision of the Council of

65 Ibid (84). The importance of the public interest has an impact on the level of rights infringement by a public authority that the court is willing to tolerate (83). Here, the balance is about the necessity of the decision, not its proportionality in the narrow sense.

66 Ibid (69).

67 We have mentioned that the cost-benefit analysis is the control of proportionality in the strict sense. But when it is used at the stage of the control of the precautionary principle, this is different. The control of the precautionary principle and of the public utility of a planning decision are two related, but distinct, operations. They have two different objects. See A Bouveresse, 'Du bon usage du principe de précaution' (2013) *RTDE* 880: this scholar explains why it is possible to consider the control of the precautionary principle as the second step of the proportionality test. See Alexandre Lallet (n 64).

68 *Stop THT* (n 61) (63).

69 (1978) rec. 245 (*Conseil d'État*).

State. These terms seem to be implicit in the wording of the court, which stated that 'by determining, on the basis of the facts, the compulsory retirement of Mr. Lebon, the rector has taken a decision that is not vitiated by a manifest error'. The Council of State considered in this case that the sanction was proportionate. In this decision, we can identify an application of the proportionality test since the court checks whether the administrative authority has imposed an adequate sanction that meets a factual situation described as 'misconduct'. The sanction has been applied 'on the basis of these facts', which can be interpreted in the sense that the sanction was justified by the facts, and is therefore proportional. The extreme seriousness of the facts justified the application of the most severe sanction, which was chosen by the administrative authority. In contrast to *Lebon*, in the *Vinolay* case, a member of a local agricultural chamber was dismissed because of his delay in sending a report to the ministry.[70] There, the Council of State agreed that the facts constituted a fault but that the sanction applied – in this case the most severe sanction available – would have implied manifest error. The court stated that the error made by the civil servant 'could not legally justify a dismissal without [the presence of] manifest error'. The seriousness of the facts was not sufficient to justify such a sanction. In other words, the sanction was too severe with regard to the error committed by the civil servant.

The review of administrative sanctions reveals another side of the control of the Council of State, one that demonstrates that the entire review of the Council of State is permeated with the idea of proportionality. While judicial review is presented as a way of protecting individuals against arbitrary and excessive decisions of the state,[71] the control of proportionality has also been used by courts to sanction the leniency of public bodies. In this case, it is not a question of excessively limiting rights or freedoms, but to regard as illegal an act that is insufficient and that does not allow correct functioning of the public service. This is particularly clear with regard to the review of hospital services' decisions.

In 2010, an administrative court considered in the case *Assistance publique – Hôpitaux de Paris* that the sanction imposed by the administration was illegal because it was not severe enough.[72] In this case, a childcare assistant on probation was punished by a two-month suspension for an error in medication given to an infant that resulted in his death. The sanction meted out by a disciplinary committee was judged insufficient by the hospital. The Council of State decided that 'considering the seriousness of the errors that were committed by Miss L and the consequences that these facts may have had on the hospital's mission of public service', the committee 'had compromised

70 (1978) rec. 315 (*Conseil d'État*).

71 See chapter 2 on Germany and the historical roots of the principle of proportionality.

72 (2010) rec. 826 (*Conseil d'État*); R Bonnefont 'Contentieux disciplinaire hospitalier: quand la gravité des conséquences de la faute l'emporte sur les circonstances atténuantes' (2010) *L'Actualité Juridique: Droit Administratif* 2329.

its appreciation of the facts by a manifest error' by not choosing the most severe sanction, i.e., the dismissal of Miss L. It is important to emphasize two aspects of this decision.

First, the decision, *Assistance publique – Hôpitaux de Paris*, indeed reflects a control of proportionality. As noted by Rémi Bonnefont, the court had to decide whether there was 'a manifest lack of proportionality between the error committed [by Miss L] and the sanction inflicted.'[73] The expression 'lack of proportionality' does not mean excessive but sufficient in this case. The court had to inquire whether the sanction was sufficient in view of the fact; it was not. Such assessments are performed in view of both the sanction and the seriousness of the error. The decision that the sanction was not sufficient meant that the fault had not been assessed correctly. By linking both components – seriousness of the fault and gravity of the sanction – the court checked the proportionality of the decision. In addition, one should note that before this decision, administrative courts were able to carry out a similar control by assessing only the seriousness of the fault. In the case *Centre hospitalier général de Toulon*, the Council of State specified that by lowering the sanction 'the review committee has underestimated the errors committed by Mr X', and that 'this misjudgement created a manifest error in the assessment of the seriousness of the facts blamed on the party'.[74] The sanction is indeed insufficient because of the inappropriate appreciation of the seriousness of the fault.

Second, the control of the lack of proportionality expresses a wish to safeguard the good functioning of the public service. The court notes this clearly in the case *Assistance publique – Hôpitaux de Paris*. If the sanction is not sufficient, it is due to the inappropriate appreciation of the seriousness of the facts and of the consequences that the fault will have on the hospital's mission of pursuing the public interest.[75]

Often presented as a method to avoid the excesses of public administration, the control of proportionality is used in the mentioned case to mitigate the leniency of the administration. The control of the proportionality of an administrative decision is not simply the control of 'the excess', it is the implementation of the principle of proportionality, in favour or against the citizen.[76] This specific use of the principle of proportionality relates more to the 'user of the tool' than the tool itself. The Council of State as the guardian of legality, and also as the guardian of good administration, has conferred an additional dimension to the principle of proportionality. While this concept of the proportionality test might sound strange to lawyers from other jurisdictions, this case law has not led to significant debates, meaning that this dimension of the proportionality control is accepted without controversy.

73 Ibid 2331.
74 (1986) rec. 675 (*Conseil d'État*).
75 *Assistance publique – Hôpitaux de Paris* (n 74).
76 M Guibal 'De la proportionnalité' (1978) *L'Actualité Juridique: Droit Administratif* 477.

Finally, it is important to note that the proportionality test is applied in a unique way in the 'administrative sanction-fault' balance when the court reviews the dismissal of employees protected by law, such as union representatives. Although cases brought by an employee against an employer are matters for the civil courts, dismissal of protected employees must be brought before the administrative courts because such dismissals must be authorised by the public administration. The court has applied the proportionality test in this type of case. This occurred for example in the *Bernette* decision where the Council of State ruled that the administrative authority had to check 'whether the allegations against the employee were sufficiently serious to warrant his dismissal in light of all the rules applicable to the employment contract and elements for the normal execution of the mandate entrusted to him'.[77]

In a word, the sanction had to be proportionate to the fault alleged against the employee.[78]

In conclusion, although the proportionality test was imposed later in the field of disciplinary or administrative sanctions that had long been reserved for the discretion of the administration, this test has even permeated areas that used to be outside the jurisdiction of administrative courts. The field of administrative sanctions is thus particularly interesting since it reveals the evolution of the intensity of the proportionality test.

3.4 Proportionality test and modulation of the effects of annulment

More recently, it has been argued that the proportionality test applies to the modulation of the effects of judicial decisions in time.[79] The Council of State established this power in 2004.[80] This power gives courts the option to decide that the annulment of a measure will only come into effect after the publication of the judicial decision, or, that the effects of the administrative act that has been annulled remain valid, in the event that the judicial decision places an excessive burden on the rights of individuals. This was meant to deal with the problems created by the retroactivity of annulments pronounced by the administrative courts. The disappearance in the past of an administrative measure had created difficult situations for citizens who

77 *Société d'aménagement foncier et d'établissement rural d'Auvergne et Ministre de l'Agriculture c Bernette* (1976) rec. 232 (*Conseil d'État*).

78 There is another application of the proportionality test in this case. If the offence is sufficient to justify the dismissal of the employee, the public authority may refuse to order it because of its impact on the general interest. However, in this case, the administrative court may annul this refusal, if the impact on the interests at stake is excessive. Again, the idea of conciliation is at the centre of the proportionality test.

79 A-C Bezzina, '2004–2014: les dix ans de la jurisprudence AC!' (2014) *Revue Française de Droit Administratif* 735, 740.

80 *Association AC!*, (2004) rec. 197 (*Conseil d'État*).

had applied or relied upon the measure and who had witnessed its complete and sudden annihilation.

In the decision *Association AC!*, the collective agreements negotiated between employers and employees were in the spotlight. The validity of the ministerial agreement – the administrative measure necessary for the legality of the collective agreement – was contested. Once the court had decided that the ministerial agreement was illegal, the question of the effect of this decision needed to be addressed. The standard – i.e., the retroactive—annulment of the agreement would have had some considerable and adverse effects, notably with regard to unemployment benefit and social security contributions. To tackle these issues, the court, in a long statement of principle, noted that if the retroactive effect of the annulment appears to have manifestly excessive consequences, it is then possible to modulate the effects of the decision.[81] This modulation will be put into practice after the court has taken into account:

> on the one hand, the consequences of the retroactivity of the annulment for various relevant public or private interests; and on the other, the disadvantages that would create a limitation in time of the effect of the annulment with regard to the principle of legality and the right to effective remedy.[82]

In the opinion of Anne-Charlène Bezzina, the *AC!* case constitutes a new form of proportionality test.[83] According to this scholar, the court undertakes a double control of the cost-benefit analysis. The first consists of determining the need to modulate the effects of the decision by comparing the advantages and disadvantages of this modulation, while the second consists of establishing the exact nature of the modulation that the court will be using, so that 'it will only choose the most appropriate effect in time.'[84]

In the two controls depicted by the aforementioned scholar, we find, in fact, the three classical steps of the proportionality test. The first is a balance that ensures the annulment is neither excessive nor disproportionate[85] when compared to the advantages. This is a concretisation of the proportionality test *stricto sensu*. On the level of the second control, the court tries to balance the problems created by the late enforcement of its decision in contrast to those caused by the validation of past effects of the administrative act. We can identify here *a control of the necessity* – regarding the most appropriate solution – and *a control of the 'adequacy' or 'fit'* – in search of the best solution for the aim in question.

81 *Ibid.*

82 *Ibid.*

83 A.-C Bezzina (n 79) 737.

84 *Ibid* 740.

85 The word 'disproportionate' is used by the *Commissaire du Gouvernement* Devys in his conclusions in the case *Association AC!*. He argued that 'it was not possible not to be struck by the disproportionate consequences of the decision to quash' (211) and 'that the court should have had the possibility to put aside the retroactivity of the annulment only when the consequences of this annulment would appear to him to be disproportionate having regard to the requirements of legality' (216).

While Bezzina's argument is interesting, it is not fully convincing.[86] First, the reference to the proportionality test does not seem to be adapted here. In our opinion, it is not a proportionality test that is resorted to in this case law, but simply the application of the principle of proportionality. Second, the principle of proportionality is not used to review the legality of a measure but to determine the effects of a judicial decision. It is used more to frame the reasoning of the judge, particularly with regard to subsequent cases that may need this modulation, than as a means of ensuring legality. Therefore, it is difficult in our opinion to refer to a proportionality test in the strict sense. In fact, this is reflected in the methodology followed by the court: it resorts to proportionality *stricto sensu* before determining the appropriate measure. This does not correspond to a classical and logical application of the proportionality test.[87]

3.5 Intensity of the proportionality test

While disciplinary sanctions is an interesting field of study to highlight the possible intensity variations in the proportionality test, it is also necessary to refer to other fields in order to fully understand the intensity of the proportionality test in French administrative law. In this subsection, the emphasis is placed on the analysis of the factors affecting the intensity of the control. This subsection finds support in various examples to show that the proportionality test is structured around two main degrees of different intensity.

3.5.1 The two degrees of the proportionality test

The variation in the intensity of the proportionality test is not easily demonstrated due to a simple reason: the authors traditionally present the proportionality test as a control called 'maximum'.[88] By equating 'proportionality test' to 'the intensity' of control, the literature has been unable to identify degrees in the proportionality test. Despite this, it is possible to show that the courts vary the intensity of the test. They use various formulations showing various levels of intensity in the test.[89] In this chapter, two degrees of control are identified: 'limited control of proportionality' and 'normal control of proportionality'.[90]

86 See also the criticisms of Olga Mamoudy, 'D'AC! à M6 en passant par Danthony. 10 ans d'application de la jurisprudence AC! – Bilan et perspectives' (2014) *L'Actualité Juridique: Droit Administratif* 501, 506–507.

87 See chapter 2.

88 On this point, see also P Serrand (n 11) 919–921; P Wachsmann (n 52) 738–741.

89 The distinction between the proportionality test and the intensity of the control has been explicitly admitted by the *Commissaire du Gouvernement* Yann Aguila *Syndicats des avocats de France* (2007) rec. 384 (*Conseil d'État*), also in (2014) *Revue Française de Droit Administratif* 1191.

90 See Appendix I.

The 'limited control of proportionality' is often characterized by the use of the word 'obvious' or the word 'manifest'. These adjectives are applied, for instance, when the judge controls differences in treatment that are not 'grossly disproportionate' with respect to the principle of equality,[91] or, until recently, in the monitoring of administrative sanctions.[92] The judge used to annul sanctions that were 'manifestly disproportionate'. However, the limited control of proportionality can be used implicitly, for example, in the context of the cost-benefit analysis. As previously explained, the court can repeal projects when their disadvantages outweigh the benefits. A simple imbalance is not enough to compromise the legality of the project.[93] The limited control of proportionality uses the method of the proportionality review but with tempered requirements. Only manifest errors of assessment are sought. Therefore, the intensity of the control is reduced. The goal of this reduced intensity is to leave more discretion to the administration.

The second degree is the normal control of proportionality. It cannot be identified by the use of a particular word, in contrast with the first type. Its application stems from the requirements imposed by the court at the end of its control. Illustrations can be found in the field of administrative sanctions. In the *Dahan* decision of 13 November 2013, the court extended the normal control of proportionality to the disciplinary sanctions of civil servants.[94] This is the latest development in an evolution that started with the *Arfi* case.[95] The court has gradually replaced the limited control of proportionality with normal control.[96]

In the *Dahan* case, the court merely stated that it will 'consider whether the facts held against a public official who is subjected to disciplinary action constitute a misconduct that justifies a sanction and whether the chosen sanction is proportionate to the seriousness of the misconduct.' The absence of the word 'manifestly' is a sign of the transition to the normal control of proportionality. But it is only that: a sign or a clue. It is the careful judicial examination of the facts and the appreciation that the administration has brought to the case that shows an increase in the demands by the court. In fact, placing too much emphasis on the words used by the court might actually be deceiving in assessing the intensity of the control. For example, in the *Mattely*

91 *Villemain* (n 45); *Duvignères* (n 16).

92 *Touzard* (2006) rec. 36 (*Conseil d'État*).

93 See P Wachsmann (n 52) 741–748. See also the conclusions of Guy Braibant on *Ville Nouvelle-Est* (n 53) (421)-(422).

94 (2013) rec. 279 (*Conseil d'État*). This case moves away from the low intensity of review found in Lebon (n 69).

95 (2007) rec. 263 (*Conseil d'État*).

96 This evolution is still ongoing as the Council of State still refuses to control the sanctions of prisoners with normal intensity: *Letona Biteri*, (2011) rec. 246 (*Conseil d'État*). On that judicial trend, see F Melleray 'De l'erreur manifeste d'appréciation au contrôle entier en matière de contentieux des sanctions', (2010) 5 *DA* 41.

decision, the Council of State was able to use the word 'manifestly' while undertaking a very thorough control of the choice of sanction imposed by the administration.[97]

Although it is not yet clearly recognised in France, the proportionality test is a control technique in itself. This control is applied independently from other existing techniques. This does not mean that other considerations will not influence the court when deciding the case. However, the proportionality control, as a control technique, implies a very different legal and intellectual process. While the control may be limited or normal, this binary classification does not hide the fact that it is not easy to identify with certainty the intensity of review used by the court. Undeniably, the Council of State court does not operate in two ways only, and even within a given intensity, the control does change. Each case is unique and has its own characteristics that determine the requirements of the court.

3.5.2 Factors affecting the intensity of the proportionality test

Many factors influence the intensity of the proportionality test. While the proportionality test is identical in structure, the courts adapt their reasoning with regard to various elements. Some elements are found in the limited control, others in the normal control.

With regard to the cost-benefit analysis, limited control is justified by the technical context of the measures and the need to leave some discretion to the administration. The limited control results in these cases from the large number of details pertaining notably to the cost of the project, and the difficulty of assessing them properly. The Council of State only strikes down the gravest errors and most noticeable imbalances, thus leaving more leeway to the administration. This logic also dominates the control of proportionality of measures taken by the administration on the ground of the precautionary principle.[98]

Similarly, the limited control of disciplinary sanctions may be justified by the lack of precision with which the texts define the conduct constitutive of a fault. The administration is often limited in the choice of sanctions and the statutory provisions rarely provide details or further guidance on the type of behaviour that justifies them. Much is left to the discretion of the administrative authority.[99]

Finally, the control of the court may be restricted by the 'theory of exceptional circumstances'. This judge-made theory allows an increase of the powers of public authorities in specific circumstances and decisions that would

97 (2007) rec. 263 (*Conseil d'État*).

98 See the *conclusions* of Alexandre Lallet (n 64). The *rapporteur public* founded his position on the complexity and the political dimension of the matter (n 89).

99 P Serrand (n 11) 919.

normally be illegal.[100] This theory is used when a serious crisis requires extraordinary measures. In this case, the judge reviews strictly the measures that infringe the rights and freedoms of individuals, but leaves a wider margin of appreciation to the administration because of the particularly challenging circumstances.[101]

Conversely, some factors will influence the court to increase the intensity of its control. First, the court takes into account the legal background of the case. In the *Belgacem* case, the recourse to the normal proportionality test is justified by article 8 of the European Convention on Human Rights.[102] This evolution of the case law was necessary at the time, considering the numerous decisions taken by the European Commission on Human Rights against France because of the weak judicial review of the deportation of foreigners.[103] Similarly, in its opinion on the *Dahan* case, Rémi Keller explained that a normal control of proportionality of sanctions would be more consistent with the requirements of the ECHR.[104] The court also takes into account the judgments of the Court of Justice of the European Union, and its influence can also explain the better control of proportionality in some cases.[105]

It is important to note that when a case deals with human rights, the court will seek to impose a greater protection. Such is the case with the control of police measures: these are subject to normal control since the *Benjamin* case. The court's control may vary, however, with the nature of the right in question. In some circumstances, the freedom of trade and commerce may be restricted by an administrative measure,[106] but not the general principles

100 Belaïd, Essai sur le pouvoir créateur et normatif du juge (LGDJ, 1974) 241–248; F Batailler, Le Conseil d'État, juge constitutionnel (LGDJ 1966) 210–215.

101 *Dames Dol et Laurent* (*Conseil d'État*), February 28. 1919 (rec. 208, GAJA 19 éd, 2013, n° 33). See the observations on the *Heyriès Case* (*Conseil d'État*), June 28, 1918, *Heyriès* (rec. 651, GAJA, 19e éd, n° 31).

102 *Belgacem* (n 44).

103 *Djeroud c France* (1989) DR n° 61, 244 (Comm); *A. c France* (1991) DR n° 68, 319 (Comm). The European Commission of Human Rights was abolished in 1998.

104 R Keller, 'Le contrôle normal des sanctions disciplinaires par le juge de l'excès de pouvoir' (2013) *Revue Française de Droit Administratif* 1175, 1177–1178. See also J-C Bonichot 'Les sanctions administratives en droit français et la Convention européenne des droits de l'homme' (2001) *L'Actualité Juridique: Droit Administratif* 73. On the influence of the ECtHR on proportionality control, and the difference see K Grabarczyk, *Les principes généraux dans la jurisprudence de la Cour européenne des droits de l'homme* (PUAM 2008) 416–418 (about foreign publications), 466–472 (more general remarks).

105 J Petit (n 10). The recent recognition of the application of the Charter of Fundamental Rights of the European Union should increase its impact, especially if the ECJ continues in the way of an autonomous interpretation of the rights from the decision of the ECtHR (A Bailleux 'Entre droits fondamentaux et intégration européenne, la Charte des droits fondamentaux de l'Union européenne face à son destin', (2014) *Revue Trimestrelle des Droits de l'Homme* 215; D Ritleng 'De l'articulation des systèmes de protection des droits fondamentaux dans l'Union. Les enseignements des arrêts *Akerberg Fransson* et *Melloni*' (2013) RTDE 267).

106 *Dames Dol et Laurent* (n 101).

of criminal law.[107] Nevertheless, the presence of a right may lead the judge to increase its control. The opinion of Alexandre Lallet on the *Stop THT* decision is particularly revealing of this. When the precautionary principle is applied to declarations of public utility, the court resorts to a limited control. This occurs because individuals do not have a right to a declaration of public utility. However, when the administration refuses the exercise of a right to an individual because of the precautionary principle, the court will review the measures through a normal control of proportionality.[108]

It would be possible to list other factors that play a more or less explicit or important role in the variation of the intensity of judicial review.[109] However, we have focused on those that seem to be more often behind the court's reasoning. In this context, a final factor must be considered: the will of the court.

As to the will of the court, it is important to note two points. First, the elements that influence the control of the court are seldom imposed. Most of the time, the court is free to decide upon the type of control that will be applied in a concrete case. Second, the proportionality test has a particular nature: it is a method that requires an assessment of various elements of fact and law. This assessment is also rarely dictated by national legislation or by another authority. When the court weighs the level of threat to public order, the seriousness of an offence, or the public utility of a planning project,[110] this assessment decision is made discretionarily according to the circumstances of each case. The proportionality of the administrative measure will depend on this assessment. The court may feel more or less bound by elements external to its control, but the assessment of the facts of the case carries a strong element of discretion. The court can thus decide to increase the intensity of its control in some cases. The importance of 'external' factors is largely dependent on the will of the court. Therefore, each case will be casuistically assessed by the court, and will be resolved by a pragmatic application of the proportionality test.

3.6 Interesting thoughts and food for thought on the proportionality test

In this subsection, the proportionality test is placed in a less judicial context and more emphasis is placed on its place in the literature. Interestingly, the academic assessment of this control is ambiguous: while some scholars are critical of the powers of the court, others demand more control. A common

107 *Canal, Robin et Godot* (1962) rec. 552 (*Conseil d'État*).

108 *Stop THT* (n 61) (89)–(90).

109 M Guibal (n 76) 483–484.

110 See, for example, *Association SOS Rivières et environnement* (2003) rec. 417 (*Conseil d'État*) in which the court quashed the decision of public utility due to the weak interest of the project by reference to the aims it was meant to pursue.

criticism is shared, however: the language used by the Council of State is not precise enough. While analysing these academic assessments of the control of proportionality, one realises that these scholars themselves lack a rigorous use of terminology.

3.6.1 Thoughts on the control of proportionality

The French literature on administrative law appears to be facing a contradiction regarding the proportionality test. On the one hand, a number of opinions are being given and proposals for changes or reviews are made. On the other, none of these are actually being used to conceptualise the proportionality test.

It is possible to distinguish three positions on the proportionality test: some scholars criticise the excesses of the proportionality test; others plead for a distinction between the control of proportionality and merits review; and yet others are critical of the inadequacies of proportionality review.

Some authors criticise recent developments, particularly with regard to the field of sanctions. According to Hervé Rihal, the *Dahan* case law is not a positive evolution of judicial review.[111] The transition to normal control will limit administrative sanctions. The aforementioned scholar mostly criticises the court for fettering the discretion of public authorities. However, some *rapporteurs publics* have already stated that the normal proportionality test will not compel the administration to choose the best sanction.[112] It is primarily aimed at compelling the administration to decide on proportionate sanctions. This does not mean that there is only one possible result. The transition to normal control does not question the discretion of the administration.

Rihal's criticism may open the door to a question of conceptual nature. In principle, the court should only review the legality of administrative measures.[113] Hence, a court cannot control the merits, i.e., 'the overall considerations of interests, utility and justice that bring an authority to decide on a measure or to give a solution to a specific case'.[114] Increasing the intensity of the proportionality test raises the question of its nature: is it still judicial review or merits review? Some scholars choose the first answer,[115] others

111 H Rihal 'Dans la jurisprudence *Lebon* . . . il y avait du bon' (2014) *L'Actualité Juridique: Droit Administratif* 817.

112 See the *conclusions* of Guyomar on the *Arfi* case (n 98), see the *conclusions* of Remi Keller (n 104).

113 G Cornu, *Vocabulaire Juridique* (10e éd. PUF 2014) 598–599.

114 Ibid 710.

115 G Kafleche, 'Le contrôle de proportionnalité exercé par les juridictions administratives' (2009) 46 *Les Petites Affices*, 46. B Seiller (n 52); P Moor (n 14) 337–340. See also the 'conclusions' of Lallet on the case *Stop THT* (n 61) (87): 'not because it would lead you to exceed the limits of your role as judge of legality, and enter in the realm of merits; because it is you who delineated the frontiers between both'.

embrace the second.[116] The question itself depends on the position of each scholar: those who embrace the former consider proportionality review a part of the legality review; those who criticise it, label it as merits review. If by merits review, we mean that a public authority considers all aspects of a factual situation before taking an appropriate measure/solution on this basis, we must admit that the proportionality test indeed allows the court to review the merits of the measure/solution. By controlling the necessity, the court may require the administration to adopt the 'best' measure in the sense of the 'most appropriate solution' to the facts.

Other critical scholars highlight the shortcomings of the proportionality test. For instance, Bertrand Seiller defended the introduction of a control on the 'extrinsic legality' of the declarations of public utility.[117] The proportionality test of these administrative decisions falls short because it does not allow the court to impose on the administration the project that has the best cost-benefit ratio. The court should make an 'assessment of the cost-benefit analysis'.[118] The author therefore advocates a review of the necessity between projects of public utility. Currently, this proposal has not been followed by the court, and has even been analysed with scepticism in a recent *rapporteur public's* opinion. In fact, Alexandre Lallet considered in the case *Stop THT*[119] that it would be difficult to give effect to such a test. In addition, the test would be of little use. This statement is interesting for three reasons.

First, the very fact that Bertrand Seiller mentions the term 'extrinsic legality' to cover the possibility of comparing alternatives reflects the hesitation of scholars with regard to the terminology specific to proportionality. It would be preferable to resort to the terminology used in Germany with regard to the three stages of the proportionality test.[120] The 'extrinsic legality' would then become the control of necessity of the planning project.

Second, the necessity control of the public utility of the project is partly undertaken already. This is clear from the judgment in *Commune de Levallois-Perret*. In this case, the Council of State checked that the public authority did not own any land in the area. Otherwise, it would have been able to realise the project without resorting to compulsory purchase.[121] The Council of State compared the original project with others where it was not necessary to resort to compulsory purchases.

Therefore, Bertrand Seiller's suggestion regarding an extension of this necessity control is not useful or innovative. In addition, an increase in the

116 P Serrand (n 10) 921–923. See also *Vocabulaire Juridique* (n 116) 818 in which it is said that the proportionality test is an 'arbitration *in casu* comparable to a conciliation of legal rules with the resulting interest of the appreciation of the merits of factual situations'.

117 B Seiller (n 52).

118 *Ibid.*

119 See the conclusions of Lallet in the case *Stop THT* (n 61 87–88). The same fears were highlighted by the *Commissaire du Gouvernement* Dondoux in *Malardel* (n 27, 298–299).

120 See chapter 2.

121 Supra 3.2.2.; *Commune de Levallois-Perret* (n 26).

scope of proportionality control would not result in a higher number of annulments. What is more, by resorting to such a test, the court would take the place of the administration and assume the position of a decision-maker. The court would undoubtedly review the merits of the initial decision. While this may be welcome in some areas, such as in the context of public order measures, this should not be extended to all areas. For instance, planning decisions are complex, technical and have a sizeable political dimension. While the control undertaken in *Commune Levallois-Perret* can be explained by the wish to protect property rights, it needs to remain limited.[122] The court must remain in its 'control territory' and avoid crossing over to a form of control that would imply comparing the choice of the administration to any other possible variations. Not only would the court review the merits of the decision, but such an expansive review would require time and knowledge of a technical and political nature that the court does not have.[123] Considering these elements, the Council of State has already refused to review alternative projects put forward by the plaintiffs.[124]

3.6.2 The shortcomings of the literature on proportionality

As mentioned above, in recent years, administrative courts have been mainly using the proportionality test implicitly. As a result of this, scholars have not shown much interest in providing an accurate definition of the proportionality test. From this, stem errors regarding the nature of this control and its mere equation to an intensity of control. It is necessary to stop considering proportionality as a degree of intensity and to study it instead as a *method of control*. The proportionality test is distinct from the characterisation of the facts. It is another stage in the control of the measure and it refers to the consequences of the measure. As a result, proportionality is not an additional stage of the characterisation of the facts but an additional one after the characterisation of the facts. For example, with regard to sanctions, when the court decides whether the behaviour of someone was faulty, it controls the characterisation of the facts. However, when the court decides whether the sanction was 'the right one', it controls its proportionality by checking the link between the seriousness of the fault and the severity of the sanction.

Having said this, how can we explain that in urban planning, the court seems to be undertaking a control of proportionality from within the control of the facts? In those cases, the control of the court focuses on the nature of the project, inquiring whether it has public utility. Once this is confirmed,

122 *Commune de Levallois-Perret* (n 26).

123 For a similar criticism, see the conclusions of Lallet in *Stop THT*, (n 61, 87).

124 *Malafosse et Fédération des comités de défense contre le tracé et de l'autoroute A28* (1997) rec. 123 (*Conseil d'État*).

there is nothing else for the court to analyse. If we look again at the administrative sanctions cases, after an infringement is verified, one still needs to determine the sanction to be applied. Indeed, this second step does not exist in planning cases since compulsory purchase decisions are exclusively bound to the legal characterisation of the project's public utility.

On a different note, it is important to emphasise that the scope of the control and its intensity should be distinguished in the control of proportionality. These elements are often mixed up in academic writing.[125] Further inaccuracies can be found in the literature. While some authors simply discuss the proportionality review and the cost-benefit analysis separately,[126] others refuse to accept that the cost-benefit analysis can be an expression of proportionality review.[127] These problems reveal inaccurate definitions and a poor systematisation of the proportionality test. The cost-benefit analysis expresses a control of proportionality *stricto sensu*, while at the same time, ensuring that the disadvantages of a decision do not surpass its advantages.

Comparative law can play an important role in assisting the French literature to solve the aforementioned misperceptions with reference to the proportionality test. A more systematic control of proportionality in three stages would help to address the issues identified above.[128] Indeed, the Council of State seems to walk slowly in that direction and scholars should follow suit. So far, the complete lack of a systematic approach to proportionality is multiplying uncertainties and misunderstandings, if not errors. A three-stage approach is certainly not perfect, but it is a necessary basis to ensure a common terminology when using the term 'proportionality'. We can only encourage the court to do so and also to seize the opportunity to systematize and clarify its control.

3.6.3 Food for thought and reflections on the proportionality test

French administrative courts are not particularly organised when using the proportionality test. Both judges and commentators have long dealt with this in an almost anarchic manner. Some commentators even deny the autonomy of this method. The proportionality test may have been developed too silently. Paradoxical as it may seem, this silence helps us to understand the attitude of the court. The control of proportionality is actually a very good example of the 'ingenuity' of judges. Almost without a legal basis, the Council of State has developed a judicial control and technique that now permeates much of administrative law. While its effectiveness is not always obvious,

125 See Appendix I.

126 P Serrand (n 10); J-P Costa (n 10) 434–437.

127 M. Fromont 'Le principe de proportionnalité' (1995) *L'Actualité Juridique: Droit Administratif* 156. The Dieudonné (n 17) et M C (n 18) cases are recent examples. These are all the more interesting when compared to the solution adopted in Benjamin (n 8).

128 See chapter 2.

especially with regard to the cost-benefit analysis, it has imposed limits on the administration. In doing this, the proportionality test demonstrates the liberal position of French administrative courts. Still, it might be wrong to consider the entire case law as 'liberal'. As observed above, the court may compel the administration to take more coercive decisions against individuals.

The Council of State is also known for its pragmatism, adapting its requirements to the circumstances, or not systematically annulling measures that deny the exercise of a right or freedom. The proportionality test was, in fact, forged by the court to match its function: the court is a guardian of individual rights and freedoms but it also protects the effectiveness of administrative action.

Furthermore, a study of the proportionality test brings together judicial reasoning techniques and the concretisation of the ideal of justice. Depending on the various areas of judicial review, the court has to balance conflicting demands, and those demands are different every time. The proportionality test shows the gradual extension of judicial review into the realm of the discretionary power of the administration. In this, it highlights the pervasive evolution of French administrative law, and what guides its courts.

3.6.3.1 Appendix I

Appendix 1: Table describing the different stages of proportionality control by the court regarding administrative measures.

Kind of control *Grounds of review (control of . . .)*	*Minimum*	*Normal*	*Maximum*
Aim	YES	YES	YES
Question of law	YES	YES	YES
Question of fact	YES	YES	YES
Qualification of facts	NO	Limited Full	Full
Proportionality	NO	NO	Limited Full

This table focuses on the intensity of the judicial review of administrative decisions. The table compares proportionality control to other methods of reviewing administrative decisions, showing the variations from limited to maximum control of administrative acts.

Take, for example, the case of disciplinary sanctions for the sake of this table. The control of the *purpose* allows courts to verify whether the administrative measure respected the legislative purpose. If that is not the case, then the relevant ground constitutes an abuse of power. It means that a public body is not allowed to use its discretionary power regarding the application of a sanction for personal matters. Parliament has granted such powers to the administration so that the latter can adequately sanction a civil servant who was at fault. Therefore, disciplinary powers cannot be used for other purposes.

In addition, the court checks the points of law that bunch together the questions of interpretation of the texts as well as the determination of the legal basis. If the statute enabling the public authority to impose a sanction contains the mere possibility to give a warning to the civil servant or order a temporary suspension, the public authority cannot dismiss the civil servant in this context. Such a decision would be easily annulled on the grounds of error of law.

The elements of fact enable a review of the facts to check whether the facts that justified the measure did take place. For example, if the public authority decides to adopt a disciplinary sanction against an agent who is always ten minutes late to work, the judge must verify whether this factual element is true. The ten-minute delay shall be subject to 'normal review'.

Minimum control is identified by the absence of control of the legal characterisation or of proportionality.[129] This control can be called 'normal review' when the court checks the characterisation of the facts but not 'proportionality control'. Finally, the control is 'maximum' when the court, in addition to checking the characterisation of the facts, also checks the proportionality of the administrative decision. Still, within the normal and maximum controls, there are different intensities. When a court only annuls manifest errors, it is possible to argue that the control is a limited normal control. In the former case, the public authority still has discretionary powers over the qualification, while in the latter, the judge will qualify the facts. However, when the court annuls all errors it applies a full normal control. The same observation can be put forward with regard to the maximum control and the different intensity of reviews of proportionality.

References

Bailleux A, 'Entre droits fondamentaux et intégration européenne, la Charte des droits fondamentaux de l'Union européenne face à son destin', (2014) *Revue Trimestrelle des Droits de l'Homme* 215.

Baranger D, 'Retour sur Dieudonné' (2014) *Revue Française de Droit Administratif* 525.

Batailler F, *Le Conseil d'État, juge constitutionnel* (LGDJ 1966).

Belaïd, *Essai sur le pouvoir créateur et normatif du juge* (LGDJ 1974).

Bezzina A-C, '2004–2014: les dix ans de la jurisprudence AC!' (2014) *Revue Française de Droit Administratif* 735.

Bonichot J-C, 'Les sanctions administratives en droit français et la Convention européenne des droits de l'homme' (2001) *L'Actualité Juridique: Droit Administratif* 73.

Bonnefont R, 'Contentieux disciplinaire hospitalier: quand la gravité des conséquences de la faute l'emporte sur les circonstances atténuantes' (2010) *L'Actualité Juridique: Droit Administratif* 2329.

Bouveresse A, 'Du bon usage du principe de précaution' (*RTDE* 2013) 880.

Broyelle C, 'Retour sur Dieudonné' (2014) *Revue Française de Droit Administratif* 521.

—— 'Retour sur l'affaire Dieudonné', (2014) *L'Actualité Juridique: Droit Administratif* 473.

129 In Piazza (2011) req. n° 317314 (*Conseil d'État*): no control over the merits of an application to a professorial appointment.

Chetard G, 'La proportionnalité de la répression dans la jurisprudence du Conseil constitutionnel' (2013) *Révue de Science Criminelle et de Droit Pénal* 51.

Cornu G, *Vocabulaire Juridique* (10e éd, PUF 2014).

Costa J-P, 'Le principe de proportionnalité dans la jurisprudence du Conseil d'État' (1988) *L'Actualité Juridique: Droit Administratif* 434.

Debbasch P, and Colin F, *Droit administratif* (10e éd, Economica 2011).

Delhoste M-F, 'La théorie du bilan et la protection de l'environnement' (2006) *Revue Française de Droit Administratif* 990.

Denizeau C, 'Principe de précaution et droit de l'urbanisme' (2012) *Revue Française de Droit Administratif* 864.

Eisenmann C, *Cours de droit administratif* (vol 1, LGDJ 1982).

Fromont, 'Le principe de proportionnalité' (1995) *L'Actualité Juridique: Droit Administratif* 156.

Gilbert S, 'Principe de précaution et déclaration d'utilité publique' (2013) *AJDI* 531.

Grabarczyk K, *Les principes généraux dans la jurisprudence de la Cour européenne des droits de l'homme* (PUAM 2008).

Guibal M, 'De la proportionnalité' (1978) *L'Actualité Juridique: Droit Administratif* 477.

Guyomar M, and Domino X, 'Le passeport biométrique au contrôle: empreintes et clichés' (2012) *L'Actualité Juridique: Droit Administratif* 35.

Houstiou R, 'Expropriation: précisions sur la mise en oeuvre de la théorie du bilan' (2012) *RDI* 617.

Janin P, 'La jurisprudence du bilan est-elle toujours utile?' (2011) 195 *Droit de l'environnement* 318.

Kafleche G, 'Le contrôle de proportionnalité exercé par les juridictions administratives' (2009) 46 *Les Petites Affiches* 46.

Keller R, 'Le contrôle normal des sanctions disciplinaires par le juge de l'excès de pouvoir' (2013) *Revue Française de Droit Administratif* 1175.

Mamoudy O, 'D'AC! à M6 en passant par Danthony. 10 ans d'application de la jurisprudence AC! – Bilan et perspectives' (2014) *L'Actualité Juridique: Droit Administratif* 501.

Maurer H, *Droit administratif Allemand* (LGDJ 1995).

Melleray F, 'De l'erreur manifeste d'appréciation au contrôle entier en matière de contentieux des sanctions' (2010) 5 *DA* 41.

Moor P, 'Systématique et illustration du principe de proportionnalité', *Mélanges Michel Fromont* (Presses Universitaires de Strasbourg 2001) 318.

Petit J, 'Les ordonnances *Dieudonné*: séparer le bon grain de l'ivraie', (2014) *L'Actualité Juridique: Droit Administratif* 866.

Rihal H, 'Dans la jurisprudence *Lebon* . . . il y avait du bon' (2014) *L'Actualité Juridique: Droit Administratif* 817.

Ritleng D, 'De l'articulation des systèmes de protection des droits fondamentaux dans l'Union. Les enseignements des arrêts *Akerberg Fransson* et *Melloni*' (2013) *RTDE* 267.

Seiller B, 'Pour un contrôle de la légalité extrinsèque des déclarations d'utilité publique', (2003) *Revue Française de Droit Administratif* 1472.

—— 'La Censure a toujours tort', (2014) *L'Actualité Juridique: Droit Administratif* 129.

Serrand P, 'Le contrôle juridictionnel de l'administration à travers la jurisprudence récente', (2012) 4 *Révue de Droit Public* 901.

Stirn B, 'Panorama: le mouvement de réforme de la justice administrative' (2012) *L'Actualité Juridique: Droit Administratif* 1193.

Wachsmann, 'Un bilan du bilan en matière d'expropriation. La jurisprudence Ville Nouvelle Est, trente ans après', in *Gouverner, administrer, juger. Liber amicorum Jean Waline* (Dalloz 2002) 733.

4 Proportionality in English law

A.C.L. Davies and J.R. Williams***

4.1 Introduction

Proportionality is a relative newcomer in English law. It is used in cases that fall to be decided under European Union (EU) law, and in cases arising under the Human Rights Act 1998 (HRA). But it is not generally used in judicial review cases decided outside the HRA or EU sphere. In these cases, the courts generally continue to use a version of the well-known *Wednesbury* unreasonableness test, so called because of the case in which it was first formulated in 1948.[1]

We begin this chapter by reviewing the historical development of the *Wednesbury* test and the emergence of proportionality onto the scene in more recent years (section 2). In section 3, we compare the *Wednesbury* and proportionality tests, and we develop the argument that proportionality is preferable because it helps to structure the courts' reasoning and offers more 'intense' or searching scrutiny of administrative decisions than does the *Wednesbury* test. These benefits are apparent from cases decided under the HRA. We suggest that if the English courts were to adopt proportionality instead of *Wednesbury* for all types of case, the test would probably be formulated somewhat differently outside the human rights context, but that the twin advantages of structure and intensity would continue to apply. In section 4, we consider the incommensurability objection: an argument that the objectivity offered by proportionality is an illusion because the courts are being called upon to balance individual rights against public policy goals that cannot be weighed against each other using the same scales. We argue that this is a problem facing judicial review generally and is neither particular to the proportionality test nor insurmountable. Then, in section 5, we turn to the issue of 'deference'. Once the court has chosen the test to be used in a particular case, whether *Wednesbury* or a form of proportionality, there is still scope for varying the intensity of *application* of the test in practice, by varying the weight to

* Professor of Law and Public Policy, University of Oxford; Garrick Fellow and Tutor in Law, Brasenose College, Oxford.

** Lecturer in Law, Brasenose College, Oxford.

1 *Associated Provincial Picture Houses v Wednesbury Corporation* (1948) 1 KB 223 (CA).

be afforded to the initial decision-maker's decision in the court's reasoning process. Although some commentators challenge the idea of deference, we argue that a separate doctrine of deference improves the transparency of judicial decision-making and is thus to be welcomed.

4.2 Background

In this section, we introduce the debate by offering a brief explanation of judicial review in English law. We define the two tests – proportionality and reasonableness – that are central to our discussion, and explain their current status in English law.

4.2.1 Judicial review

We are concerned in this chapter with judicial review of administrative decision-making.[2] Judicial review in English law traces its history back to the seventeenth century. Its development slowed somewhat in the first half of the twentieth century, when judges were confronted with a significant increase in statutory regulation and war-time emergency measures, and then enjoyed a considerable revival after 1945, which continues to the present day. It is a jurisdiction developed by the judges as a matter of common law. Until the creation of the Administrative Court in 2000, there was no special court for judicial review cases, and even today, it is possible to raise issues of administrative law in other courts and other types of proceedings.

It is often said that the judicial review jurisdiction concerns itself with three main 'grounds' of review: procedural impropriety, illegality, and irrationality.[3] The first of these, which is concerned with the procedure followed by the administrative decision-maker leading up to the decision, need not detain us here. The distinction between illegality and irrationality may be less obvious to the outside observer. Under the illegality head, the court seeks to determine whether the decision-maker has applied the law correctly in reaching his or her decision. Failures here might include: acting outside the scope of the power granted to the decision-maker by the applicable legislation,[4] failing to exercise a discretion altogether,[5] taking into account irrelevant considerations or failing to take account of relevant considerations when reaching the decision,[6] or acting for improper purposes not permitted by the relevant legislation.[7] Under the irrationality head, the court is concerned with the substance

2 See, generally, William Wade and Christopher Forsyth, *Administrative Law* (11th edn, OUP 2014), chapter 1.

3 *Council of Civil Service Unions v Minister for the Civil Service* (1985) AC 374 (HL), 410 (Lord Diplock).

4 *R v Lord President of the Privy Council, ex p Page* (1993) AC 682 (HL).

5 *R (Corner House Research) v Director of the Serious Fraud Office* (2008) UKHL 60, (2009) 1 AC 756.

6 *Tesco Stores Ltd v Secretary of State for the Environment* (1995) 1 WLR 759 (HL).

7 *Padfield v Minister of Agriculture* (1968) AC 997 (HL).

of the decision. Assuming that the decision-maker has followed a fair procedure and acted within the law, should the decision nevertheless be struck down because the outcome reached is unreasonable? In theory at least, the judge should consider procedural impropriety and illegality first, and only if the decision passes those tests should he or she turn to consider irrationality as a last resort. However, in practice, judges are often less systematic and may simply pick up on the most appealing argument from the many presented by the applicant, whether it pertains to illegality or irrationality.

Because the irrationality head of review addresses the substance of the decision, it gives rise to particular concerns about the proper constitutional role of the judiciary. The task of the courts in judicial review is, in broad terms, to protect the rights and interests of citizens by ensuring that the executive governs in accordance with the law and does not abuse its powers. If the judges overturned administrative decisions simply because they disagreed with them, or started taking such decisions for themselves, they would be overstepping the proper boundaries of their own role and usurping that of the executive. The point is well-explained by Laws J (as he then was) in the *Fewings* case:

> The court does not ask itself the question, 'Is this decision right or wrong?' Far less does the judge ask himself whether he would himself have arrived at the decision in question. The only question for the judge is whether the decision taken by the body under review was one which it was legally permitted to take in the way that it did.[8]

Thus, the courts' approach to the irrationality head of review is particularly sensitive because it must strike a balance between enabling the courts to scrutinise the merits of an administrative decision while restraining them from interfering on the basis of disagreement alone. This issue overshadows the debates surrounding the test to be applied by the courts under this head of review and, in particular, whether the unreasonableness test should be replaced by proportionality.

4.2.2 The Wednesbury *test and its progeny*

The irrationality head of review first emerged in the decision in *Associated Provincial Picture Houses v Wednesbury Corporation*.[9] An administrative decision that satisfied the requirements of the illegality and procedural impropriety heads of review could nevertheless be struck down if, in Lord Greene MR's famous words, it was 'so unreasonable that no reasonable authority' could have made it.[10] It is clear, both from the reasoning structure and the test laid down by Lord Greene MR, that review on this ground was intended to be

8 *R v Somerset CC, ex p Fewings* (1995) 1 All ER 513 (QB), 515.

9 Above n 1.

10 Ibid 234.

exceptional, reserved for cases in which the decision-maker had taken leave of his or her senses. On the face of it, the high threshold of traditional *Wednesbury* review might lead the outside observer to suppose that *Wednesbury* cases would be very rare indeed. As Craig puts it: 'If the courts really were to restrict irrationality review to such manifest absurdity then we would all be out of business, in this area at least. There would be almost no successful challenges of this kind.'[11]

However, *Wednesbury* has not fallen into disuse.[12] The courts have modified the test in various ways to fit different types of case, so that now the term '*Wednesbury*' is used by English lawyers in two senses: to denote Lord Greene's traditional test, and to denote the various modifications that have emerged in the subsequent case law.

Some judges have reformulated the test into one of 'reasonableness'. For example, in the *ITF* case, Lord Cooke suggested that it was sufficient to ask 'whether the decision in question was one which a reasonable authority could reach'.[13] In a subtle way, this reformulation lowers the threshold for a finding of unreasonableness. Rather than looking for a 'crazy' decision, courts are encouraged to consider whether the decision-maker could justify his or her choice. The *Rogers* case provides a good example of this approach in operation.[14] In that case, a health authority adopted a policy of providing patients access to a particular drug treatment for breast cancer only in 'exceptional' cases. However, it could not identify what might constitute an 'exceptional' case within the category of people who would derive clinical benefit from the drug. As the Court of Appeal explained:

> a policy of withholding assistance save in unstated exceptional circumstances . . . will be rational in the legal sense provided that it is possible to envisage, and the decision-maker does envisage, what such exceptional circumstances might be. If it is not possible to envisage any such circumstances, then the policy will be in practice a complete refusal of assistance: and irrational as such because it is sought to be justified not as a complete refusal but as a policy of exceptionality.[15]

Where this approach is adopted, the key point for our purposes is that the courts are willing to impugn decisions that may not be absurd in Lord Greene's traditional *Wednesbury* sense. In *ITF* itself, Lord Cooke was clearly of the view that substantive review of administrative decision-making was appropriate even in less extreme cases, and would not trespass on the proper

11 Paul Craig, 'Unreasonableness and Proportionality in UK Law' in Evelyn Ellis (ed), *The Principle of Proportionality in the Laws of Europe* (Hart 1999), 95.

12 See, for example, R *(McDonald) v Royal Borough of Kensington and Chelsea* (2011) UKSC 33, (2011) 4 All ER 881, and R *(Ahmad) v Newham London Borough Council* (2009) UKHL 14, (2009) 3 All ER 755.

13 *R v Chief Constable of Sussex, ex parte International Traders' Ferry Ltd* (1999) 2 AC 418 (HL), 452.

14 R *(Rogers) v Swindon NHS PCT* (2006) EWCA Civ 392, (2006) 1 WLR 2649.

15 Ibid (62).

province of the executive: '. . . judges are entirely accustomed to respecting the proper scope of administrative discretions. In my respectful opinion they do not need to be warned off the course by admonitory circumlocutions.'[16]

Another important development in the case law has been the courts' willingness to vary the intensity of their application of the reasonableness test according to the circumstances of the case. As the courts began to recognise and enforce certain human rights at common law, it was decided that the reasonableness test could be applied more rigorously in such cases. The leading authority on this is the *Smith* case, in which Lord Bingham MR cited the following submission of counsel with approval:

> The court may not interfere with the exercise of an administrative discretion on substantive grounds save where the court is satisfied that the decision is unreasonable in the sense that it is beyond the range of responses open to a reasonable decision-maker. But in judging whether the decision-maker has exceeded this margin of appreciation, the human rights context is important. The more substantial the interference with human rights, the more the court will require by way of justification before it is satisfied that the decision is reasonable in the sense outlined above.[17]

By contrast, the reasonableness test could be applied with a lighter touch in non-rights cases, and an extremely light touch in cases of particular sensitivity. For example, in the *Nottinghamshire* case, the House of Lords was faced with a challenge to the secretary of state's decision on expenditure targets for local authorities.[18] The decision was politically controversial, involved complex financial questions and had been approved by parliament. Despite noting that judicial review had moved on since *Wednesbury*, the House of Lords held that the secretary of state's decision could only be reviewed if the applicants could show bad faith, improper motive or absurdity.

4.2.3 The proportionality test

In 1998, the UK Parliament enacted the HRA, which entered into force in 2000. For the first time, this gave effect in domestic law to most of the rights contained in the European Convention on Human Rights (ECHR). For administrative law purposes, the most important section of the Act is s. 6, which empowers the courts to review administrative decisions for their compatibility with the claimant's Convention rights. The enactment of the HRA brought about a transformation in the judicial review jurisdiction, with many cases now being argued as human rights claims against the executive under the Act. In this section, we will explain how the HRA introduced the principle

16 Above n 13, 452.

17 *R v Ministry of Defence, ex p Smith* (1996) QB 517 (CA), 554.

18 *Nottinghamshire County Council v Secretary of State for the Environment* (1986) AC 240, 247 (Lord Scarman).

of proportionality into English administrative law and how that principle has since been defined.[19]

Most of the rights in the ECHR are 'qualified' rather than absolute rights. This means that the government may infringe them where it is 'necessary in a democratic society' to do so for the pursuit of certain public interest goals listed in the Convention itself. The ECtHR has, over many years, used the proportionality test as a means of assessing governments' interferences with the Convention rights. Under s. 2 HRA, the English courts are obliged to 'take into account' the decisions of the ECtHR, although they are not bound to follow them in the traditional common-law precedential sense. But since one of the central purposes of the HRA was to resolve more human rights cases in the domestic courts, instead of forcing claimants to take the costly and time-consuming step of taking a case to the ECtHR, it was perhaps unsurprising that the English courts chose to adopt the proportionality test under the HRA.[20]

The precise formulation of the proportionality test has proved controversial.[21] In the early cases, including *Daly*,[22] the English courts defined proportionality as a three-stage test using a formulation from the *de Freitas* case.[23] Lord Clyde said that the court should ask whether:

> (i) the legislative objective is sufficiently important to justify limiting a fundamental right; (ii) the measures designed to meet the legislative objective are rationally connected to it; and (iii) the means used to impair the right or freedom are no more than is necessary to accomplish the objective.[24]

In the later case of *Huang*, the House of Lords expressed concern that this three-stage formulation omitted any element of 'balancing' between the individual's right and the government's policy objective.[25] The latest Supreme Court authorities appear to have settled on a fourfold test. For example, in *Bank Mellat*, Lord Sumption summarised the effect of the previous case law in the following terms:

> . . . the question depends on an exacting analysis of the factual case advanced in defence of the measure, in order to determine (i) whether

19 The English courts were also familiar with proportionality from EU law, on which see Gráinne de Búrca, 'The Principle of Proportionality and its Application in EC Law' (1993) 13 YBEL 105, and *ITF* (n 13).

20 *R (Daly) v Secretary of State for the Home Department* (2001) UKHL 26, (2001) 2 AC 532.

21 Tom Hickman, 'Proportionality: Comparative Law Lessons' (2007) 12 *JR* 31.

22 *Daly* (n 20), (27) (Lord Steyn).

23 *De Freitas v Permanent Secretary of Ministry of Agriculture, Fisheries, Lands and Housing* (1999) 1 AC 69 (PC).

24 Ibid 80.

25 *Huang v Secretary of State for the Home Department* (2007) UKHL 11, (2007) 2 AC 167, (19) (Lord Bingham).

> its objective is sufficiently important to justify the limitation of a fundamental right; (ii) whether it is rationally connected to the objective; (iii) whether a less intrusive measure could have been used; and (iv) whether, having regard to these matters and to the severity of the consequences, a fair balance has been struck between the rights of the individual and the interests of the community.[26]

We will examine this test and its application in much greater detail later in the chapter.

4.2.4 The Wednesbury/*proportionality split*

In simple terms, then, we can say that the proportionality test is applicable to cases arising under the HRA and in EU law, and a variable reasonableness test (probably not in the classic *Wednesbury* formulation) is still good law for cases arising outside these areas. But before we turn to a detailed comparison of the two tests, it is worth problematising this simple picture to some extent.

One claim made by some commentators is that the courts have been using proportionality, more or less explicitly, in cases that are technically governed by the reasonableness test.[27] This claim was sometimes made in relation to cases decided under the 'heightened scrutiny' reasonableness test used in cases involving common-law rights but, as we shall see below, the subsequent case law has rendered this argument untenable. However, there are some more plausible examples to support the claim. We will consider two. First, there are some human rights cases at common law in which the judges have abandoned any claim to be applying a reasonableness test. The judgment of Lord Bingham in the *Daly* case is a good example.[28] The applicant prisoner argued that his common-law right to the confidentiality of his correspondence with his legal advisers was infringed by a policy of routinely searching prison cells in the absence of the prisoners. Lord Bingham held that the right had been infringed but that there could be good reasons for searching cells in the prisoners' absence. He went on to say:

> It is then necessary to ask whether, to the extent that it infringes a prisoner's common law right to privilege, the policy can be justified as a necessary and proper response to the acknowledged need to maintain security, order and discipline in prisons and to prevent crime.[29]

26 *Bank Mellat v HM Treasury* (2013) UKSC 39, (2014) AC 700, (20).

27 For example, Jeffrey Jowell and Anthony Lester, 'Proportionality: Neither Novel nor Dangerous', in Jeffrey Jowell and Dawn Oliver (eds), *New Directions in Judicial Review* (Stevens & Sons 1988); though cf Sophie Boyron, 'Proportionality in English Administrative Law: A Faulty Translation?' (1992) 12 *OJLS* 237.

28 Above n 20.

29 Ibid (18).

Lord Bingham concluded that the policy could not be justified. Lord Bingham's approach – which was based expressly on the common law and not the HRA – seems very similar to proportionality. This suggests that, in cases where a claimant invokes a right at common law rather than under the HRA, the proportionality test may sometimes be used instead of the heightened scrutiny reasonableness test. A second example relates to the doctrine of legitimate expectations. In broad terms, this applies where a public authority has made a representation to the claimant that it will act in a particular way and subsequently seeks to resile from the representation. In order to assess whether the public authority can justify its change of position, the Court of Appeal in the *Coughlan* case rejected the reasonableness test in favour of one of 'abuse of power'.[30] It is often suggested that this was because the claim would have failed under a reasonableness test that would not have given sufficient weight to the claimant's expectation.[31] The 'abuse of power' test is inherently vague and in *Nadarajah*, Laws LJ suggested, *obiter*, that proportionality should be used as the standard of review in legitimate expectations cases.[32] His approach has since been endorsed by the Privy Council.[33]

The blurring of the straightforward distinction between EU and HRA cases using proportionality and non-HRA cases using reasonableness has been accompanied by a significant change in attitudes towards proportionality, at least among some members of the judiciary. In *ex p Brind*, the House of Lords was invited to review an executive decision on the broadcasting of the words of members of certain proscribed terrorist organisations using Article 10 ECHR and the proportionality test, many years before the enactment of the HRA.[34] It was held that this was impermissible because, as Lord Ackner put it, it would amount to incorporating the ECHR into English law (which takes a dualist approach to international treaties) 'by the back door'.[35] For our purposes, what is interesting about the decision is the concern expressed by some of the judges that the proportionality test would involve inappropriate intrusion into the proper sphere of the executive.[36] By 2003, the Court of Appeal in the *ABCI* case was prepared to state that it had 'difficulty in seeing what justification there now is for retaining the *Wednesbury* test',[37] although it held that it was for a higher court, the Supreme Court, to bring about any change in the law because the test was so well-established.[38]

30 *R v North and East Devon HA, ex p Coughlan* (2001) QB 213 (CA).

31 Paul Craig and Soren Schonberg, 'Substantive Legitimate Expectations after *Coughlan*' (2000) *PL* 684.

32 *R (Nadarajah) v Secretary of State for the Home Department* (2005) EWCA Civ 1363, (68).

33 *Paponette v Attorney General of Trinidad and Tobago* (2010) UKPC 32, (2012) 1 AC 1, (38).

34 *R v Secretary of State for the Home Department, ex p Brind* (1991) 1 AC 696 (HL).

35 Ibid 762.

36 Ibid 766–7 (Lord Lowry).

37 *R (Association of British Civilian Internees) v Secretary of State for Defence* (2003) EWCA Civ 473, (2003) QB 1397, (34).

38 Ibid (35).

4.3 Proportionality and *Wednesbury* compared

In this part of the discussion, we turn to consider the advantages of proportionality review, both in themselves and, inevitably, in comparison to traditional *Wednesbury* review in English law. The literature identifies two main advantages. First, proportionality offers the courts a more structured method of reasoning when deciding a case. *Wednesbury* is often criticised for expressing a conclusion rather than guiding the courts' decisions. On this view, it should be easier for those examining a case decided on a proportionality basis to understand how the judges reached a particular result, with all the obvious benefits of transparency and accountability that this brings. Second, proportionality is generally regarded as a more 'intensive' standard of review than *Wednesbury*, enabling the courts to scrutinise government action more rigorously. This is particularly appropriate in the human rights context, but may also be a potential advantage in other settings, given that judicial review has moved on significantly since the *Wednesbury* test was formulated in 1948. However, as will be seen, this higher intensity is not necessarily seen as an advantage by all commentators, particularly when it is used across the entire spectrum of substantive review. While there is some merit to the concerns expressed by these commentators, it will be suggested below that there are numerous strategies by which to overcome these concerns.

4.3.1 The problems with Wednesbury *review*

We saw above that the *Wednesbury* test was formulated by Lord Greene MR as a 'back-stop' to be used if a particular administrative decision had received a clean bill of health under the other grounds of review, procedural impropriety and illegality, but still seemed to the court to be substantively wrong in the sense of being unreasonable.[39] It has been the subject of a barrage of scholarly criticism.[40]

First, the *Wednesbury* test as originally formulated does not tell the court when the required threshold of unreasonableness is met in order for the decision to be struck down. It tells us that a decision is *Wednesbury* unreasonable when 'no reasonable authority' would have taken it. As many commentators have pointed out, this is clearly tautologous.[41]

The second criticism is closely related to the first. Because the test offers no guidance, it is open to judges to apply their own views of what constitutes a bad administrative decision under the guise of the *Wednesbury* test. Even if this criticism is put too strongly, the *Wednesbury* approach at least gives rise to the *suspicion* that the judges' own prejudices or policy preferences are

39 Above n 1.

40 For example, Paul Craig, 'The Nature of Reasonableness Review' (2013) 66 *CLP* 131; Anthony Lester and Jeffrey Jowell, 'Beyond *Wednesbury*: Substantive Principles of Administrative Law' (1987) *PL* 368.

41 Lester and Jowell (n 40) 372.

'hiding beneath *Wednesbury's* ample cloak'.[42] An oft-cited example of this is the decision in *Wheeler.*[43] In that case, a local council leased a sports ground to a rugby club. It banned the club from using the ground for twelve months because some of its players took part in a tour of South Africa during the apartheid era. The council argued that it was pursuing its statutory duty to promote good race relations in its multicultural area. The club argued that its players had not acted unlawfully. Two speeches were given in the House of Lords. Lord Roskill argued that the council had acted *Wednesbury* unreasonably but gave no explanation for this conclusion; Lord Templeman stated that it was unlawful for the council to punish the club when it had done nothing wrong without relating this to any particular precedent. Whatever one's view of the outcome of the case, the speeches are unsatisfactory. They do not enable the council to understand why it lost the case, nor do they offer clear guidance for future cases.

A third criticism of the *Wednesbury* test is that it purports to set the bar of unreasonableness very high. This led Lord Cooke in *Daly* to claim that *Wednesbury* was 'an unfortunately retrogressive decision . . . in so far as it suggested that there are degrees of unreasonableness and that only a very extreme degree can bring an administrative decision within the legitimate scope of judicial invalidation'.[44] Thankfully, decision-makers rarely take leave of their senses entirely, so true cases of *Wednesbury* unreasonableness are likely to be rare. In his judgment, Lord Greene MR quoted the example of a teacher being dismissed from her job for having red hair.[45] However, as he noted, it is hard to see how this example would have reached the *Wednesbury* stage: having red hair is clearly an 'irrelevant consideration' and would thus fall foul of one of the central tests for illegality review.

We saw above that, in practice, the test is rarely applied nowadays in the traditional *Wednesbury* form. Instead, the courts generally ask whether the administrative decision is 'reasonable', and vary the intensity of their scrutiny according to whether fundamental rights are at stake, in which case more intensive scrutiny applies, or matters of high policy, in which case a light-touch approach will be used. However, the three criticisms of the traditional formulation remain relevant to these newer versions of the test. First, although a 'reasonableness' test is not necessarily tautologous, it does not offer any guidance as to what constitutes a decision that is not reasonable (or, given the variable intensity of review, not sufficiently reasonable under the circumstances). Daly argues that it is possible to discern the courts' approach to reasonableness through an examination of the case law.[46] He suggests that the courts look out for certain 'indicia' of unreasonableness, which trigger an

42 Ibid.
43 *Wheeler v Leicester City Council* (1985) AC 1054 (HL).
44 *Daly* (n 20), [32].
45 Above n 1, [229].
46 Paul Daly, '*Wednesbury*'s reason and structure' (2011) *PL* 238.

obligation on the part of the decision-maker to justify the decision. But even he is forced to admit that this is not obvious from the judgments themselves. Again, then, there is a risk that judges conceal their own preferences under the guise of reasonableness review (the second criticism noted above). In relation to the third criticism, the 'heightened intensity' reasonableness test used in *Smith* was found to be insufficient to protect the applicants' rights under the ECHR when the case progressed to the Strasbourg court, and many commentators argue that reasonableness tests of any kind also offer insufficiently intensive scrutiny of executive decision-making in non-rights cases.[47] We will explore these issues in greater detail below.

4.3.2 The advantages of proportionality

Having considered the criticisms of *Wednesbury* broadly defined, we are now in a position to consider its competitor: proportionality. Two main advantages are claimed for this principle: that it offers a more structured reasoning approach to guide the judges' decisions, and that it offers greater intensity of review. We will examine each in turn. Our focus in this section will be on cases under the HRA, where proportionality is already in use in English law.

4.3.2.1 Structure

As we saw above, proportionality as commonly defined has four component parts: legitimate aim, rational connection, necessity, and balance (proportionality *stricto sensu*). The claim that proportionality is a more structured test than *Wednesbury* flows from the need for judges to work through these stages when deciding a case.[48]

While it may be possible simply to label a decision '*Wednesbury* unreasonable', as *Wheeler* demonstrates, it is not possible simply to declare a decision 'disproportionate'.[49] As Lord Steyn put it in *Daly*, '[c]learly, these criteria are more precise and more sophisticated than the traditional grounds of review'.[50] The advantage of this is the obvious one that judges are forced to explain their decisions in a more transparent way and have less opportunity to give effect to their own (unexpressed) preferences.[51]

The *Bank Mellat* case offers a useful illustration of these advantages in action.[52] The Treasury made an order under anti-terrorism legislation banning

47 *Smith and Grady v UK* (2000) 29 *EHRR* 493.

48 For example, Paul Craig, 'Proportionality, Rationality and Review' (2010) *NZLR* 265.

49 Above n 43.

50 Above n 20, (27).

51 See Aharon Barak, 'Proportionality and Principled Balancing' (2010) 4 *Law & Ethics of Human Rights* 1; 'Proportionality (2)', in Michel Rosenfeld and András Sajó (eds), *The Oxford Handbook of Comparative Constitutional Law* (OUP 2012).

52 Above n 26.

financial institutions operating in the UK from having any dealings with the applicant Iranian bank, with the objective of disrupting Iran's pursuit of a nuclear weapons programme. The bank challenged the order on various grounds, including infringement of its Article 1 Protocol 1 rights under the ECHR. It is instructive to compare the judgments of Lord Sumption (in the majority) and Lord Reed (dissenting). Both agreed that nuclear non-proliferation was a legitimate aim for the government to pursue, and both agreed that the (relatively low) threshold for a rational connection between the policy and the aim was met, in the sense that the elimination even of one Iranian bank from the UK financial sector would have the potential to hinder the weapons programme. The disagreement between them emerged at the third and fourth stages of the test. Lord Sumption argued that there were other comparable banks with Iranian connections that had been subject to lesser sanctions, such as warnings, so that order failed the 'least restrictive alternative' test.[53] Lord Reed took the view that the other banks were not comparable because they were not significant market players, so that the Treasury was justified in taking stringent action against Bank Mellat.[54] At the fourth stage, Lord Sumption held that the order was disproportionate overall because the problem of financial connections with Iran's nuclear programme affected the international banking sector as a whole, so the decision to single out Bank Mellat in particular was discriminatory and likely to be ineffective in achieving the Treasury's goals.[55] By contrast, Lord Reed would have decided that the measure was proportionate because of the importance of the government's objective and because it infringed property rights rather than other more fundamental rights.[56] The decision in *Bank Mellat* is in marked contrast to some of the reasonableness decisions we considered above. Although there was significant disagreement between the judges hearing the case, the structure of their reasoning is apparent and it is easy to identify the exact points on which they disagreed. This makes the decision much more transparent.

Arguably, a further advantage of a clearer judicial reasoning process is that it may encourage clearer reasoning on the part of administrative decision-makers. If they know that the court will analyse their decisions in a particular way, this may prompt them to explain and justify their decisions using a similar process in case they are faced with a legal challenge. While it is probably important not to overstate the impact of the prospect of judicial review on day-to-day administrative decision-making,[57] this may have a beneficial effect

53 Ibid (27).
54 Ibid (100)–(117), (125).
55 Ibid (27).
56 Ibid (126)–(129).
57 For an overview of the literature, see Genevra Richardson, 'Impact Studies in the UK', in Marc Hertogh and Simon Halliday (eds), *Judicial Review and Bureaucratic Impact: International and Interdisciplinary Perspectives* (CUP 2004).

on the way in which administrative decisions are taken, thus contributing to good administrative practice.

4.3.2.2 Intensity

A second advantage claimed for proportionality is that it offers more 'intense' scrutiny of administrative decision-making than the *Wednesbury* test.

We saw above that, prior to the enactment of the HRA, the English courts had adopted a more intense version of the reasonableness test in cases in which the claimant's rights (as recognised by the common law) were at stake. The difference between this test and the proportionality test adopted by the ECtHR became apparent in the *Smith* litigation. The applicants in that case challenged a ban on gay people serving in the UK armed forces. The Court of Appeal applied the 'heightened scrutiny' reasonableness test but nevertheless held that the government had done enough to justify the policy.[58] The applicants pursued their case to the ECtHR, where it was held that the ban was a disproportionate interference with their rights.[59] This highlighted the difference in intensity of the two approaches. The Court found that the inability of the domestic courts to assess the government's infringement of the claimants' Article 8 rights using a proportionality test amounted to a violation of Article 13, the right to an effective remedy:

> . . . the threshold at which the High Court and the Court of Appeal could find the Ministry of Defence policy irrational was placed so high that it effectively excluded any consideration by the domestic courts of the question of whether the interference with the applicants' rights answered a pressing social need or was proportionate to the national security and public order aims pursued . . .[60]

Once the HRA came into force, a change in the English courts' approach was obviously required, and the House of Lords formally adopted the proportionality test as a means of assessing governmental interference with rights under the HRA in its decision in *Daly*.[61] Since this approach is, in effect, required by statute, it is uncontroversial. More generally, since rights carry special weight in moral and legal discourse, it can be argued that the application of the more intense proportionality test is an acknowledgement of that weight.

While most commentators have welcomed the greater intensity of proportionality in human rights cases, the use of the test has triggered a fresh set of concerns: that its greater intensity might blur the constitutionally important

58 Above n 17.
59 Above n 47.
60 Ibid (138).
61 Above n 20.

line between *reviewing* an administrative decision (the judges' role) and *taking* the decision (the executive's role). The judges themselves have (perhaps inadvertently) fuelled these concerns in some instances. In the *Miss Behavin'* case, Baroness Hale said:

> The role of the court in human rights adjudication is quite different from the role of the court in an ordinary judicial review of administrative action. In human rights adjudication, the court is concerned with whether the human rights of the claimant have in fact been infringed, not with whether the administrative decision-maker properly took them into account.[62]

This characterisation suggests that proportionality review under the HRA is much more intense than reasonableness review because it is not a form of review at all: the court is, on this view, itself a decision-maker because it is responsible for determining the question about the infringement of the claimant's rights. It also suggests that the role of the court in 'ordinary' judicial review is to engage in procedural rather than substantive review. However, it is wrong on both counts.

The first claim is that the proportionality test turns the court into a primary decision-maker. It is, of course, correct to state that the HRA in general terms gives the court certain primary decision-making functions, for example, in deciding on the definition and scope of application of particular Convention rights.[63] But at the proportionality stage of the enquiry, the court does not function as a primary decision-maker. This is because it does not gather the evidence itself and evaluate it afresh without regard to the initial decision-maker's decision. As Kavanagh explains, the focus in the literature and case law on 'substantive' or 'outcomes' review masks an important point: that the initial decision-maker's decision cannot be considered in isolation from the *reasoning process* that led it to take that decision.[64] This enables us to understand Baroness Hale's quotation above in a more nuanced way. The court decides whether a proportionate outcome has been reached by evaluating the decision-maker's reasoning process. While this may be afforded more or less weight by the court, depending on the circumstances (as we shall explore below), it is never irrelevant to the court's decision. This is what ensures that the proportionality test remains within its proper boundaries as a form of review.

The relationship between the outcome and the reasoning process has two further important consequences for decision-makers. First, because the court is concerned with whether the decision-maker's reasoning process led to a

62 *Miss Behavin' Ltd v Belfast City Council* (2007) UKHL 19, (2007) 1 WLR 1420, (31).

63 Aileen Kavanagh, 'Reasoning about Proportionality under the Human Rights Act 1998: Outcomes, Substance and Process' (2014) 130 *LQR* 235, 251.

64 Ibid 246–249.

proportionate outcome, it will not strike down the decision because of flaws in the reasoning process if a proportionate outcome was reached. This is illustrated by *Miss Behavin'* itself. The decision-maker in that case had not apprehended that the claimant's Convention rights might be affected by the decision it was taking and had not therefore referred to them in its reasoning process. But this was not a ground for quashing the decision. While some have welcomed this 'non-technical' approach to decisions affecting human rights, others have expressed the concern that this undermines the incentive noted in the previous section for decision-makers to adopt a more careful reasoning process in which they themselves follow structured proportionality reasoning.[65] However, this brings us to the second important consequence for decision-makers. As Kavanagh explains, since the outcome and the reasoning process must be considered together, the more thorough the initial decision-maker's reasoning, the less likely it is that the court will strike down the decision.[66] This is illustrated by the *Quila* case, in which the government had decided not to grant marriage visas to people under the age of 21 as a means of combating forced marriage.[67] The Supreme Court accepted that combating forced marriage was a legitimate policy aim but the government's decision was found to be disproportionate because it could not produce any evidence of the prevalence of forced marriages among young people and thus of how many forced marriages the decision would prevent. It is clear, therefore, that if the decision-maker wants its decision to stand, it has a strong incentive to explain and justify its decision in a careful way.

The second claim made in the quotation above was that proportionality review was different to reasonableness review because the former is concerned with 'substance' or 'outcomes' whereas the latter is concerned with 'procedure'.[68] This claim – though commonly made – is also incorrect. The reasonableness test does require the court to evaluate the initial decision-maker's decision. It simply does so in a less intensive way than proportionality by setting the bar for judicial intervention at a much higher level. This is made clear by Lord Steyn in a well-known quotation from the *Daly* case:

> First, the doctrine of proportionality may require the reviewing court to assess the balance which the decision maker has struck, not merely whether it is within the range of rational or reasonable decisions. Secondly, the proportionality test may go further than the traditional grounds of review inasmuch as it may require attention to be directed to the relative weight accorded to interests and considerations.[69]

65 For example, David Mead, 'Outcomes Aren't All: Defending Process-based Review of Public Authority Decisions under the Human Rights Act' (2012) *PL* 61.

66 Kavanagh (n 63), 250.

67 R *(Aguilar Quila) v Secretary of State for the Home Department* (2011) UKSC 45, (2012) 1 AC 621.

68 Kavanagh (n 63), 246–249.

69 Above n 20, (27).

Endicott sums up the point neatly when he says that the reasonableness test brings with it a 'presumption of non-interference' that does not apply when proportionality is in use.[70]

In this section, we have focused on the intensity of proportionality under the HRA relative to the reasonableness test used elsewhere in English law. However, it is also important to be aware that the proportionality test can, itself, be applied more or less intensively depending on the circumstances, even in human rights cases. We return to this issue in section 5 below.

4.3.2.3 Should proportionality replace reasonableness in non-rights cases?

The adoption of proportionality review under the HRA has, not surprisingly, given rise to another fierce debate in the literature as to whether proportionality should also be used in 'ordinary' judicial review cases or, as Taggart puts it, cases involving 'public wrongs' rather than rights.[71] These cases are currently subject to the variable reasonableness test described above. Some judges have expressed the view that it would be preferable to extend proportionality to these cases but, because the reasonableness test is long-established in English law, it has been suggested that a decision of the Supreme Court would be required to bring about the change.[72]

There are both descriptive and normative dimensions to the controversy. On a descriptive level, there is a debate about the relative intensity of reasonableness and proportionality when the proportionality test is being used in non-rights cases. Some argue that proportionality is inappropriately intense outside the rights context, whereas others suggest that, because proportionality is likely to be used in a less intense form in these circumstances, there is not much substantive difference, except in methodology, between the two tests. On the normative level, there is a disagreement about whether, assuming proportionality *is* more intense than reasonableness even in non-rights cases, it would be legitimate for the courts to utilise it. Some theorists view the reasonableness test as expressing the proper boundaries of the judicial function in non-rights cases. We will examine each of these sets of controversies in turn.

We will begin by considering how the proportionality test might work in 'public wrongs' cases. It is clear that it must operate somewhat differently to the way that it operates in rights cases because the infringement of the claimant's right – the 'motor' that 'propels' proportionality, as Taggart puts it, is missing.[73] To choose a different metaphor, the proportionality test is often thought of in terms of weighing scales with the individual's right on one side and the government's policy on the other. In simple terms, because of the weight attaching to rights, the starting point of the court's inquiry is that the

70 Timothy Endicott, *Administrative Law* (2nd edn, OUP 2011) 280.

71 Michael Taggart, 'Proportionality, Deference, *Wednesbury*' (2008) *New Zealand Law Review* 423.

72 Above n 37.

73 Above n 71, 472.

right is pre-weighted and the scale is tipped towards the individual unless the government can come up with sufficiently strong counter-balancing arguments. In a 'public wrongs' case, there may be a multiplicity of different interests at stake. Each interest must be assigned a particular weight by the court and added to a scale that is not tipped in any particular direction. This has the potential to make the court's task much harder.

One useful source of ideas as to how the proportionality test might work in non-rights cases is provided by EU law. The ECJ uses the proportionality test in all types of case, including when reviewing discretionary policy decisions that do not engage an individual's rights. In these cases, it continues to maintain the four-stage structure of proportionality discussed above, but formulates the test in a less intensive way. This is apparent from the *Fedesa* case.[74] The Court set out the stages as follows:

> The Court has consistently held that the principle of proportionality is one of the general principles of Community law. By virtue of that principle, the lawfulness of the prohibition of an economic activity is subject to the condition that the prohibitory measures are appropriate and necessary in order to achieve the objectives legitimately pursued by the legislation in question; when there is a choice between several appropriate measures recourse must be had to the least onerous, and the disadvantages caused must not be disproportionate to the aims pursued.[75]

However, since the case concerned review of legislation adopted under the Common Agricultural Policy, a highly discretionary area of activity, the Court said that the measure could only be struck down if it was 'manifestly inappropriate having regard to the objective which the competent institution is seeking to pursue'.[76] Thus, the test is often referred to using the shorthand of 'manifest disproportionality' to capture the higher threshold that the claimant must meet in order to persuade the Court to strike down the contested measure.

It is clear that, as used by the ECJ, the proportionality test – even in a non-rights case – retains the features of structured reasoning and greater intensity identified in the previous section. As Craig puts it:

> The reality is that proportionality even when cast in terms of the need to find manifest disproportionality, is more searching than *Wednesbury* irrationality, precisely because the EU courts look hard at the evidence, facts and arguments adduced by the parties in order to determine whether the measure should be regarded as manifestly disproportionate.[77]

74 Case C-331/88 *R v Minister for Agriculture, Fisheries and Food, ex p Fedesa* (1990) ECR I-4023.
75 Ibid (13).
76 Ibid (14).
77 Craig (n 40), 166.

However, it is important to apply appropriate caution when considering how a test used in one legal system might work when used in another, even if (as here) the English courts are familiar with the EU law version of proportionality through their decisions in cases involving EU law.

One important difference is that although rights are not at stake in the leading EU cases on 'manifest disproportionality', there is usually a significant economic impact on the claimant bringing the case. For example, in cases like *Pfizer* and *Omega Air*, the claimant firms were challenging measures that would have eliminated or significantly reduced sales of their products.[78] This economic impact can be used to anchor the proportionality test in much the same way as a right. Indeed, in EU law, a claimant can only challenge a measure that is addressed to, or of 'direct and individual concern' to, him or her.[79] In English law, the standing test is much more relaxed and allows claimants to bring cases in the public interest even if they are not personally affected.[80] This means that the EU case law can be anchored to the burdens placed on the individual by the contested measure, whereas in English law, the courts may be faced with challenges to polycentric discretionary decisions with no particular 'victim'.

A second important difference is the much greater emphasis on access to information[81] and reason-giving in EU law.[82] The Court engages in detailed scrutiny of the costs and benefits of the contested measure, but this may be as much a reflection of the materials placed before it as it is of its use of the proportionality test. Judicial review in English law has traditionally been conceived as a mechanism for resolving legal disputes in cases in which the facts are agreed. Access to information is much more restricted. For example, there is no *general* duty to give reasons for an administrative decision, although there are potentially broad exceptions in which reasons are required.[83] Only in very recent cases have the courts begun to recognise that there may be a need for somewhat greater disclosure of evidence in cases in which the proportionality test falls to be applied.[84] Of course, the adoption of a proportionality test in 'public wrongs' cases in English law might trigger a greater willingness on the part of the courts to scrutinise the evidential basis of executive decisions, but it seems equally plausible to suggest that the courts would not be confident about doing so for reasons of institutional competence. In the recent

78 Case T-13/99 *Pfizer Animal Health SA v Council* (2002) ECR II-3305; Case C-27/00 R *(Omega Air Ltd) v Secretary of State for the Environment, Transport, and the Regions* (2002) ECR I-2569.

79 Art 263 TFEU, and see Case 25–62 *Plaumann & Co v Commission* (1963) ECR 199.

80 For example, *R v Secretary of State for Foreign and Commonwealth Affairs, ex p World Development Movement Ltd* (1995) 1 WLR 386.

81 See Articles 41 and 42 EU Charter of Fundamental Rights; Article 15(3) TFEU; Case C-51/92 P *Hercules Chemicals NV v Commission* (1999) ECR I-4235; Case C-204/00 P *Aalborg Portland A/S v Commission* (2004) ECR I-123.

82 Art 296 TFEU, and see Case C-367/95 P *Commission v Sytraval* (1998) ECR I-1719.

83 *R v Secretary of State for the Home Department, ex p Doody* (1994) 1 AC 531.

84 *Tweed v Parades Commission for Northern Ireland* (2006) UKHL 53, (2007) 1 AC 650.

Carlile case, an attempt was made to challenge the executive's decision not to permit a dissident Iranian politician to enter the UK.[85] Lord Sumption noted that, since the facts were not in dispute, the Supreme Court had 'absolutely no evidential basis and no expertise with which to substitute our assessment of the risks to national security, public safety and the rights of others for that of the Foreign Office'.[86] This suggests a very different 'mindset' to that of the ECJ, one that might not easily be altered by the wholesale adoption of proportionality.

The French courts also make use of proportionality or an analogous concept (*le bilan*) in non-rights cases. The French case law seems to focus attention on what would be the final step in the English courts' four-stage proportionality test, the balance between the costs and benefits of the contested policy. Indeed, it might be summed up as a form of cost-benefit analysis. For example, in the case of *Ville Nouvelle-Est*, which concerned an objection to a planning decision for the site of a stretch of motorway, the *Conseil d'État* conducted a full judicial inquiry into the notion of the public benefit (*utilité publique*) of the scheme; this inquiry involved weighing public gain against private loss.[87] The *Conseil d'État* adopted and applied the criteria proposed by the *commissaire du gouvernement* in the case, Braibant, in holding that 'an operation cannot be legally declared *d'utilité publique* unless the interference with private property, the financial cost, and, where it arises, the attendant inconvenience to the public is not *excessive having regard to the benefits of the operation*' (our emphasis). The *Conseil d'État* thus ultimately decided that the results of a similar process undertaken by the administration were unobjectionable. The concept of *le bilan* has since become well-established: in *Grassin*, a development plan for an airfield was declared illegal on grounds that the expense involved would have been disproportionate to the funds available to the relevant municipality;[88] in *Societé civile Sainte-Marie l'Assomption*, a plan for a road was quashed on the basis of it being contrary to the interests of patients treated in a psychiatric institution located in the area concerned;[89] and in *Drexel-Dahlgren*, the *Conseil d'État* quashed a proposed compulsory acquisition of a townhouse on the basis that the cost of purchasing and refurbishment outweighed any advantages.[90]

Interestingly, the French approach has some similarities with the 'fair balance' version of the proportionality test described by one of the leading English textbooks on judicial review, *de Smith*, as 'not . . . alien to English law'.[91] This would require the decision-maker to achieve a 'fair balance', presumably between competing considerations of whatever kind. The decision

85 R *(Carlile) v Secretary of State for the Home Department* (2014) UKSC 60, (2014) 3 WLR 1404.
86 Ibid (49).
87 *Conseil d'État* 28 Mai 1971, *Ville Nouvelle-Est*, 409 concl. Braibant.
88 *Conseil d'État* 26 Octobre 1973, Grassin.
89 *Conseil d'État* 20 Octobre 1972, *Société civile Sainte Marie de l'Assomption*, 657 concl. Morissot.
90 *Conseil d'État* 27 Juillet 1979, Mlle Drexel-Dahlgren, 349.
91 Harry Woolf et al (eds), *De Smith's Judicial Review* (7th edn, Sweet & Maxwell 2013), (11–076).

would be struck down if it gave 'manifestly disproportionate weight' to relevant considerations or was 'onerous or oppressive'.[92] This seems to combine a simple cost-benefit analysis, like that used in French law, with the 'manifest disproportionality' threshold used by the Court of Justice. It seems likely that a test of this type would be adopted by the English courts were they to move to proportionality in non-rights cases, rather than the 'human rights' version of proportionality analysed above. This is for two main reasons. First, the less formal structure of the cost-benefit analysis is easier to apply in non-rights cases where the decision-maker is weighing up a range of competing considerations. The court simply has to identify the relevant factors and assign them to the 'cost' side or the 'benefit' side before assessing how the decision-maker has weighed them against each other. Second, the 'manifest disproportionality' formulation is generally less intense (although, like all formulations, it could be applied flexibly) and allows the court to give due regard to the complexity of the decision-maker's task in cases where a strong justification for judicial intervention, in the form of the claimant's right, is absent.

It is worth noting that the English courts are familiar with the idea that the proportionality test can be varied from their decisions in cases involving EU law. For example, in the *Sinclair Collis* case, the Court of Appeal dispensed with the requirement from the human rights cases to show that the policy choice was the least restrictive alternative and applied the 'manifest disproportionality' test.[93] Lord Mance's judgment in the recent *Kennedy* case appears to offer some support for our position:

> In the context of fundamental rights, it is a truism that the scrutiny is likely to be more intense than where other interests are involved. But . . . proportionality review may itself be limited in context to examining whether the exercise of a power involved some manifest error or a clear excess of the bounds of discretion . . .[94]

Lord Mance appears to suggest that the proportionality test is to be preferred to reasonableness, but at the same time it is clear that he is seeking to offer reassurance that the intense human rights version of the test would not be applicable if proportionality were to be used in 'public wrongs' cases.

If we are right about this, our argument inevitably begs the question whether a less structured and less intense version of proportionality in 'public wrongs' cases would in fact bring any benefits when compared with the reasonableness test currently in use in these cases in English law. It is important to acknowledge at this point, as many judges have done, that the outcomes of cases might well be the same under the two approaches. As Dyson LJ (as

92 Ibid (11–075).
93 *R (Sinclair Collis Ltd) v Secretary of State for Health* (2011) EWCA Civ 437, (2012) QB 394.
94 *Kennedy v Charity Commission* (2014) UKSC 20, (2014) 2 WLR 808, (54).

he then was) put it in *ABCI*, 'it is true that the result that follows will often be the same whether the test that is applied is proportionality or *Wednesbury* unreasonableness. This is particularly so in a case in the field of social and economic policy'.[95] However, there are two important differences, both of which can be regarded as advantages for proportionality. First, in terms of structure, the cost-benefit analysis at least requires the court to identify the costs and benefits and to consider their weight. We saw above that the reasonableness test does not generate clear reasoning in any of its guises. Second, in terms of intensity, Elliott makes a powerful argument that the choice of a particular approach to review *in itself* says something important about the extent of the court's scrutiny, because different tests have different levels of intensity 'hard wired' into them.[96] From this perspective, a choice of proportionality over reasonableness is a more intense 'starting-point' for review, even though it may be *applied* with varying degrees of intensity (as we shall see below).

Before concluding this section, we should address the two main objections that have been made in the literature to the adoption of proportionality in 'public wrongs' cases in English law.[97] First, some commentators have argued that it is only legitimate for the courts to scrutinise administrative decisions to the extent required by proportionality where their aim in doing so is to safeguard rights.[98] In non-rights cases, the less intense reasonableness standard captures the appropriate boundaries of the judicial role. This argument accepts that proportionality is more intense than reasonableness and places great emphasis on the special weight attaching to rights in moral and legal reasoning. Although we have argued that proportionality is generally more intense than reasonableness, we have suggested that the courts would use a less intense formulation of the test in non-rights cases, so our argument is less prone to this objection. Nor do we accept that proportionality carries with it a risk of the judges usurping the proper role of the executive in any type of case, since it remains (as we argued above) a method of review and does not turn judges into primary decision-makers. More generally, it is important to acknowledge that the distinction between rights and non-rights cases does not necessarily correspond neatly to a distinction between severe and minor impact of the contested decision upon the claimant.[99] The use

95 Above n 37, (33) (Dyson LJ).

96 See Mark Elliott, 'Justification, Calibration and Substantive Judicial Review: Putting Doctrine in its Place', *UK Const L Blog* (17 September 2013).

97 See also Tom Hickman, 'Problems for Proportionality' (2010) *New Zealand Law Review* 303.

98 James Goodwin, 'The last defence of *Wednesbury*' (2012) *Public Law* 445; Lord Irvine of Lairg, 'Judges and Decision Makers: the Theory and Practice of *Wednesbury* Review' (1996) *PL* 59. For a nuanced 'middle way' argument see Jeff King, 'Proportionality: A Halfway House' (2010) *New Zealand Law Review* 327.

99 See Murray Hunt, 'Against Bifurcation' in David Dyzenhaus, Murray Hunt and Grant Huscroft (eds), *A Simple Common Lawyer: Essays in Honour of Michael Taggart* (Hart 2009); David Mullan, 'Proportionality – a Proportionate Response to an Emerging Crisis in Canadian Judicial Review Law?' (2010) *New Zealand Law Review* 233.

of a proportionality test in non-rights cases as well as rights cases – given its flexibility in terms of formulation, as discussed above, and application, to be considered below – allows the courts to respond appropriately to the case before them.

A second objection is the technical one that the change from reasonableness to proportionality could only be brought about by statute and not by judicial decision.[100] We saw above that the English courts use the proportionality test when deciding cases under the HRA, and that they were prompted to do so by the jurisprudence of the ECtHR, which they were obliged to take into account by virtue of s. 2 of the HRA. For this reason, it can be argued that the use of proportionality in human rights cases has some statutory support, albeit of an indirect kind. However, the HRA is the exception rather than the rule: in judicial review, the vast majority of development takes place through judicial decisions at common law and not through statute. The judges develop new doctrines incrementally in the case-law by interpreting and re-interpreting the requirements of the Rule of Law, a point generally accepted in the academic commentary on the subject.[101] The reasonableness test was, in effect, invented by Lord Greene MR in 1948, so there is no reason why it could not be replaced with a different test by a court at an appropriate level in the hierarchy today. Writing extra-judicially, Sir Philip Sales has argued that a change from reasonableness to proportionality would be too big a step to amount to an incremental development of the common law and would therefore be an illegitimate foray into the legislative function.[102] However, it is not clear why this particular development would be too big when the courts have introduced many other innovations at common law, including reasonableness itself and its modifications over time, and other new doctrines such as legitimate expectations.[103] If parliament took exception to the development, it could – as with any other aspect of the common law – reverse it by statute. There is no need for the courts to 'second-guess' parliament's views.

While it is a useful shorthand to speak of the adoption of proportionality 'across the board' in English law, we have argued in this section that if the courts were to use a proportionality test in non-rights cases, it would probably look rather different, both in terms of structure and intensity, to the proportionality test in use under the HRA. In all likelihood, it would involve the use

100 Goodwin (n 98); Philip Sales, 'Rationality, Proportionality and the Development of the Law' (2013) 129 *Law Quarterly Review* 223.

101 See, for example, Paul Craig, 'Competing Models of Judicial Review' (1999) *PL* 428; Mark Elliott 'The Ultra Vires Doctrine in a Constitutional Setting: Still the Central Principle of Administrative Law' (1999) *CLJ* 129.

102 Sales (n 100).

103 See Mark Elliott, 'Does the Ultra Vires Doctrine Prevent Courts from Replacing *Wednesbury* Review with Proportionality?', available at: http://publiclawforeveryone.com/2013/03/15/does-the-ultra-vires-doctrine-prevent-courts-from-replacing-wednesbury-review-with-proportionality/ last accessed 8 December 2014.

of a simple cost-benefit analysis of the administrative decision, which would only be struck down by the courts if the balance struck between competing considerations was 'manifestly disproportionate'. This approach would be both workable and legitimate in non-rights cases. Even though it would not offer quite such dramatic advantages when compared with reasonableness as proportionality does in human rights cases, it would still be an improvement on the English courts' current approach.

4.4 The incommensurability objection

We have just discussed, and refuted, two particular criticisms of applying a proportionality test in non-rights cases. There is, however, a broader criticism of applying a proportionality test in both non-rights *and* rights cases.[104] Some commentators have challenged the argument that proportionality offers a more structured reasoning process, noting that, particularly at the final 'balancing' stage, the judges simply have to make a choice between the competing factors: the claimant's rights and the government's policy. It is argued that these competing factors are 'incommensurable' in two senses: first, that it is impossible to assign precise values to rights and interests, and, secondly, that the rights and interests in question are not capable of being weighed using the same common scale. Together these form the so-called 'incommensurability problem': if there is no rational basis for deciding one way or another, then the result seems to represent 'a departure from the rule of law, in favor [sic] of arbitrary rule by judges'.[105]

However, the incommensurability problem can be challenged and overcome in a number of ways.[106] First, incommensurability is a problem with substantive review in rights cases generally. Whatever test is used, the judges ultimately have to make a choice at some point. If the incommensurability problem is being used to argue for reasonableness review in rights cases over proportionality, then proponents of this view need to clarify how reasonableness does not suffer from the same problem (in addition to the others stated above).

104 See, for example, Grégoire CN Webber, *The Negotiable Constitution* (CUP 2009), and Stavros Tsakyrakis, 'Proportionality: An Assault on Human Rights?' (2009) 7 *I•CON* 468.

105 Timothy Endicott, 'Proportionality and Incommensurability', in Grant Huscroft, Bradley W Miller and Grégoire Webber (eds), *Proportionality and the Rule of Law: Rights, Justification, Reasoning* (CUP 2014), 311.

106 There is a large literature on this topic and only a summary of the ways in which proportionality can be defended from the incommensurability problem can be offered here. For a particularly robust defence of proportionality, see Mattias Kumm, 'Political Liberalism and the Structure of Rights: On the Place and Limits of the Proportionality Requirement' in George Pavlakos (ed), *Law, Rights and Discourse: Themes from the Legal Philosophy of Robert Alexy* (Hart 2007); 'The Idea of Socratic Contestation and the Right to Justification: The Point of Rights-Based Proportionality Review' (2010) 4 *Law & Ethics of Human Rights* 142; (with Alec D Walen), 'Human Dignity and Proportionality: Deontic Pluralism in Balancing', in Huscroft et al (n 105).

Second, the incommensurability problem might be overstated. As Craig rightly points out,[107] incommensurable values have to be weighed in a range of public law situations, including, for example, negligence liability of public authorities,[108] the fettering of discretion doctrine,[109] and legitimate expectations.[110]

Third, the proportionality test does not depend upon assigning exact mathematical quantifications.[111] Instead the proportionality test is a formal framework which requires substantive discourse to fill it. The balancing stage might thus be seen not so much as interest balancing *per se*, but as balancing of substantive reasoning.[112] In this way it might be possible to assign values or weights to different interests without requiring precise and identical values. Proportionality does not work in a mechanical, push-button fashion separate from substantive argumentation as presented to the courts by the litigants themselves. As Endicott himself recognises, there is a distinction between radical incommensurability (where there is no rational basis for comparing two objects at all) and vague incommensurability.[113] Most of the time radical incommensurability is not present and a rational choice is not precluded merely because goals are valued in different ways. One should not, therefore, confuse incommensurability with incomparability; the proportionality test requires only comparability. In a similar vein, one should also not conflate uncertainty with indeterminacy – the latter is rarer, and more problematic, than the former.

Fourth, as well as not requiring precise weights for each interest, there might not need to be a precise, common scale of measurement for both rights and public interests. Instead, there might be strategies to overcome this. For instance, it would be possible to delineate between 'light', 'moderate' and 'serious' infringements of rights and to create a 'balancing formula' whereby the greater the degree of non-satisfaction or detriment to one interest, the greater must be the importance of satisfying the other.[114] A similar, but alternative, solution would be to create a common base for comparison such as 'marginal social importance' – instead of balancing the two competing interests themselves together, the judges apply a single criterion to evaluate both interests.[115]

Finally, even if we accept that incommensurabilities will inevitably exist in substantive review of any sort, then, as Endicott himself suggests, one could argue that the Rule of Law actually demands a system in which judges reconcile these incommensurable interests. This is based on what Endicott calls

107 Craig (n 40), 151.

108 For example, *Barrett v Enfield LBC* (2001) 2 AC 550 (HL).

109 For example, *R (Sandiford) v Secretary of State for Foreign and Commonwealth Affairs* (2014) UKSC 44, (2014) 1 WLR 2697.

110 *Coughlan* (n 30).

111 Matthias Klatt and Moritz Meister, 'Proportionality – a Benefit to Human Rights? Remarks on the I•CON Controversy' (2012) 10 *I•CON* 687.

112 Kai Möller, 'Proportionality: Challenging the Critics' (2012) 10 *I•CON* 709.

113 Endicott (n 105), 319–320.

114 Robert Alexy, 'Balancing, Constitutional Review, and Representation' (2005) 3 *I•CON* 572.

115 See Barak (n 51).

an 'institutional premise' – the respect that all public authorities must have for certain human interests can best be secured by an independent tribunal, i.e., the courts.[116]

4.5 The application of proportionality and the deference debate

We noted above that there is debate among theorists about whether proportionality is inappropriately intense, particularly outside the rights context, and how some theorists see the use of proportionality – as an inherently more intensive tool of review – as stepping outside the proper boundaries of the judicial function in these non-rights cases. Thus, for these academics, the greater intensity of proportionality review is more of a vice than a virtue. We have seen, however, that one way of allaying these concerns is to modify the proportionality test, as a doctrinal tool, so that it is configured at the *outset* more or less intensively in certain situations. This section focuses on a second way in which the same concerns can be allayed, namely by modifying the *application* of the proportionality test. This can be framed in terms of a separate concept of 'deference': the court should, when applying the limbs of the proportionality test to the decision in question, decide what degree of respect to accord to the initial decision-maker's determination. This hinges upon a clarification of the proper respective roles of judges and decision-makers. This deference approach is most clearly seen in the English cases, although there is controversy as to whether an independent doctrine of deference should even exist.

4.5.1 Definition and application

It is important to clarify what we mean when we use the word 'deference'. It is probably easier to start by outlining what we do *not* mean. First, deference is not to be understood in 'spatial'[117] terms by which we mean creating 'no-go zones' for judges wherein review of any sort does not lie, e.g., regarding national security. A spatial approach proceeds on an incorrect assumption that cases can be neatly classified into distinct categories, once and for all, according to their subject matter. This clearly cannot be achieved in practice, and is not what the English courts generally attempt to do.[118] Any particular case may contain a mix of factors that point in different directions and can be dealt with differently in turn. For example, in *A v Secretary of State for the Home Department*, the House of Lords struck down secondary legislation after

116 Endicott (n 105), 326.

117 Murray Hunt, 'Sovereignty's Blight: Why Contemporary Public Law Needs the Concept of Due Deference', in Nicholas Bamforth and Peter Leyland (eds), *Public Law in a Multi-layered Constitution* (Hart 2003).

118 Some *dicta* appear to support a 'spatial' approach, for example, *R v Director of Public Prosecutions, ex p Kebilene* (2000) 2 AC 326 (HL), 380 (Lord Hope).

intensive review on human rights grounds despite the fact that the government attempted to justify its actions by reference to national security concerns.[119] Deference is not, then, a concept of non-justiciability.

This was confirmed in the recent Supreme Court case of *Carlile*.[120] The majority judges, Lord Sumption,[121] Lord Neuberger[122] and Baroness Hale,[123] all expressed the concept of deference in terms of ascribing weight to the decision-maker's (i.e., executive's) judgments. Indeed, Lord Sumption expressly rejected the spatial concept of deference, and thus 'forbidden areas'[124] for judges, by saying that 'there can be no absolute constitutional bar to any inquiry which is both relevant and necessary to enable the court to adjudicate'.[125] This does not mean, however, as Lord Sumption continued, that even 'in human rights cases a court of review is entitled to substitute its own decision . . . it stops short of transferring the effective decision-making power to the courts'.[126] Second, deference is not the same thing as the ECtHR's margin of appreciation doctrine.[127] The twin rationales for that ECHR concept are that interests and contextual circumstances vary from state to state and that the ECtHR is somewhat removed or distant from those local circumstances. These rationales simply do not apply to a domestic doctrine of deference, and the English courts have expressly distinguished the two doctrines.[128] For example, in the recent Supreme Court case of *Nicklinson*, all nine judges distinguished the (domestic) doctrine of deference from the (international) doctrine of the margin of appreciation on similar grounds to those stated above.[129] Thus, the Supreme Court concluded that it was not prevented from considering the compatibility of the Act with the ECHR by the fact that the matter fell within the state's margin of appreciation. Lord Mance expressly stated that a matter could be 'incompatible at the domestic level, when it is compatible at the international level'.[130] The fact that legislation is within the margin of appreciation does not also mean that domestic courts are more ready to hold that it is proportionate.[131]

Instead, what we *do* mean by 'deference' is that the court will attach an appropriate amount of weight to the views of the initial decision-maker

119 (2004) UKHL 56, (2005) 2 AC 68 (commonly known as the 'Belmarsh' case).

120 Above n 85.

121 Ibid (n 22).

122 Ibid (n 80).

123 Ibid (n 98).

124 *R (Abbasi) v Secretary of State for the Foreign and Commonwealth Affairs and Secretary of State for the Home Department* (2002) EWCA Civ 1598, (2003) UKHRR 76, (106).

125 Above n 85, (30).

126 Ibid (31).

127 *Handyside v UK* (1976) 1 EHRR 737, (48).

128 For example, *Kebilene*, above n 118; *Re G (Adoption: Unmarried Couple)* (2008) UKHL 38, (2009) 1 AC 173, (118)–(119) (Baroness Hale).

129 *R (Nicklinson) v Ministry of Justice* (2014) UKSC 38, (2014) 3 WLR 200.

130 Ibid (188).

131 Ibid (75) (Lord Neuberger).

in relevant circumstances. In the literature, this has been called 'due deference',[132] or 'adjudicative deference'[133] to denote that it is utilised when the court is applying the doctrinal mode of review (whatever that may be). In proportionality, this is most obviously seen at the third and fourth limbs of the test when, respectively, evaluating whether the measure was necessary and in balance with the legitimate aim sought to be achieved. The answers to these questions are still the court's, but the judges will have arrived at their conclusions with greater reliance on the position of the decision-maker.

The effect of the court utilising the deference doctrine in this sense is that the proportionality test can be applied more or less intensively depending on the circumstances by giving more or less respect to the initial decision-maker's views. The relevant circumstances exhibited in the case law are varied, but broadly fall into two categories: institutional competence grounds (relating to the *capacity* of a body) and constitutional grounds (relating to the normative *legitimacy* of a body). Where either of these two grounds for deference applies, the utilisation of a deference doctrine means that replacing reasonableness review with proportionality would not have a necessary consequence of creating a uniformly more intensive standard of review. That there are two sources of the deference doctrine was confirmed by Lord Sumption in *Carlile*:

> In some circumstances, 'deference' is no more than a recognition that a court of review does not usurp the function of the decision-maker, even when [ECHR] rights are engaged. Beyond that elementary principle, the assignment of weight to the decision-maker's judgment [sic] has nothing to do with deference in the ordinary sense of the term. It has two distinct sources. The first is the constitutional principle of the separation of powers. The second is no more than a pragmatic view about the evidential value of certain judgments [sic] of the executive, whose force will vary according to the subject matter.[134]

This acknowledges the two forms of due deference that we identified above: deference on constitutional grounds, and deference on institutional grounds. The former hinges upon a principled view of the proper respective roles of judges and decision-makers (e.g., the latter may be accountable, or closer, to the electorate and thus have greater democratic credentials, or the type of decision might lend itself better to one branch over the other, such as broad social economic policy decisions to the executive), while the latter acknowledges practical limits on what a court can achieve compared to the initial decision-maker (the executive might have access to more expertise or information, for example). We shall discuss each form in turn.

132 Hunt (n 117).
133 Elliott (n 96).
134 Above n 85, (22).

With regards to institutional competence reasons for deference, the courts have acknowledged that the decision-maker may possess, or be able to access, expertise or information that is unavailable to the court. This is most pertinent at the necessity stage of the proportionality test when it is questioned whether the measure restricts the right in the least intrusive way compatible with achieving the legitimate aim in question. Here, the court is reliant on the public authority, for example, in order to know how effective either measure might be. The clearest example of deference on expertise grounds is *A v Secretary of State for the Home Department*.[135] In that case, the legality of the indefinite detention of foreign prisoners in Belmarsh prison without trial under section 23 of the Anti-terrorism, Crime and Security Act 2001 was in question. There were two issues to be decided: first, whether there was a risk of future terrorist attacks, and, second, whether the alleged violation of Convention rights by statutory provisions that treated nationals and non-nationals unequally infringed upon the right to liberty. In relation to the first question as to whether there was a public emergency and whether it threatened the life of the nation, the judges held that this was a question predominantly for the executive so that the government's decision should not be overturned.[136] Here, the government, unlike the court, had access to intelligence and expert evaluation. With regards to the second question regarding whether the claimants' indefinite detention without charge or trial was necessary, however, this was more than capable of being answered by the judges themselves – the executive was in no special position to answer this as compared to the judges. It was therefore ultimately decided to be a question for the court.

Lord Sumption in *Carlile* summarised the considerations relevant to deference on institutional grounds: (i) the nature of the decision; (ii) the expertise and sources of information of the decision-maker; (iii) whether there are predictive and judgmental assessments to be made, particularly regarding the future impact of alternative courses of actions; and (iv) the risks of making a mistake so that in some circumstances responsibility for a wrong judgment might lend itself better to political accountability.[137] However, it must be noted that the claim to have expertise has to be reliable,[138] and the expertise itself must have been used in the case in question.[139] In evaluating the relative institutional competence between the branches of government, the courts will also look at the quality of the initial decision-maker's reasoning process: if a decision-maker carefully balances the relevant issues, the court will usually be more reluctant to hold that its conclusion was disproportionate.[140]

135 Above n 119.

136 Ibid (29) (Lord Bingham); (115)–(119) (Lord Hope).

137 Above n 85, (32).

138 Above n 119, (154) (Lord Scott).

139 Above n 62, (37) (Baroness Hale).

140 R *(SB) v Governors of Denbigh High School* (2006) UKHL 15, (2007) 1 AC 100, (34) (Lord Bingham).

With regards to constitutional reasons for deference, the courts have acknowledged two circumstances in which it is appropriate to defer. First, the courts will look at the identity of the decision-maker (in particular, whether it is the legislature or an administrative decision-maker). If that decision-maker boasts democratic credentials, then the courts will be more likely to defer on constitutional grounds. For example, in *International Transport Roth GmbH v Secretary of State for the Home Department*, Laws LJ stated that greater deference would be paid to an Act of Parliament than to a decision of the executive,[141] and in R *(Farrakhan) v Secretary of State for the Home Department*, concerning a challenge to the Home Secretary's decision to exclude a non-national from the UK on the basis that he would make speeches risking the public order, Lord Phillips MR looked at the fact that the Secretary of State was better placed to reach an informed decision and was democratically accountable for the decision.[142] These sorts of questions represent a broader debate, based on the separation of powers, about the appropriate respective roles of courts and decision-makers. Thus, where the decision-maker is accountable, or closer, to the electorate and thus has greater democratic credentials, the courts are more willing, in certain situations, to be more deferential on constitutional grounds. Second, the courts will look at the subject-matter and context of the decision (especially its policy content) and defer more readily when it is the type of decision that might be more constitutionally appropriate for the executive to make such as in broad social economic policy decisions. This was seen earlier in *A v Secretary of State for the Home Department* with regards to the first question.[143] As Lord Hoffmann said in *Alconbury*:

> . . . in a democratic country, decisions as to what the general interest requires are made by democratically elected bodies, or persons accountable to them . . . [In cases where Parliament has delegated such questions to ministers,] the only fair method of decision is by some person or body accountable to the electorate.[144]

It follows that in some contexts the judiciary will defer on democratic grounds to the opinion of the elected body or accountable person. This will be more readily found in cases of social and economic policy, and is less likely to be found when a right of constitutional importance, which the courts are well-placed to assess, is in question.[145]

141 (2002) EWCA Civ 158, (2003) QB 728, (83).

142 (2002) EWCA Civ 606, (2002) QB 1391, (73)–(74).

143 Above n 119.

144 R *(Alconbury Developments Ltd) v Secretary of State for the Environment, Transport and the Regions* (2001) UKHL 23, (2003) 2 AC 295, (69)–(70).

145 Above n 119.

There has, however, been particular controversy in the literature regarding whether deference on constitutional grounds is ever appropriate.[146] This is neatly encapsulated by the differing approaches of, on the one hand, the majority, and on the other hand, Lord Kerr in the minority in the case of *R (Carlile) v Secretary of State for the Home Department.*[147] The question for the court was whether the Secretary of State for the Home Department (SSHD) had breached the applicant's right to freedom of expression by her decision to refuse to allow him to enter the UK on the grounds that, as a dissident Iranian politician, his presence would not be conducive to the public good. By a 4–1 majority, the Supreme Court held that the SSHD's decision was lawful.

Lord Kerr, dissenting, concluded that the SSHD's decision was disproportionate. He was led to such a conclusion after dismissing the appropriateness of deference on constitutional grounds. For example, he stated:

> . . . the word of the Secretary of State cannot hold sway . . .[148]

> . . . courts are there to examine whether that interference is justified. That examination must focus on the proffered reason of the decision-maker but the inquiry necessarily extends beyond that. The courts, charged with the solemn duty by Parliament of deciding whether the political reasons that have actuated the decision to interfere with the particular Convention right justify the interference, have a clear obligation to have proper regard to the importance of the right which has been interfered with. That exercise requires the courts not only to examine the reasons for the interference but also to decide for themselves whether that interference is justified.[149]

Thus, for Lord Kerr (unlike for the majority) deference is acceptable only on institutional grounds, as opposed to on constitutional grounds. The debate between the majority and Lord Kerr centres on broader normative opinions about questions such as what one means by 'democracy', and whether legitimacy requires a connection with 'representativeness', or whether the legitimacy of the judiciary from other sources (such as public argumentation and reasoning) is alone sufficient to legitimise broader control of executive action. This debate has strong parallels to that in *R v Secretary of State for the Home Department, ex parte Brind* and the concerns in that case of Lords Ackner, Lowry and Roskill about the appropriateness of a more intensive standard of substantive review more generally.[150]

It is submitted that the majority's position in *Carlile* is preferable to that of Lord Kerr's: the necessity and balancing stages of proportionality potentially

146 See, for example, Jeffrey Jowell, 'Judicial Deference: Servility, Civility or Institutional Capacity?' (2003) *PL* 592, 598.

147 Above n 85.

148 Ibid (150).

149 Ibid (152).

150 Above n 34.

require the judges to ascribe values to a multitude of different factors that might be in tension with one another (private interests vs public interests, for example) and may also be hard to quantify. There is no clear-cut constitutional reason why the (unelected) court's views – which might, in the end analysis, be no more than value judgements – should necessarily prevail without due regard to another (elected or accountable) branch of government that draws on other sources of legitimacy. Broadly speaking, judges' and administrators' roles should remain distinct.

4.5.2 Deference as a doctrine?

Despite the increasing references to deference in the case law, there is lively academic discussion as to whether an independent doctrine of deference should exist at all. This partly stems from the overtones of 'judicial servility'[151] or 'cringing abstention in the face of superior status'[152] to which the concept of deference might give rise. However one phrases the concept – whether in terms of deference, weight, respect etc. – it is nevertheless clear from what we have said already that in substance the approach outlined above is in widespread use in English case law. But should this be the position?

We have already seen above that a 'spatial' concept of deference is to be deprecated. We therefore concluded that deference, in terms of assigning appropriate weight to the decision-maker's assessment, was not a concept of non-justiciability. However, Allan (one of deference's greatest critics) argues that even if deference is conceived in the sense we have used it, it still 'turns out, on close inspection, to be non-justiciability dressed in pastel colours'.[153] He continues:

> The illegitimate species of deference, involving an abdication of judicial responsibility for the protection of rights, is marked precisely by reliance on the expertise or experience or public visibility of the decision-maker as opposed to the apparent quality of the decision itself. Here the judges' reliance on the supposedly superior qualifications of the decision-maker effectively divests the court of its role as independent scrutineer . . . Undermining the impartiality and independence of judicial review, such deference is no more legitimate when employed as one doctrinal consideration among others than when constituting the sole basis of the court's decision.[154]

Allan therefore questions whether the limbs of proportionality should be determined by courts giving 'external' (or independent) weight to the

151 *R (ProLife Alliance) v BBC* (2003) UKHL 23, (2004) 1 AC 185, (75) (Lord Hoffmann).

152 Above n 85, (22) (Lord Sumption).

153 TRS Allan, 'Human Rights and Judicial Review: A Critique of Due Deference' (2006) 65 *CLJ* 671, 689. See further, TRS Allan, 'Judicial Deference and Judicial Review: Legal Doctrine and Legal Theory' (2011) 127 *LQR* 96.

154 Ibid.

deference factors (whether institutional or constitutional) considered above. Instead, he argues, the question should be discharged by deciding whether the measure is lawful or unlawful based only on 'internal' (or intrinsic) matters relevant to the merits of the case:

> The relative expertise of the decision-maker and the excellence of its procedures are relevant insofar as they generate convincing arguments – good reasons for curtailing rights grounded in reasonable policies and supported by clear evidence. The court must be persuaded by the reasons, however, rather than impressed by expertise or procedural competence.[155]

For Allan, a doctrine of due deference is thus either 'empty' or 'pernicious':

> It is empty if it purports to implement a separation of powers between the courts and other branches of government; that separation is independently secured by the proper application of legal principles defining the scope of individual rights or the limits of public powers. A doctrine of deference is pernicious if, forsaking the separation of powers, correctly conceived, it permits the abdication of judicial responsibility in favour of reliance on the good faith or good sense or special expertise of public officials, whose judgments about the implications of rights in specific cases may well be wrong. A judge who allows his own views on the merits of any aspect of the case to be displaced by the contrary view of public officials . . . forfeits the neutrality that underpins the legitimacy of constitutional adjudication.[156]

However, a number of points in rebuttal can be made.[157] First, deference (as we have conceived it) is not to be seen as a trump such that any mention of expertise or democratic credentials automatically means that the courts defer to the decision-maker. As was mentioned above, these claims need to be both reliable and utilised by the decision-maker. Second, there are many advantages of explicitly utilising the 'external' factors that Allan deprecates merely bundling these, logically separate, factors within a merits calculus would distort the advantages of structure and transparency with which proportionality is accredited. Openly articulating the deference factors while applying the proportionality limbs allows everyone to see, and understand, what considerations were in play in aiding the judges to reach the conclusions they made. Third, according respect is not the same thing as submission and

155 Ibid.

156 Ibid, 675.

157 In a large literature, see Hunt (n 117); Aileen Kavanagh, 'Defending Deference in Public Law and Constitutional Theory' (2010) 126 *Law Quarterly Review* 222; Jeff A King, 'Institutional Approaches to Judicial Restraint' (2008) 28 *OJLS* 409; Alison L Young, 'In Defence of Due Deference' (2009) 72 *MLR* 554.

neither does it mean judicial abdication of responsibility. Instead, it is reflective of often hotly contested definitions and weights given to certain rights or interests, some of which are difficult in themselves to assign a precise weight, which are reasonably contested within contemporary society at large. It is only right that the courts give some value to others' points of view on these, often controversial, arguments. Finally, and in a similar vein, giving some additional weight to the argument merely because it stems from an expert or democratic decision-maker, for example, is a necessary implication of the courts having not one, but two, roles. As Kavanagh states:

> There is an alternative understanding of the nature of judicial reasoning in constitutional adjudication [to that of Allan], which fits better with contemporary constitutional practice. On this understanding, judges have not one but two obligations. The first (and primary) duty is to carry out the substantive evaluation, i.e. to evaluate the legal issues on their merits and to uphold rights, scrutinising Parliament and the executive for compliance with them. Their second duty is to consider questions of relative institutional competence, expertise and legitimacy vis-a-vis the elected branches of government. The latter duty engages concerns about the constitutional separation of powers, including judges' views about the extent and limits of their own role. Thus, alongside a consideration of the merits of the substantive legal issue before them, they must also reflect on the constitutional and pragmatic limits of their role.[158]

Allan's arguments may therefore have more purchase in rights cases, where the courts are constitutionally well-placed to adjudicate on serious rights infringement, than across the whole spectrum of review and in 'public wrongs' cases especially.

We have therefore seen in this section that, when applying the separate limbs of the proportionality test, there are means to ensure that the greater intensity of proportionality can be tempered in appropriate circumstances. This is done by applying a concept of due deference: when the court is asking itself whether the measure is necessary or in balance to the legitimate aim in question, for example, it can accord an appropriate degree of respect or weight to the initial decision-maker's appraisal of these matters when it is either practically (on institutional competence grounds) or constitutionally (on separation of powers grounds) proper to do so. In order to retain the advantages of structure and transparency, which we have suggested a proportionality test provides, it is necessary to conceive the deference factors as independent (or 'external' in the language of Allan) to the substantive issues on the merits. In this way, one avoids the application of the proportionality test itself becoming a 'cloak' to hide judicial value judgements much in the same way the reasonableness test does.

158 Kavanagh (n 157) 231.

4.6 Conclusion

The proportionality test is now a well-established feature of English administrative law in cases concerning human rights brought under the HRA and when applying EU law. It has significant benefits – a clearer reasoning structure and greater intensity of scrutiny – when compared with the traditional reasonableness test. We have suggested that, were the courts to decide to adopt proportionality for 'public wrongs' cases as well as rights cases, they would probably use a modified version of the test. Nevertheless, we have argued that this modified version would still retain advantages over reasonableness. It would still have some structure and it would be somewhat more intense, but not inappropriately so. Finally, we have argued that a separate doctrine of deference is a useful tool to enable the courts to apply tests like proportionality with varying degrees of intensity depending on the circumstances, while ensuring that their decisions on this issue are explained in a transparent fashion.

In developing these arguments, we have identified some significant differences between English law and both French law and EU law. In EU law, the proportionality test retains its structure even when dealing with cases not involving fundamental rights, and a separate doctrine of deference would be an alien concept for both the Court of Justice of the European Union and the French courts. In concluding, we offer some brief reflections on the reasons for these differences. One significant difference is the English judges' lack of executive experience.

The English judiciary is, for the most part, recruited from among senior barristers. Few judges have any experience within government other than (depending on their specialism) arguing cases for the government in court. This may explain their greater propensity to defer to the executive than, for example, the *Conseil d'État*, which has a much closer relationship with the executive and a much greater depth of understanding of its workings. Another significant difference is the constitutional background. Although there are many – and well-rehearsed – flaws in the relationship between parliament and the executive in the UK, judicial review is not the only mechanism by which the executive can be called to account for its decisions. The merits of government policy are scrutinised through mechanisms of political accountability. Arguably, this contrasts with the position in EU law in which there are concerns about the vast administrative powers given to the Commission and about the possible 'democratic deficit' within the legislative process. The ECJ may regard itself as playing a central role in tackling these concerns through in-depth judicial review scrutiny, whereas the English courts regard themselves as one part of a bigger constitutional picture.

In a seminal article on comparative law, Kahn-Freund famously warned of the risks of inappropriate transplantation from one legal system to another.[159] He singled out constitutional and administrative law as one of

159 Otto Kahn-Freund, 'On Uses and Misuses of Comparative Law' (1974) 37 *MLR* 1.

the fields in which the greatest dangers lay, and highlighted the need to have regard to the social context within which a particular legal doctrine operated before attempting to deploy it in another jurisdiction. The principle of proportionality has proved to be a successful transplant from EU law and the jurisprudence of the ECtHR into English law and could, we have argued, be employed more widely in our system. This reflects one of proportionality's great strengths: its *adaptability* to facts and circumstances, and to legal systems more generally.

References

Alexy R, 'Balancing, Constitutional Review, and Representation' (2005) 3 *I•CON* 572.

Allan TRS, 'Human Rights and Judicial Review: A Critique of Due Deference' (2006) 65 *CLJ* 671.

—— 'Judicial Deference and Judicial Review: Legal Doctrine and Legal Theory' (2011) 127 *LQR* 96.

Barak A, 'Proportionality and Principled Balancing' (2010) 4 *Law & Ethics of Human Rights* 1.

—— 'Proportionality (2)', in Michel Rosenfeld and András Sajó (eds), *The Oxford Handbook of Comparative Constitutional Law* (OUP 2012).

Boyron S, 'Proportionality in English Administrative Law: A Faulty Translation?' (1992) 12 *OJLS* 237.

Craig P, 'Competing Models of Judicial Review' (1999) *PL* 428.

—— 'Unreasonableness and Proportionality in UK Law' in Evelyn Ellis (ed), *The Principle of Proportionality in the Laws of Europe* (Hart 1999).

—— 'Proportionality, Rationality and Review' (2010) *NZLR* 265.

—— 'The Nature of Reasonableness Review' (2013) 66 *CLP* 131.

Craig P and Schønberg S, 'Substantive Legitimate Expectations after *Coughlan*' (2000) *PL* 684.

Daly P, '*Wednesbury*'s reason and structure' (2011) *PL* 238.

Elliott M, 'The Ultra Vires Doctrine in a Constitutional Setting: Still the Central Principle of Administrative Law' (1999) *CLJ* 129.

—— 'Justification, Calibration and Substantive Judicial Review: Putting Doctrine in its Place', *UK Const L Blog* (17 September 2013).

—— 'Does the Ultra Vires Doctrine Prevent Courts from Replacing *Wednesbury* Review with Proportionality?', available at: http://publiclawforeveryone.com/2013/03/15/does-the-ultra-vires-doctrine-prevent-courts-from-replacing-wednesbury-review-with-proportionality/ last accessed 8 December 2014.

Endicott T, *Administrative Law* (2nd edn, OUP 2011).

—— 'Proportionality and Incommensurability', in Grant Huscroft, Bradley W Miller and Grégoire Webber (eds), *Proportionality and the Rule of Law: Rights, Justification, Reasoning* (CUP 2014).

Goodwin J, 'The last defence of *Wednesbury*' (2012) *PL* 445.

Hickman T, 'Proportionality: Comparative Law Lessons' (2007) 12 *JR* 31.

—— 'Problems for Proportionality' (2010) *New Zealand Law Review* 303.

Hunt M, 'Sovereignty's Blight: Why Contemporary Public Law Needs the Concept of Due Deference', in Nicholas Bamforth and Peter Leyland (eds), *Public Law in a Multi-layered Constitution* (Hart 2003).

—— 'Against Bifurcation' in David Dyzenhaus, Murray Hunt and Grant Huscroft (eds), *A Simple Common Lawyer: Essays in Honour of Michael Taggart* (Hart 2009).

Jowell J, and Lester A, 'Proportionality: Neither Novel nor Dangerous', in Jeffrey Jowell and Dawn Oliver (eds), *New Directions in Judicial Review* (Stevens & Sons 1988).
—— 'Judicial Deference: Servility, Civility or Institutional Capacity?' (2003) PL 592.
Kahn-Freund O, 'On Uses and Misuses of Comparative Law' (1974) 37 *MLR* 1.
Kavanagh A, 'Defending Deference in Public Law and Constitutional Theory' (2010) 126 *LQR* 222.
—— 'Reasoning about Proportionality under the Human Rights Act 1998: Outcomes, Substance and Process' (2014) 130 *LQR* 235.
King J, 'Institutional Approaches to Judicial Restraint' (2008) 28 *OJLS* 409.
—— 'Proportionality: A Halfway House' (2010*) New Zealand Law Review* 327.
Klatt M, and Meister M, 'Proportionality – a Benefit to Human Rights? Remarks on the I•CON Controversy' (2012) 10 *I•CON* 687.
Kumm M, 'Political Liberalism and the Structure of Rights: On the Place and Limits of the Proportionality Requirement' in George Pavlakos (ed), *Law, Rights and Discourse: Themes from the Legal Philosophy of Robert Alexy* (Hart 2007).
—— 'The Idea of Socratic Contestation and the Right to Justification: The Point of Rights-Based Proportionality Review' (2010) 4 *Law & Ethics of Human Rights* 142.
—— (with Alec D Walen), 'Human Dignity and Proportionality: Deontic Pluralism in Balancing', in Grant Huscroft, Bradley W Miller and Grégoire Webber (eds), *Proportionality and the Rule of Law: Rights, Justification, Reasoning* (CUP 2014).
Lester A, and Jowell J, 'Beyond *Wednesbury*: Substantive Principles of Administrative Law' (1987) PL 368.
Lord Irvine of Lairg, 'Judges and Decision Makers: the Theory and Practice of *Wednesbury* Review' (1996) *PL* 59.
Mead D, 'Outcomes Aren't All: Defending Process-based Review of Public Authority Decisions under the Human Rights Act' (2012) *PL* 61.
Möller K, 'Proportionality: Challenging the Critics' (2012) 10 *I•CON* 709.
Mullan D, 'Proportionality – a Proportionate Response to an Emerging Crisis in Canadian Judicial Review Law?' (2010) *New Zealand Law Review* 233.
Richardson G, 'Impact Studies in the UK', in Marc Hertogh and Simon Halliday (eds), *Judicial Review and Bureaucratic Impact: International and Interdisciplinary Perspectives* (CUP 2004).
Sales P, 'Rationality, Proportionality and the Development of the Law' (2013) 129 *Law Quarterly Review* 223.
Taggart M, 'Proportionality, Deference, *Wednesbury*' (2008) *NZLR* 423.
Tsakyrakis S, 'Proportionality: An Assault on Human Rights?' (2009) 7 *I•CON* 468.
Wade W, and Forsyth C, *Administrative Law* (11th edn, OUP 2014).
Webber GCN, *The Negotiable Constitution* (CUP 2009).
Woolf H et al (eds) *De Smith's Judicial Review* (7th edn, Sweet & Maxwell 2013).
Young AL, 'In Defence of Due Deference' (2009) 72 *MLR* 554.

5 Proportionality in Dutch administrative law

Boudewijn de Waard

5.1 Introduction

For a good understanding of the position and meaning of 'proportionality' (*evenredigheid*) in Dutch administrative law, it is necessary to start by providing some information about the development of judicial review. The reason for this is that the Dutch equivalent of the proportionality test – as it is used in EU law and in German administrative law – has been used and has evolved as an instrument of judicial review of administrative action.

This chapter therefore starts with some history. This historical background is divided into two parts: the divide between the two parts is set in 1994. In that year, the Dutch General Administrative Law Act (hereinafter 'GALA') entered into force. The enactment of this statute had a major impact on the principle of proportionality since the GALA codified it, giving rise to the question as to whether the codification had changed the meaning of proportionality.

5.2 Towards a definition: a brief history of judicial review

5.2.1 Control of administrative action in the first half of the twentieth century

In the first half of the twentieth century there were no general administrative courts in the Netherlands and the ordinary courts were very reluctant to interfere with decisions made by the public administration.[1]

The debate about legal protection against administrative action was dominated by several questions that could be considered as 'universal' legal questions. The first of those questions was of a substantive nature: should the

1 There was a specialised administrative court, dealing with social security matters, established in 1902. In 1935, another specialised court was introduced, dealing with cases about the legal position of civil servants. The decisions made by this court could be appealed at the same appeal court as social security matters (the *Centrale Raad van Beroep*).

legal standards that rule relations between ordinary people apply to the actions of the public authorities? Should procedural rules be different in cases about administrative action? And the third and last question addressed an organisational matter: who shall be entrusted with dealing with cases against public authorities? Should that be a hierarchical control by a higher public body or a court? And, if it should be a court, should that be the ordinary court (that deals with private law and criminal law cases), or a separate administrative court?

In this period, organisational questions were predominant in the debate. Scholars were divided as to the answers, explaining why the legislator did not succeed in providing a coherent framework for legal protection against administrative action.

Nowadays, it is generally accepted in the Dutch literature that there are good reasons to entrust independent courts – as established in Article 6 of the ECHR – with the task to protect the rights of citizens in case these rights are endangered by administrative action. But in the first half of the twentieth century, this was not such a common view among Dutch scholars.[2] There was strong support for the idea that the legislator should choose an appeal within the administration instead of judicial review. One could argue that this is a token of naive faith in public administration.[3] However, it would be too simplistic to accuse scholars of holding a 'governmental' position by advocating a bigger role for the administration, based on the confidence that administrative bodies would 'do the right thing' and should not be impeded by judicial decisions.

The other side of the story is the true fear that courts would not be able to offer adequate protection because of the limitations set by the idea of separation of powers. The problem that was perceived was linked to the spectacular rise of the volume of administrative law statutes and regulations that started in the first half of the twentieth century. As a consequence of the massive legislative efforts that were made, the legislator refrained from giving clear and detailed criteria for the actions of the administration. Hence, statutes often contained only general and comprehensive rules. Details were left to be dealt with in regulations, drawn up by administrative bodies. In such a situation, where statutes hold little substantive criteria, courts would not be able to offer the required level of protection.[4] Courts would have to act in accordance with the doctrine of separation of powers. Therefore,

2 GJ Wiarda, 'De betekenis van art. 6. lid 1 van het Europese Verdrag tot bescherming van de rechten van de mens voor de Nederlandse administratieve rechtsgangen' in P Abas and others (eds) *Non sine causa* (WEJ Tjeenk Willink 1979) 459–474.

3 HD van Wijk, Willem Konijnenbelt and Ron M. van Male, *Hoofdstukken van Bestuursrecht* (16th edn, Kluwer 2014) 17.

4 This argument was put forward by AAH Struycken, *Administratie of rechter* (1910). Struycken referred to a 'withdrawal of the legislator'. This idea was picked up and elaborated on by HD van Wijk, *Voortgaande terugtred* (inaugural lecture VU 1959, also published in *Besturen met recht* (VNG 1974) 99ff).

without clear statutory criteria, the courts would be left empty-handed. For this reason, scholars argued that the best way to protect the position of citizens was to entrust the protection against administrative decisions to higher administrative bodies. That was 'a better idea' than having courts dealing with administrative decisions: courts did not have the right instruments to exercise control over administrative actions, and for that reason the result could only be that they would offer hardly any protection. Another imaginable scenario would be one of excessive protection, which would disrupt the balance of power. In fact, in the first decades of the twentieth century, the courts had hardly any instruments other than the criterion of 'violation of the law'. This changed, however, during the twentieth century.

The history of the development of instruments of judicial review shows that these instruments were first developed in case law – stimulated by debates in legal doctrine – and were only later laid down in legislation. Although a few steps had already been taken before 1945, it was just after World War II that these instruments were truly developed.[5]

In January 1949, the Dutch Supreme Court took an important step by recognising the standard of *détournement de pouvoir* (abuse of power) in the case *Zandvoortse woonruimtevordering*. This standard forbade administrative bodies to use a statutory power for a purpose other than the one intended by the legislator.[6] The decision of the Supreme Court implied that the court had the power to determine that such abuse had taken place and could conclude that this produced a violation of the civil rights of the individuals that were affected.

A second major step was taken by the Supreme Court only a few weeks later, in *Doetinchemse woonruimtevordering*. In that case, the Supreme Court formulated a test that would be similar to the traditional 'reasonableness test' in the UK (the *Wednesbury* test, see chapter 4). In the Dutch legal literature, the criterion is referred to as 'the prohibition of arbitrariness'. In case law, courts used to assess whether any alleged 'arbitrary action' was 'not (manifestly) unreasonable'. The formula to describe the test performed by the courts is as follows: 'The court has to investigate whether it can be said "that the administrative body in weighing the interests involved, could not reasonably have reached the contested decision."'[7]

The case was decided just a few years after World War II.[8] At the time, the Netherlands was facing a major housing shortage. A statute provided local authorities with the power to claim a house, or part of a house, which could

5 On the history of the general principles of good administration in Dutch doctrine see P Nicolaï, *Beginselen van behoorlijk bestuur* (Kluwer 1990) 11–72.

6 *Zandvoortse woonruimtevordering* HR 14 January 1949, *NJ* 1949/557 (note Veegens), *ARB* 1949, 751.

7 This was also codified in several statutes that were replaced when the GALA was enacted. One of those statutes was the *Wet administratieve rechtspraak overheidsbeschikkingen* (*Wet Arob*). The cited formula is a translation of Article 8 *Wet Arob*.

8 *Doetinchemse woonruimtevordering* HR 25 February 1949, *NJ* 1949/558.

subsequently be allocated to other people. From the point of judicial review, this statute contained a very interesting element. The statute held a provision that the claim made by the local authorities was 'considered to advance an opportune distribution of housing', and that 'no evidence of the opposite was admissible in court'.[9] Therefore, it was evident that the legislator did not want the courts to interfere with the way local authorities exercised their power to claim housing.

In the particular case of *Doetinchemse woonruimtevordering,* the local authorities had claimed a part of a large house that was inhabited by just two people, a married couple. The couple contested the claim in court. Their lawyer stated that the mental health of the couple was very unstable and their having to live with other people in the same house would probably harm their health and lead to serious conflicts with the other inhabitants. It would become inevitable that they would have to be hospitalised. A psychiatric report supported these arguments. The couple argued that it was very important for them to be able to continue to live in this house together, that they had a right to do so, and that the administrative decision that claimed a part of their house violated this right.

This case could not be treated the same way as the case *Zandvoortse woonruimtevordering*, mentioned above.[10] The second case could not be labelled as a case of 'abuse of power', because the decision to claim the housing space was based on no other motive than the promotion of the objectives of the relevant statute: to advance an effective housing policy. The case fed the idea that the court should be able to intervene when the outcome of a weighing of interests seemed unacceptable, even if the court accepted that the court itself should not 'redo' the process of administrative decision-making. But how should such a judicial control be constructed? Is the balancing of interests not predominately and exclusively the task of the administration? The court reasoned as follows:[11]

1 balancing the interests that are involved in a case like this, has to be left to the policy of the administrative body. The court cannot reach another conclusion on the basis of another (its own) appreciation of these interests;
2 therefore, the appeal is well-founded, because the high court has articulated the opposite interests in this case and concluded that it is reasonable

9 *Woonruimtewet 1947*, Article 32. The Dutch legal system is not unique here. In other countries, examples can be found in which the legislator tries to make administrative decisions 'judge proof', *and* in which the legislator fails, because the courts react by exercising at least a minimum of control. See, e.g., Simona Rodriquez 'Traditional Model vs. Dialogue Model in US Legal System', in Roberto Caranta and Anna Gerbrandy (eds), *Traditions and Change in European Administrative Law* (Europa Law Publishing 2007) 267–303.

10 *Zandvoortse woonruimtevordering* (n 6).

11 *Doetinchemse woonruimtevordering* (n 8).

that the interests of the couple that already lived in the house should prevail;

3 however, the court might intervene, if the act of the administration would have to be qualified as arbitrary (een daad van willekeur);

4 such a qualification is in place in case it could be said that the administrative body, in balancing the relevant interests, could not reasonably have reached the contested decision;

5 and therefore there is a situation as if no weighing of interests has taken place;

6 such a situation is not at hand here, because in this case people that are judging reasonably could come to different results.

In this case, we see the court taking an important step in the development of an instrument to control administrative action. But the court operates in a very precautious way. It chooses to stay very close to a check on the conformity with statutory requirements. In the above-mentioned *Zandvoortse woonruimtevordering*, the court did so by accepting the criterion 'abuse of power'. That is a criterion that could also be described as a check on the conformity with the relevant statute *as it was intended by the legislator*. In *Doetinchemse woonruimtevordering*, the court stayed close to checking statutory requirements by:

a) starting with an explicit emphasis on the fact that the weighing of interests should be left to the administration,
b) criticising the Court of Appeal on the ground that it performed a weighing of interest itself;
c) introducing the formula that expresses that the court should only use a 'marginal control';
d) and, adding that the outcome of the administrative decision leaves no other conclusion than that a (serious) *weighing of interests has not taken place.*[12]

By expressing this last consideration, the court again stayed very close to a control of statutory requirements. In fact, it is obvious that the legislator, when it created a power like the one mentioned, intended the administrative body to perform a weighing of the relevant interests. The court links up with the statutory requirement and uses a *procedural* instead of a substantive criterion, in saying that there is ground for courts to interfere if no balancing of interests has taken place.

In the Dutch literature, the formula that an administrative act constitutes tort when the administrative body *could not reasonably have reached the contested decision* is often paraphrased by saying that (the outcome of) administrative decisions may not be *manifestly* unreasonable. If a decision is manifestly unreasonable, the 'prohibition of arbitrariness' is being violated.

12 This is an element that is often overlooked in comments on the court's decision.

5.2.2 Introduction of the GALA in 1994

The conclusion of the former paragraph is that until the introduction of the GALA, Dutch law did not hold a test on proportionality as it is used in EU law (see chapter 6) and in German law (see chapter 2). Instead, Dutch case law used a prohibition of arbitrariness, a criterion similar to the *Wednesbury* test in the UK.

It should be noted, however, that Dutch administrative law did hold a standard called 'proportionality' (*evenredigheid*) before the GALA was enacted, but that standard was only used in the context of punitive sanctions. This standard was codified in the Civil Servants Act of 1929 (*Ambtenarenwet 1929*). Article 58 of this act contained the grounds for appeal. Section 3 of Article 58 stated that, should the appeal involve the application of a disciplinary sanction, a ground for appeal was that there was disproportionality between the sanction imposed and the offence committed.

Because the word 'proportionality' traditionally had a specific meaning in Dutch Law, related to administrative sanctions, for a long time the use of the word 'proportionality' was avoided in the broader context of administrative action in general. This changed with the implementation of the GALA. The concept of 'proportionality' can be found in Article 3:4, Section 2 of the GALA.[13] It reads as follows: '[t]he adverse consequences of an order for one or more interested parties may not be disproportionate to the purposes to be served by the order.'

This provision had two objectives: on the one hand, it created a statutory basis for the case law on 'arbitrariness' (*willekeur*), and on the other, it established a standard of conduct for the administration. The term 'proportionality' could very well serve both purposes. The fact that proportionality had a special meaning in the domain of administrative sanctions was, at that time, not considered problematic. Another objective of this disposition was to connect to developments in EU law by introducing the word proportionality into Dutch administrative law.[14]

The fact that the provision has a double function creates some complexity. The explanatory memorandum that accompanied the draft of the GALA mentions the difficulty that would arise if an attempt were made to codify 'the prohibition of arbitrariness'.[15] It explains that the GALA could not hold a section that read: 'the administrative decision[16] has to be based

13 GALA stands for: General Administrative Law Act (*Algemene wet bestuursrecht Wet van 4 juni 1992, Stb* no 315). It was enacted in 1994.

14 See the explanatory memorandum on Article 3:4 GALA, in EJ Daalder and GRJ de Groot (eds), *De parlementaire geschiedenis van de Algemene wet bestuursrecht, Eerste Tranche* (HD Tjeenk Willink 1993) 211. The committee that drafted the GALA had commissioned comparative research on the matter, subsidised by the Ministry of Justice. For the results of the research see AJC de Moor-van Vugt, *Algemene beginselen van behoorlijk bestuur en buitenlandse equivalenten* (WEJ Tjeenk Willink 1987).

15 Commissie wetgeving algemene regels van bestuursrecht, *Voorontwerp Algemene wet bestuursrecht, Eerste deel* (Staatsuitgeverij 1987) 72.

16 The English version of the text of the GALA does not use the words 'administrative decision', but 'order'. 'Order' is defined in Article 1:3, Section 1, of the GALA as: 'a written decision of an administrative authority constituting a public law act'.

on a balancing of interests that is not manifestly unreasonable'. Such a formulation would give the impression that it is acceptable if an administrative decision is *somewhat* unreasonable, as long as the unreasonableness is not 'manifest'. However, the provision in the GALA could not mention that an administrative decision has to be 'reasonable' either, since that could generate a more intensive judicial control than the one considered appropriate. For these reasons, the criterion of proportionality was introduced.

The memorandum also analyses the case law concerning the prohibition of arbitrariness and concludes that in all those cases, the legal question that had to be answered was whether the conduct of the administration has shown a manifest mismatch between the purpose the administration had, and the means that it used to reach that purpose. That is why Section 2 of Article 3:4, which has already been quoted above, uses the double negative: 'The adverse consequences . . . may *not* be *dis*proportionate'. By using this formulation, the GALA tries to combine the functions of an instrument for judicial control and a standard for conduct. The explanatory memorandum says that the use of the double negative indicates a type of control that fits within the limits of the judicial role. The judiciary is perfectly able to determine that a 'reasonable' relationship between purpose and means is missing. When the court performs such a control, it does not assess what contents of the decision at hand would be fair. The memorandum says that an assessment such as the latter would exceed the limits of the judicial role.

The analysis performed in the preparatory documents of the GALA explains that the prohibition of arbitrariness in case law had often been used in situations where, in essence, an evaluation of a relationship between means and ends was at stake.[17] I will come back to this point. However, first I will describe how the test, demanded by the principle of proportionality as it is laid down in Section 2 of Article 3:4 GALA, should be performed, according to the case law and literature in the Netherlands.

5.2.3 Case law after the introduction of Article 3:4, Section 2, GALA

5.2.3.1 Maxis and Praxis

The main reason why there is not much focus on proportionality in Dutch case law seems to be that courts have not fully embraced the concept of proportionality. Instead, they hold on to the 'old' criterion of 'arbitrariness' (*willekeur*). The leading case on the subject in the Netherlands is a case called *Maxis and Praxis.*[18]

17 Adrienne de Moor-van Vugt, *VUGA Commentaar, Comments on Art. 3:4* (Reed Business Elsevier), referring to EMH Hirsch Ballin & AJC de Moor-van Vugt, 'Doel en middel in het bestuursrecht', in *AA* (1986) 783.

18 *Maxis & Praxis* ABRvS 9 May 1996, *AB* 1997/93; *JB* 1996/158; *AA* 1997 43; *Gst* 1997, 7053, 9 (*Maxis & Praxis*. The case is sometimes called *Kwantumhal Venlo*).

Kwantum is a company that owns a chain of stores. The Kwantum stores sell low-priced furniture and household goods. At a certain point, Kwantum decided to open a new store in the city of Venlo. A permit from the municipal board of Venlo was required in order to use a building for commercial purposes. However, Kwantum found out that, for the site chosen for the new store, the local rules held that the use of buildings to sell goods directly to end-users (consumers) was not allowed. The rules held, nonetheless, that local authorities had the authority to derogate from this prohibition, under certain conditions. Kwantum got the administrative exemption but this decision was challenged in the administrative court of first instance. The plaintiff (Maxis and Praxis) argued that the exemption should not have been given, because the plans did not fit the local rules at that time. In fact, new rules were being discussed at the time: the city council were shortly to decide on the plan. However, the Kwantum store did not fit in that new plan either.

The court of first instance quashed the administrative exemption. It considered that at the time the dispensation order was issued, the revision of the local rules was in such an advanced phase that, in the opinion of the court, it was legally not acceptable to enable the establishment of the Kwantum store on that site by granting an exemption of the applicable rules. The court especially disapproved of the fact that the dispensation order even referred to the decision of the town council regarding the future revision of the plan, which decision was expected to be taken in the near future. Indeed, by issuing the administrative exemption, the town council was confronted with an accomplished fact, and the procedural guarantees that the Town and Country Planning Act offered to third parties, proved to be illusory.

The court concluded that for *Maxis and Praxis*, the disadvantages of the exemption were disproportionate to the purposes to be served by that order. The court quashed the administrative decision: it violated Article 3:4, section 2, of the GALA, which holds the criterion of proportionality. In appeal, the Council of State considered that the court of first instance had applied a wrong interpretation of the concept of proportionality contained in that article. The Council of State first went into the parliamentary history of the provision in the GALA. It said that the legislator did not intend to intensify the judicial control, in relation to the case law formed before the GALA was enacted. The Council of State then considered that, according to the parliamentary history of the provision:

> courts are not meant to assess which consequences are, and which are not proportional, or that the courts will assess which outcome of the weighing of interests is to be considered as the most balanced.[19] This view of the legislator is based on the different positions the independent judge and the politically accountable administration have in

19 *Kamerstukken II*, 1990–1991, 21 221 no 5 55ff.

> the constitutional system. From the [parliamentary history] it is also apparent that the wording of Article 3:4, Section 2, GALA, with the double negation ('not unreasonable') intends to oblige the courts to a restrained control of the weighing the interests the administration has performed.

These considerations render the doctrine on the prohibition of arbitrariness, as it is taught in the Netherlands, very adequately. Part of that doctrine is on the importance of the double negative 'not unreasonable'. The double negative refers to the method of testing, which is called 'marginal testing' or 'marginal control'. I will go into this method of testing in the next section. However, before that, a few more words are still necessary on the *Maxis and Praxis* case.

The Council of State considered that the court of first instance had failed to appreciate that, because a discretionary power was at stake, it was up to the public authority to weigh the interests involved in the administration of the authority and to decide whether it would use its power. The court should have confined itself to answering the question whether there was such an imbalance in the way the interests had been weighed. In addition, it should have been concluded that the administration could not reasonably have reached the decision to grant the requested dispensation.

The Council of State made it very clear, in this case, that the introduction of the word 'proportional' in the GALA was not intended to *intensify* judicial control. Moreover, the Council of State decided that there should be no change in the *method* of judicial control of the use of discretionary powers by the administration: the administrative court should apply the 'old' test of reasonableness.

5.2.3.2 Exception: punitive sanctions

The rule in *Maxis and Praxis* that the court, when examining the balancing of interests, should confine itself to a marginal control is the main rule. There is an important exception. In case a punitive administrative sanction is challenged before the court – the case law qualifies this as a 'criminal charge' in the sense of Article 6 of the ECHR – the court itself should decide whether there is a right balance between the gravity of the offence and the gravity of the sanction that has been applied by the administration.[20] In the case of administrative fines, the GALA holds that, if the court concludes that a contested fine, imposed by an administrative body, is justified but disproportionate, the court is obliged to determine the amount of the fine itself.[21]

20 *Keuringsplaats Scheerwolde* ABRvS 4 June 1996, *RAwb* 1996, 110, *JB* 1996/172. CRvB 5 November 1998, *AB* 1999/75 (note Hennekens).

21 Art 8:72a GALA.

In the field of compliance, matters of proportionality or reasonableness emerge frequently. This extends far beyond the realm of *punitive* sanctions. For example, suppose a car was parked under a sign that only allowed parking for loading and unloading on that spot. The car was towed away and the owner had to pay for the towing costs. The owner of the car protested: arguing that there was a mistake. Under the sign that prohibited parking should have been an additional sign that limited the prohibition to certain hours during the day. The additional sign used to be there, but it had been removed during restoration works on the pavement. By accident, the additional sign had not been put back. The authorities agreed that this was a correct representation of what had happened.

Nevertheless, the local authorities argued that the car owner should have obeyed the sign, or, if in doubt, made inquiries about the situation. The owner had not done this. Therefore, the authorities argued that they had the power to have the car towed away and have the owner pay the costs for the removal of the car. The court agreed to the first argument: the authorities were allowed to have the car towed away, but not to the second. The authorities had failed to show that they were aware of the fact that the statutory system discriminated between the decision to end an offence and the decision to have the offender pay the costs. The court quashed the decision of the administrative body, on the ground that it lacked sound and sufficient reasons.[22]

Note that in this case, the court did not choose 'disproportionality' or 'unreasonableness' as a ground to quash the decision. But it could have done. In other cases about the recovery of costs, the test of unreasonableness is applied.[23] The cited example shows that in some Dutch cases in which the court quashes the contested decision, one could say that the line of reasoning of the court is much like that in the UK: that the administrative body fettered its discretion.[24]

To summarise, in cases where the contested administrative decision has the character of a punitive sanction, the administrative court is not limited to a restraint control. It should form its own judgment of whether the weight of the sanction is in accordance with the gravity of the offence. More generally speaking, one can say that the courts exercise a stricter control when punitive sanctions are at hand. The field of sanctions in general – that is to say, regardless of whether they have a punitive or a restorative character – is a field where plaintiffs relatively often complain that a decision is unreasonable.

22 *Weggesleept uit de Gerard Doustraat* ABRvS 17 June 2009, *AB* 2010/65 (comment by Damen).

23 ABRvS 31 October 2012, *AB* 2013/72 (note Spijker & Van Mil). In addition, the GALA explicitly holds that the costs to end an offence can be recovered from the offender, unless that would not be 'reasonable' (Art 5:25 GALA).

24 See, e.g., Carol Harlow and Richard Rawlings, *Law and Administration* (CUP 2009) 217. Timothy Endicott, *Administrative Law* (2nd edn, OUP 2011) 269.

5.2.3.3 Case-law: after Maxis and Praxis *comes silence?*

In the period that followed *Maxis and Praxis*, there are few cases about 'arbitrariness' or proportionality outside the field of sanctions that appear to have attracted the attention of scholars. No developments regarding the method or intensity of judicial control of administrative action can be reported. No steps towards adopting the method that is used in EU law or German law to perform a proportionality test are visible. Elements of such a test are rare in Dutch case law.[25] Is there only silence after *Maxis and Praxis*?

It is true that cases are rather exceptional in which the court finds that a decision of an administrative body violated the prohibition of arbitrary decisions. I will give two examples.

The first example refers to a case in which a minister had originally awarded a subsidy, but after the activities had taken place, the same authority decided to award no money after all. A company that utilised a slaughterhouse had been granted a subsidy for architectural provisions that would improve hygiene. These provisions should be ready on a certain date, because of new regulations that would enter into force by then. In order to have the provisions ready on time, the company had calculated that it would have to contract a builder before the end of July. And so it did. However, the possibility to apply for the subsidy opened only two weeks later.

The minister decided to use his power to reduce the amount of the subsidy (in this case to zero), because the company had violated a condition: by contracting the builder in July, it had started the project before the ministry confirmed receipt of the application. The court decided that the decision to reduce the subsidy to zero was disproportionate.[26]

The second example is about a row of trees, planted to block the view in the applicant's back garden. The applicant complained that there was a violation of a prescription of a building permit. The prescription held that the trees should be planted one metre from the wall that separated the plots. According to the complaint, the actual distance was only sixty centimetres. The court considered that the administrative body could reasonably have decided that issuing an order to move the row of trees would be disproportionate.[27]

Apart from the control of punitive sanctions, there is not much debate about proportionality in Dutch case law. Maybe it is for that reason (i.e., too little focus on the subject) that recent research shows that the Dutch administrative courts are not very precise about the way they perform their control of discretionary powers.[28]

25 See for an incidental example below, in para 5.7.3.

26 ABRvS 8 May 2002, *AB* 2003/137 (note Verheij).

27 *Leiplatanen Nederweert* ABRvS 21 July, 2004, *AB* 2004/293. *Hekwerk Anna Poulowna* ABRvS 19 January 2005, *AB* 2005/50 (comments by Blomberg).

28 See the series of about twenty-five case notes (all labelled '*marginale toetsing*') by LJA Damen in *AB*, during the period of 2012–2013.

5.2.4 Approach to proportionality in the literature

The literature holds that the principle of proportionality relates to the balancing of interests the administration has to perform. This balancing has to be performed on two levels. The first level is an abstract, general level. The second is the concrete, specific level of the individual case. To start with, the public body has to determine which goals are to be pursued and to investigate which legal basis provides the competence to do so. The actual proportionality test consists of three steps.

The first step is to determine with which means – that fit within the framework of the competences – the goals can be achieved (criterion of *suitability*). The second step purports a confrontation of these means with the interests that are involved. In other words, which of the means will least harm the involved interests (criterion of *necessity/subsidiarity*)?

The third step holds an assessment of whether the chosen means are proportional to the goal that is pursued, regarding the nature of the interests involved and the extent to which these interests will be harmed (criterion of *proportionality in the narrow sense*).

With this description of the proportionality test according to the Dutch doctrine, I follow the work of Adrienne de Moor-van Vugt. This scholar has written extensively on the topic[29] and performed comparative research on criteria for judicial control of administrative action, commissioned by the Dutch Ministry of Justice, in the context of the preparation of the draft of the GALA.[30] The aforementioned presentation of the proportionality test can be said to be authoritative, at least in the sense that it represents the intentions of the text of Section 2 of Article 3:4 of the GALA. Moreover, the description is in line with the three-step approach in EU law. Dutch authors are familiar with this approach.[31] But does the description truly reflect the position of *Dutch* literature in the field of administrative law?

The abovementioned presentation of the principle of proportionality also builds on comparative research, including the legal systems of the Federal Republic of Germany, France, and Belgium and includes the legacy of EU case law. In that respect, this description of proportionality is certainly not a doctrine of Dutch origin. What is more important, it does not seem to be quite representative of the prevailing view on proportionality in the Netherlands as a methodology used by the Dutch courts. Gerards has advocated that the Dutch administrative courts should apply the method used by the

29 AJC de Moor-van Vugt, *Maten en gewichten. Het evenredigheidsbeginsel in Europees perspectief* (WEJ Tjeenk Willink 1995). I used AJC de Moor-van Vugt, *VUGA Commentaar* (n 17) E 3.2.3–11.

30 See above (n 14).

31 See i.e., Janneke Gerards, 'Het evenredigheidsbeginsel van art. 3:4 Awb en het Europees recht', in Barkhuysen, Den Ouden and Steyger (eds), *Europees recht effectueren* (Kluwer 2007) 73. Janneke Gerards refers to O Koch, *Der Grundsatz der Verhältnismäßigkeit in der Rechtsprechung des Gerichtshofs der Europäischen Gemeinschaften* (Duncker & Humblot 2003) 48ff.

European Court of Justice (ECJ) to test on proportionality (implying that the Dutch courts do not do so yet).[32]

The principle of proportionality has not captured extensive attention in leading Dutch administrative law textbooks. One of the textbooks, *Van Wijk/Konijnenbelt & Van Male*, has a paragraph with the heading 'proportionality' (*evenredigheid*). It mentions the three-step test the ECJ uses (which was described above). Subsequently, it is noted that case law still uses the criterion of the prohibition of arbitrariness that is subject to marginal control: only if the court assesses an *apparent* unreasonableness, will it conclude that Section 2 of Article 3:4 GALA is violated.[33]

Another textbook, written by Damen and other scholars, seems to avoid the word proportionality (*evenredigheid*) as much as possible. It only uses the word in excerpts citing Section 2 of Article 3:4 GALA. For the remainder of the paragraph, it speaks of the demand that interests are properly balanced. The term 'principle of proportionality' (*evenredigheidsbeginsel*) is reserved for the context of administrative sanctions that can be considered a 'criminal charge' in the sense of Article 6 of the ECHR.[34]

Schlössels and Zijlstra's textbook takes 'the prohibition of arbitrariness' as a starting point in discussing judicial control in substantive matters. However, the principle of proportionality is not given a prominent place in this textbook either.[35]

This quick scan of the leading textbooks shows that none of them presents a three-(or four-)[36] step approach as a model that is used by courts in Dutch administrative law.

5.2.5 Conclusion on the definition of proportionality

Dutch (statutory) law contains the term 'proportionality', and this term can refer to one of two things. The main rule is that it refers to a 'marginal' test on reasonableness, and that this test does not imply a test of means and ends. The second possibility is that proportionality is used in the context of a punitive sanction (criminal charge). In that case, proportionality means that there

32 Janneke Gerards (n 31).

33 *Hoofdstukken van Bestuursrecht* (n 3) 329–330 (para 51). The same chapter of the book holds a separate – more extensive – paragraph on the prohibition of arbitrariness and marginal testing (para 53).

34 LJA Damen and others, *Bestuursrecht. Deel*, 1 (3rd edn, *BJu* 2009) 392–397. However, in the 4th edition of 2013 the word 'balanced' (*evenwichtig*) is replaced by the word 'proportional' (*evenredig*). See 392ff. of that edition. I presume these changes have a didactic background, because the word 'proportional' has a more direct link to the text of the GALA.

35 RJN Schlössels and SE Zijlstra, *Bestuursrecht in de sociale rechtsstaat* (Kluwer 2010) 408–416.

36 Other authors advocate a *four*-step approach (see also the chapter on Germany). The first step of that approach is the one that is missing in the three-step model. It is the check that the administrative action has a legitimate aim. Aharon Barak, *Proportionality. Constitutional rights and their limitations* (CUP 2012) 131ff, also uses such a four-step approach.

should be proportionality between the severity of the sanction that is applied and the gravity of the offence committed. Dutch lawyers are familiar with the principle of proportionality as it is used in German law and in EU law, but this principle plays hardly any role in practice, and gets little attention in the leading textbooks.

5.3 Marginal control: a method of testing

Typical for marginal control is that the court does not give its own appreciation of what would be 'reasonable', or 'balanced', or 'arbitrary' in the case at hand. The court looks at the outcome of the balancing of interests the administration has performed. Only if there is an apparent *imbalance*, will the court assess a violation of the legal standards. This marginal control is different in that respect from judicial control in other cases. In most situations, judicial control is performed by assessing whether there has been a violation of a legal standard. This assessment is easily reduced to a 'yes' or 'no' question. For instance: was there an obligation to be heard? If so, is the party heard? If not, the norm is violated. Or: was there an obligation to give adequate reasons? Yes? Do the reasons that are given qualify as adequate reasons? If not, the norm is violated.

This 'yes or no' control has a 'digital', 'black or white' character. Even if the assessment may be difficult – for example, the assessment whether the given reasons are adequate – the control is presented as an answer to a 'yes or no' question: the question whether a line has been crossed or not. When the method of marginal control is used, this is different. Then, the courts do not look for a line that is crossed or not. They even refuse to tell where the line between balance and imbalance, or reasonable and unreasonable, should be drawn, because it is not their constitutional position to decide on that point. Instead, they focus on the outcome that has been reached in the specific case and simply admit that it is not up to the court to decide whether a well-balanced decision has been taken.

From a legal point of view, the administration may have discretion in the matter (or margin of appreciation), but there is a limit to that discretion and that is where the court sees an apparent unreasonableness or imbalance or disproportionality.

Law sets a limit to choices made by administrative bodies. That limit is not to be found by looking for a certain spot where proportionality is reached in a case like the case at hand. It is to be found by looking at the decision that is taken and answering the question whether the outcome exceeds the boundaries of what can be considered proportionate.

Let me give a graphic representation of what just has been argued. Figure 5.1 sketches the line drawn by the court when performing the ordinary control to assess whether there has been unequal treatment or not (yes or no) in the case:

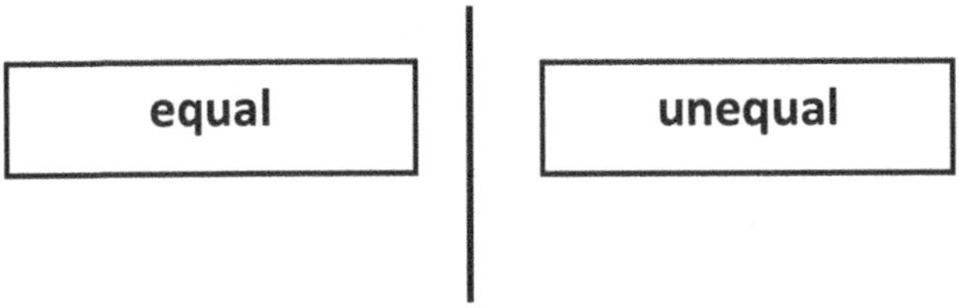

Figure 5.1 Judicial assessment of unequal treatment

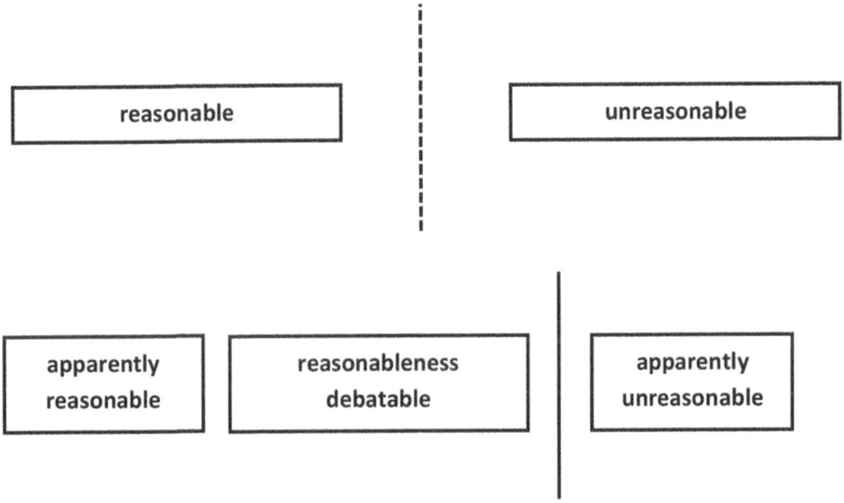

Figure 5.2 Marginal control

Figure 5.2 represents marginal control. The court does not draw a line between reasonable and not (upper half of the picture, with the dotted line in the middle). It refuses to define where reasonableness ends and unreasonableness begins. Instead, it focuses on the case at hand and expresses that it is capable of assessing whether this is a case of *apparent* unreasonableness. Note that in this type of marginal control, the *criterion* ('unreasonable', 'arbitrary', 'disproportional') is not the most dominant factor. Instead of 'unreasonable' one could use 'unfair', or 'arbitrary'. The dominant factor is the *method of control*. Furthermore, note that the fact that because we are discussing a method of control, the question of the *intensity* of control is still open. One could call the marginal control a restrained form of control. But that leaves the question: how restrained is restrained? The intensity depends on the legal framework of the topic at hand. I will come back to that.

The reason for this 'restrained' method of control is evident. The courts want to show that they know they have to respect the discretionary character of the power of the administration. On the other hand, they want to show that this discretion is not unlimited, however vaguely the exact position of that (legal) limit is situated. This dilemma is visible in the first case where the Dutch Supreme Court formulated the formula that became known as the 'prohibition of arbitrariness'.[37]

5.4 Interim conclusion

The interim conclusion can be that Dutch administrative law holds a statutory criterion of proportionality (*evenredigheid*) in the GALA, which applies to judicial control of administrative decisions. However, case law implies that this control differs from the control of proportionality that is performed under EU law or in German administrative law. In Dutch administrative law, the judicial control on proportionality is limited to a test of 'arbitrariness' or 'unreasonableness'.[38] This test comes down to a marginal (restrained) control of the acceptability of the outcome of a balancing of interests. Note that the courts are not supposed to balance these interests themselves. The question the courts have to answer is not 'what would constitute the right balance'. The question for the courts to answer is whether the outcome of the process of balancing, performed by the administration, is acceptable.

In theory, there is no reason that the control on proportionality in Dutch law could not include a *means and purpose test* as the ECJ performs. However, Dutch case law shows hardly any examples of applying such a means and purpose test. The examples that can be given all seem to figure in the field of national application of EU law.[39]

5.5 Elements of proportionality permeating other legal principles

The fact that – as a general rule – judicial control of the choices the administration makes in its decisions does not take the form of a four-step approach or a *means-ends test* resembling what the ECJ performs, does not justify the conclusion that Dutch administrative courts exercise a much more limited control than other courts that use proportionality more explicitly. Dutch administrative law doctrine holds other instruments for judicial control of administrative decisions. The equivalent for the first step in the German model (legitimate aim) is covered in Dutch administrative law by: the demands that

37 That first case is *Doetinchemse woonruimtevordering* (n 8).

38 There is an exception to the general rule that the control should be a restrained one, in case a decision qualifies as a 'criminal charge'. In such cases, the court should establish whether the severity of the sanction is in balance with the severity of the offence.

39 See below and chapter 6 for more extensive considerations on EU law.

administrative decisions need a statutory basis; that a power to decide may not be used to pursue a goal other than the goal provided in that statutory basis; and that administrative decisions may not conflict with decisions that have a higher hierarchical status. These instruments are not limited to statutory provisions. Some of them are to be found in what are called 'principles of good administration'. These principles show similarity with the French *principes généraux du droit*. Brown and Bell state that these French principles can be compared to the English principles of natural justice. But 'unlike English Law, *droit administratif* has refused to confine itself to restricted procedural rules, and it has considered itself free to recognize a new "general principle" when it considers this desirable'.[40] This remark applies to the Dutch principles too: not only do principles of good administration hold procedural standards, some of them also have a substantive nature. Furthermore, over the years, doctrine and case law have brought changes in the principles that are recognised as principles of good administration, as in France.

Some of the principles of good administration are codified in the GALA. The remaining principles of good administration cannot, however, be qualified as 'unwritten' standards of law. These principles have to be considered as criteria that determine lawfulness, and not merely as an expression of requirements of good behaviour. This means that if such a legal principle is violated, courts will conclude that the decision concerned is unlawful.

Some of those principles of good administration hold elements that are considered part of proportionality control in other legal systems. In this context, the principle that prohibits an order inflicting unnecessary burdens on an interested person should be mentioned.[41] If the goal of a measure could have been reached by choosing a less burdensome way, that way should have been chosen. According to the administrative law literature, the standard that the administration should choose for the least burdensome solution – at least whenever there is a choice – is sometimes considered as a principle that stands on its own.[42] Other authors explicitly link this principle to the requirement of proportional weighing of interests.[43] An example can be given to illustrate this point.

In 1990, the Council of State was asked to decide a case about the nuisance caused by cleaning ships in a shipyard. The ship-cleaning caused a nuisance to the yard's neighbours since water spray drifted past the premises of the shipyard. The administrative authorities prohibited all cleaning on the part of the shipyard where the nuisance was caused. The court agreed with the plaintiff that other measures to prevent nuisance were available and said that the

40 L Neville Brown and John S Bell, *French Administrative Law* (5th edn, Clarendon Press 1998) 216.

41 The principle goes back more than a century. It can be found in the doctoral thesis of Boasson (JJ Boasson, *De rechter tegenover de vrijheid van de administratie* (Wolters 1911) 381ff. See Nicolaï (n 5) 35. In more recent publications, it is referred to as the obligation to choose the measure that 'inflicts the least pain' to the people involved.

42 See e.g., Nicolaï (n 5) 420–422.

43 Damen and others (n 34) 2013 414.

principle of the duty of care (*zorgvuldigheid*) demands that the administration chooses the solution that puts the lightest burden on the addressee.[44]

The remarks that were just made may show that the first step and the third step of the proportionality test as described in the chapter on Germany, are 'covered' in Dutch administrative law too, although in the Netherlands they do not figure as steps in the context of proportionality. The second step regards the suitability of administrative action; the question of whether the measures that are taken are able to contribute to the goal that is pursued. Sometimes, it is argued that this step does not play an impressive role in EU law. It is very rare that 'the hurdle of suitability . . . causes problems. After all, why should a Member State . . . adopt a measure which is not effective?'.[45] However, the German chapter in this book shows that there may be cases in which the administrative body is mistaken about the suitability of a measure taken.

The question of suitability has no clear equivalent in Dutch administrative law. I am, however, confident that a measure, which is clearly not able to contribute to the goal pursued by the administration, will not survive the control of the administrative court. I expect, nevertheless, that a slightly different problem will arise: the lack of clarity or certainty as to whether a measure is suitable. The court would then have to fall back on the principle that administrative decisions need careful preparation. In this case, it could conclude that the administrative body should have investigated better what effects could be expected from the measure. But in many cases, the court will leave the benefit of the doubt to the administration.[46] Therefore, I assume that the suitability criterion is covered in Dutch law too.

The fact that the standards – which are part of the first three steps of the proportionality test described in the German chapter – are not integrated in a step-by-step approach to proportionality in the Netherlands can be explained by the historic development of criteria for judicial control of administrative action in Dutch law. In that development, the focus was on criteria that did not touch on examining the merits of a decision. The courts only gradually developed instruments with which administrative action could be controlled.

44 ABRvS 1 November 1990, *AB* 1991/118. Example found in Damen and others (n 34) 2013 414. Note that the court did not link the principle to proportionality, but to the principle of care.

45 JH Jans, S Prechal, R de Lange, RJGM Widdershoven and others, *Europeanisation of Public Law* (Europa Law Publishing 2007) 149.

46 For example, in ABRvS 4 May 2010, *AB* 2010/183 (note O Jansen). The court concluded that a publisher of a newspaper could be qualified as the 'employer' ('*werkgever*') in the sense of a statute on work performed by foreigners. The publisher had been fined a total of €312,000, because the papers were delivered by foreigners that had no work permit. These foreigners were hired by a distributing company. The court was of the opinion that the fact that the publisher contracted a firm that was responsible for transport and distribution of the newspapers, and the fact that in practice it was impossible for the publisher to check whether the statute was observed, does not detract from the publisher being responsible for taking the necessary measures to ensure that the statute is observed. Janneke Gerards (n 31 80) gives an example from ECJ case law. The example suggests that if there is *some* effect to further the goal that is pursued by the administrative authorities, even it is a small effect, the measure will pass the test of suitability. Case C-434/04 *Ahokainen and Leppik* (ECJ 28 September 2006).

As I argued above, the first steps the Dutch courts took can be considered a control that hardly goes deeper than control of legality. This does not mean that the criteria that were developed later on were restricted to procedural standards (e.g., the right to be heard). Substantive criteria were also recognised as principles of good administration, for example, the duty to treat equal cases equally and the principle of legal certainty. A more delicate example is the principle that the reasons the administration gives for taking a certain decision must be adequate, in the sense that they are able to justify the decision. This principle is violated if, for instance, the reasoning is self-contradictory, or if the decision is based on an inadequate qualification of the facts. This principle is delicate because it allows the court to criticise the administration for its evaluation of the merits of the case. Nevertheless, this kind of judicial criticism is considered acceptable in the light of the separation of powers because the idea is that the court does not substitute its own evaluation for that of the administration, but simply points out a defect in the reasoning by the administration. By using these principles of good administration, the courts have succeeded in establishing a rather close control of administrative action, without touching on the merits.

5.5.1 Unreasonableness: ultimum remedium

If the administrative court in a certain case is presented with different grounds of review, the criterion of proportionality or 'arbitrariness' will be the last in line. The courts will first look at the question of whether all statutory requirements are fulfilled (including the question of whether the power is used in conformity with the purposes of the legislator when it created that power), and then it will look into the question of whether specific principles of good administration are observed. Proportionality comes last, because – no matter how restrained the control is – it is a criticism on the merits of the case.[47] Even if the court presents its assessment as an imbalance between means and ends – an imbalance that can be determined in a more or less objective way – the assessment comes dangerously close to the merits of the case. The courts will avoid giving the impression that they take up the role of the administrative decision-maker. In practice, it is rather rare that an administrative decision is quashed on the grounds that it did not pass the marginal control on reasonableness.[48]

5.6 Margin of appreciation, discretion and judicial control

5.6.1 Distinction between 'margin of appreciation' and 'discretion (in a narrow sense)'

I have just argued that courts prefer to investigate the possible violation of statutory requirements to controlling whether the limits of discretionary

47 BWN de Waard, *Beginselen van behoorlijke rechtspleging* (WEJ Tjeenk Willink 1987) 150ff.
48 See above, par. 5.2.3.3.

powers have been exceeded. That general rule is a simplification, because statutes in the field of administrative law do not always prescribe which decisions administrative bodies should take in which circumstances. Statutes are sometimes limited to providing the basis for administrative bodies to choose how and when to use powers that are provided by the legislator. Therefore, it is important to deal with an important question: to what extent does the legislation shed light on when courts should show restraint in controlling administrative action?

Whenever a statutory provision offers the administration the possibility to choose how to decide (for instance, to grant or refuse an application), Dutch doctrine holds that the administration has a discretionary power that is called *beleidsvrijheid* (policy freedom). If the administrative decision is challenged in court, the choice the administration has made is open to a marginal control only.

Apart from the decision whether or not to use a discretionary power, there may be another matter to decide in applying a discretionary power: the question whether the statutory conditions to use the power are fulfilled (for instance, if a statute holds that if a house is unsafe, the administration has to prohibit the use of the house as a residential building). A plaintiff in court could argue that, in the case at hand, the administration was wrong in deciding that the statutory conditions are fulfilled. How should the court operate in such a case? The answer depends on the character of the statutory conditions concerned. Sometimes, the court will find that the question the court has to answer is a matter of a mere interpretation of the meaning of the statutory provision for the specific situation. In such a case, there is no reason for the court to leave a margin of appreciation to the administration. This is the case, for instance, if the question arises as to whether a construction is 'a building' in the sense of a certain statute. In such a situation, there is no reason to distinguish between an administrative law case and any other type of case that comes to court. Rather, it is up to the court to decide what the meaning of a norm is, and to answer the question of how a specific case qualifies under that norm. The court exercises full control. To take another example, suppose there is a norm that prohibits putting chairs on a lawn. If somebody puts a bench on a lawn, it is up to the court to decide whether the bench qualifies as a chair or not. There is no need to treat an administrative law case differently from any other case.

5.6.1.1 Explicit indication that a margin of appreciation has to be left to the administration

However, sometimes a statutory provision makes clear that the court should leave a margin of appreciation to the administration as to whether the conditions of a norm are met. That is the case, for instance, when a statute allows the minister to take certain measures, if, '*to the judgment of the Minister*', there is a serious threat to public health. In such a case, the question of whether a 'serious threat to public health' is at stake, has to be answered by the minister, and the court has to leave the minister a margin of appreciation in answering the question.

To address the abovementioned situations, the Dutch literature uses the term *beoordelingsvrijheid* (margin of appreciation). It avoids the term *beleidsvrijheid* (discretion in policy) that is used to express the discretion to decide in a positive or a negative way from the point of view of the addressee. In the example of the threat to public health, the text of the statutory provision contains the explicit message that the legislator intends to create such a margin of appreciation.[49] In the context of this chapter, I have translated *beoordelingsvrijheid* as 'margin of appreciation'. '*Beleidsvrijheid*' (policy freedom) has also been called 'discretion (in a narrow sense)'.[50]

5.6.1.2 Implicit indication that a margin of appreciation has to be left to the administration

If a statute does not explicitly mention that it is the task of the administrative body to discern whether a certain situation is at hand, Dutch doctrine holds that there can be, nevertheless, a reason to assume that the administrative body has a margin of appreciation. Of course, if there is no explicit indication, it may be rather unclear whether a norm is intended to leave a margin of appreciation or not. Take, for example, the right to a benefit for unemployment. Let us suppose the statute says that a person loses the right to a benefit on refusing to accept an offer of 'suitable work'. Is the question of whether the work refused was 'suitable' a question where the court has full control? Or, should the court leave a margin of appreciation to the administration? Dutch law accepts that sometimes the court should leave a margin of appreciation – although the statutory norm does not hold an explicit indication that the court has to do so – as if the statutory text held an explicit statement that the judgment is primarily up to the administration.[51]

In cases where the courts have to leave a margin of appreciation, the method of judicial control is, in essence, the same as when there is discretion.

49 The suggestion to distinguish between *beoordelingsvrijheid* and *beleidsvrijheid* in the Netherlands goes back to W Duk, 'De zachte kern van het bestuursrecht', in *RMThemis* (1978) 564–587 and (from the same author) 'Beoordelingsvrijheid en beleidsvrijheid', in *RMThemis* (1988) 156–169. *NB1*: I see Duk as the spiritual father, although in his 1988 article, Duk himself attributes the term '*beoordelingsruimte*' to AM Donner. Donner may have first used this term, but when he talks about the concept, he refers to the 1978 article by Duk.

More about the topic of '*beoordelingsvrijheid*' and '*beleidsvrijheid*' in *Hoofdstukken van Bestuursrecht* (n 3) 147ff or Damen and others (n 34) (2013) 335–343.

50 For readers from abroad, I should clarify that Dutch authors would not hesitate to call a 'margin of appreciation' a form of 'discretion'. That is why I added 'in a narrow sense'. The real distinction advocated in Dutch doctrine, is not the distinction between 'margin of appreciation' and 'discretion', but the distinction between *beleidsvrijheid* and *beoordelingsvrijheid* as just explained. However, this distinction too is of a rather academic nature, because in both situations the courts have to show restraint.

51 It was HD van Wijk who showed that there may be quite a few cases in which it can be said that the legislator has implicitly conferred a margin of appreciation (*beoordelingsvrijheid*). Van Wijk (n 4).

The court will exercise a *marginal control.* The judges will not ask themselves 'what decision would we have taken, if were in the administrator's position?'. Instead, they will ask: 'is the choice the administration has made within the boundaries of what could have been reasonably chosen?'.

5.6.2 Leaving a margin of appreciation: within and beyond the separation of powers

The traditional answer to the question of why courts should show restraint (whether the administration has discretionary power or a margin of appreciation) is that the court should not take over the role of the administration in case the legislator had the intention to lay a certain power in the hands of the administration. This answer is based on a vision of separation of powers and/or ideas about how public administration should function in a democratic society. It is the administration that has democratic legitimation and it is a good thing that representatives of the people, often organised in political institutions, influence the administration when it is setting out policy lines.

I will call the *first* ground for restraint 'policy sensitivity'. When there is policy sensitivity, political parties may have very different ideas about how to use a statutory power. Political parties may differ in their approach of the role of public authorities in, for instance, matters of education, art or leisure facilities. In other fields, the political dimension of 'policy sensitivity' might not be so apparent.

The *second* category consists of cases that need special (non-legal) expertise to take the right decision. An old example is the question of whether there is 'a reasonable certainty' that a pesticide 'will not have damaging side-effects'.[52] Note that, in this category, the reason for allowing a margin of appreciation has little to do with the need for courts to keep out of a *political* debate.[53] As far as some subjects are concerned, the legislator has even excluded administrative decisions about them from the right of appeal to court (e.g., examinations; technical examination of vehicles or airplanes).[54] In other cases of technical expertise, the situation is more complex, for example, if a concept like 'best available practices' is decisive in obtaining an environmental permit.

In the context of environmental permits, in the past, the Dutch Council of State exercised an intensive control. Statutory provisions read that such a permit could only be refused to protect environmental interests. The statute expressly states that prescriptions can be attached to an environmental permit. The Council of State used an intense level of control of what is necessary for the environment. In 1998, the court changed its view. Since then, the

52 *Vlododex Band* CBb 31 May 1977, *AB* 1977/349; CBb 20 March 1974, *M&R* 1974 54.

53 As Duk says: 'Would "a reasonable certainty" (that no harmful side-effects will occur) have a different meaning, depending on the question of whether the ruling minister is left wing or right wing?'. Duk (n 49) (1978) 575, note 26.

54 See Article 8:4 GALA.

court has declared that a margin of appreciation has to be left to the administrative authorities. That margin of appreciation is limited by demands that are derived from the latest generally accepted environmental techniques.[55]

The *third* category concerns cases where the administration has a certain special expertise itself because it has performed research into those kinds of cases, and because it has studied many other, similar cases. For this reason, the administration is the best party to guarantee sound and consistent decision-making: better than if the court – that does not have as many sources of information and sees only incidental cases – were to exercise intense control.[56]

The *fourth* group refers to situations in which there is an administrative body that has to be able to decide quickly on whether or not action should be taken. In those cases, a certain degree of freedom of choice is needed on practical grounds. One can think of police action or measures to prevent disorder.

The *fifth* category is a group of situations where other practical factors play a role, like the situation where a seemingly 'objective' norm is intertwined with discretionary power or a margin of appreciation. To illustrate, article 3 of the *Monumentenwet 1988* holds that the minister 'can' label a 'monument' as a protected monument. The word 'can' indicates that this is a discretionary power. But in court, the debate often concerns the question of whether the building should be considered as a monument or not. The statute defines 'monument' as an object that is of general interest because of (for instance) its historical value (art. 1). One could argue that the question of whether a building is a monument is an objective matter that deserves full control by the court. But generally speaking, that would be rather artificial because the opinion that a building is worth protecting comes very close to the decision to label a monument as a protected monument. And the law is very clear on this: the minister has discretionary power to take that decision.[57]

Another example is 'in case of danger' the administrator of a waterworks can take the measures that seem fit 'as long as the situation requires such measures'. These conditions are formulated without a margin of appreciation ('danger'; 'require'), but the message of the statutory article is clear: it is for the administrator to decide whether (and which) measures are in order, and the control by the court should be limited (article 5.30, § 1, *Waterwet*).

55 *Varkenshouderij Breda* ABRvS 21 April 1998, *AB* 1998/199 (note Jurgens).

56 *Asielrelaas* ABRvS 27 January 2003, *AB* 2003/286 (comment by Vermeulen). Note that if the court exercises only a limited control on an aspect of a decision (as in this case, the credibility of the information that an asylum-seeker provides about the reasons he or she had to flee), this does not affect the other means the courts has for control, like a control on principles of good administration, like the duty to perform careful investigation and to give reasons. In the case cited, the court explicitly shows that it is aware of that.

57 BWN de Waard, 'De matigende rechter', in T Barkhuysen, W den Ouden & JEM Polak (eds), *Bestuursrecht harmoniseren* (BJu 2010) 476, inspired by AP Klap, 'Rechter en bestuur: communicerende vaten of concurrerende machten?', in *NTB* (2007) 183–194.

To recapitulate: the reasons for courts to show restraint in controlling administrative action may have different backgrounds; that background is certainly not always fear of interfering with political decisions. The following categories were listed:

a) sensitivity for policy (in a broad sense);
b) special (non-legal) expertise is needed for the decision;
c) the administrative body is better equipped to decide than the courts;
d) the administrative body has to operate in a situation that demands immediate action;
e) other practical factors, in particular when that discretionary power is intertwined with the meaning of a vague term.

Of these categories, the third one deserves further elaboration. In the aforementioned case, *Asielrelaas*, the way the Council of State controlled a decision by the minister in an asylum case was discussed. The court declared in this case that the minister should have a margin of appreciation, where it concerns the *credibility* of the grounds the asylum-seeker gives for his or her reasons to flee (the 'asylum story'). The court considered that the minister evaluates credibility on the basis of detailed questioning and by comparing the story with everything known about the situation in the country or region concerned on the basis of information gathered by embassies or consulates and other objective sources, as well as the questioning of other persons in a similar situation. This enables the minister to assess credibility by comparing information. The court is not able to conduct such an assessment.[58] There is truth in that.

It is clear that the assessment of the credibility of a story is not a matter of mere facts. It has an element of qualification of the facts, of giving meaning to facts. If there are no witnesses, or other (reliable) sources of information about what happened, there is no way to establish what truly occurred. It is then very likely that the minister will have a better picture than the court will ever be able to have. However, if the minister has to depend on a variety of sources that are difficult to control, there is a real danger that mistakes may be made.[59] In such a situation, it is very important that the person concerned has a proper basis to defend his or her case by having opportunities of rebuttal. Recent decisions by the Council of State show that the fact that the minister has a margin of appreciation does not entail that the assessment of credibility cannot be contested successfully in court. For instance, if the story of the asylum-seeker is supported by medical evidence, the minister has to go

58 Considerations from the case that was mentioned above: *Asielrelaas* (n 56).

59 Arnout Klap, *Vage normen in het bestuursrecht* (WEJ Tjeenk Willink 1994) 231–234, gives some disquieting examples of cases where the information, upon which the minister based his decisions, was deficient. The examples may now be outdated, but they are only advanced here to show that deficient information in this field is not hypothetical.

into the matter if he or she wants to hold on to the opinion that the story is not credible. It may be necessary for the minister to seek new medical advice in order to be able to stick to the conclusion that the story is not credible.[60]

Note that the point of view of the court implies that, in this field, the administrative body is even more capable of ensuring equal treatment of cases than the court. However, I am not sure it is wise to look at the matter as one where *a margin of appreciation* is appropriate. I would prefer to consider credibility as a special field where *proof* is problematic. One could say that this is not an example that is very different from those of the second category (cases that need special expertise). The reason I labelled the asylum story cases as a special category is that, in these cases, the special expertise is generated *inside* the institutions of the administrative body. What is more, the special expertise is not just a matter of 'objective' (controllable) knowledge: part of the expertise is kept secret. Both of these factors call for a high level of attention by the court as an independent and impartial guardian of rights. Granting a margin of appreciation does not help in achieving that goal. From a fair trial point of view, this might actually be disappointing.

5.7 In what circumstances is the proportionality test used?

In this section, the question is raised of whether categories of cases – or other circumstances – can be identified in which it is more likely to find examples in Dutch administrative law of a proportionality test like the test used in EU law.

5.7.1 The field of law: EU law or national law?

Earlier in this chapter, I remarked that Dutch case law shows very few examples of applying a means-ends test, such as the one performed by the ECJ. As previously mentioned, in theory, there is no reason why the control performed by the Dutch administrative courts under the GALA could not include such a test. Indeed, a few examples can be found, but they all seem to regard cases in which EU law is at stake. When discussing the approach of the Dutch Council of State, Jans *et al.* start with the remark that, according to this highest general administrative court in the Netherlands, in appraising Article 3:4(2) of the GALA, the Dutch administrative courts have to confine themselves to a test of arbitrariness. However, with regard to disputes on the compatibility of national measures with EU internal market law, the proportionality principle is applied 'EU-style', the authors claim.[61]

60 ABRvS 31 July 2013 (nr. 201211436/1/V4), JV 2013/355 (note Zwaan). ABRvS 19 February 2014, *AB* 2014/222 (note AM Reneman).

61 JH Jans, R de Lange, S Prechal and RJGM Widdershoven, *Europeanisation of Public Law* (Europa Law Publishing 2007) 145. The authors mention (just) one example of a case, decided by the Council of State: ABRvS 8 February 2001, *Milieu en Recht* 2001/7–8 no 73.

An example can be found in a case that was judged in 1996. A farmer had transformed farmland into woodland and was awarded more than €40,000 on the basis of a Dutch subsidy ordinance that was enacted to implement EC Regulation No. 2080/92. Payment of the subsidy would follow, if the applicant lodged a form holding a 'statement of completion'. This form had to be lodged before a certain date. In this case, the farmer was eleven days late. The minister had decided that, for that reason, the farmer had lost all claim. The court, however, concluded that the fact that the farmer did not comply with the ordinance led to consequences that are disproportionate (the court said: 'in no relation') to the purposes of a good administrative implementation of the subsidy programme laid down in the ordinance. The court concluded that there had been a breach of Section 2 of Article 3:4 GALA 'and the corresponding EU-Law principle of proportionality'.[62]

In the example above, the court held that the EU-law principle of proportionality was incorporated in the provision in the GALA. And it is true that the court did not use the wording typical for the marginal testing of whether the prohibition of arbitrariness was violated. But it should also be noted that the court compared the outcome, the effects, of applying a rule to the interests served by upholding the rule. In looking at the outcome in that way, the court performed a test that is very much like the test of 'apparent unreasonableness' (prohibition of arbitrariness) that the Dutch administrative courts apply in other cases.

5.7.2 The field of law: human rights?

Some human rights, notably some of those laid down in the European Convention on Human Rights, can be limited by national statutes, in case these limitations are 'necessary in a democratic society'.[63] Dutch courts do go into these questions of necessity, but they do not always expressly link their considerations to proportionality. Most probably, the courts consider this control as a matter of checking whether the conditions of the paragraph in the treaty are being respected. If the plaintiff expressly argues that the administrative act at hand is disproportional, the court tends to confine its considerations to proportionality in the narrow sense, as it is perceived in the Netherlands. It simply answers the question of whether the administrative action concerned can stand the test on arbitrariness.[64] Occasionally, however, a court does consider

62 CBB 24 July 1996, *AB* 1996/396; *RAwb* 1997, 14. See also CBB 31 January 1996, *Rawb* 1996, 63. Both cases are discussed in JH Jans and others (n 60) (2nd edn (in Dutch) 2002) 201–202.

63 For example, in Art 8, 9, and 10 ECHR. See AJ Nieuwenhuis, 'Van proportionaliteit en appreciatiemarge: de noodzakelijkheidstoets in de jurisprudentie van het EHRM', in AJ Nieuwenhuis, BJ Schueler and CM Zoethout (eds), *Proportionaliteit in het publiekrecht* (Kluwer 2005) 37–60.

64 *Dijkverbod Landvreugd* ABRvS 19 December 1996, *AB* 1997/79. In that case, the mayor of Amsterdam had prohibited a drug dealer from entering a specific district of the city. The court decided that the prohibition was not apparently disproportional.

that an administrative body, if it takes a decision that prohibits the exercise of human rights, has to investigate whether lighter measures than a prohibition would be sufficient.[65]

5.7.3 Control of regulation or of individual decisions?

The administrative courts in the Netherlands do not have jurisdiction over administrative decisions (in some jurisdictions, called regulations) that have the character of general rules.[66] Most cases that the administrative courts deal with relate to administrative decisions that are directed at *individuals* (*beschikkingen*).

Roughly speaking, the competence of the Dutch administrative courts is limited to administrative decisions in individual cases. General rules cannot be the object of an appeal. The fact that Dutch case law is, in the main, strictly about *individual* decisions (a rough estimation would be 95% of the cases), entails that the step-by-step approach of the proportionality principle, as used in EU law or German law, is often not appropriate.

The first three steps of that approach imply a check on whether the administrative action has a legitimate aim, is suitable to reach the goals that are proposed (suitability, aptitude) and is necessary (criterion of necessity; was a less damaging instrument available?). In practice, many Dutch administrative law cases concern decisions that were taken as a reaction to a demand or a request. Therefore, the questions of whether the decision is *necessary*, or whether other instruments would have better fit the purpose, are hardly ever opportune.[67]

The question of whether the goal, for which the administrative act is taken, is legitimate, whether it has a proper basis in a conferral of competence, is part of the control that Dutch courts can apply. However, in the Netherlands, this control is performed under another label, that of:

a) *détournement de pouvoir* (abuse of power); or
b) incompatibility with the statutory provisions that provide the administrative body with the competence to act.

Therefore, in Dutch administrative law, the most relevant question is the fourth step, where the question about proportionality *stricto sensu* is asked: *is the administrative decision disproportionate, all interests considered?*

65 Pres Rb Zutphen16 May, 2002, *AB* 2002/301. A prohibition of a public demonstration was set aside by the court.
66 This is according to Article 8:2 of the GALA.
67 This may be different if (detailed) prescriptions are integrated in an individual decision such as a permit. In such a case, the question can be raised as to whether (all) these prescriptions are necessary. See fi ABRvS 26 April 2011, *AB* 2001/213 (note Jongma).

In some cases, however, regulatory measures are at stake in a case before the administrative court.[68] In such cases, the court sometimes explicitly answers the question of whether the regulation is *suitable*. Think about the following case: the Council of State determined that a prohibition to feed doves serves a reasonable goal: to diminish the nuisance caused by pigeons. The court established that expert reports differ about the best way to reach this goal. The reports are not clear about the question of whether the wellbeing of the animals is damaged, or whether the wellbeing of the pigeons would be better served by other means than the prohibition of feeding them (no violation of the obligation to choose the 'lesser burden'). The court concludes that the prohibition of feeding the pigeons does not violate the statute about the health and wellbeing of animals.[69]

However, if Dutch courts have to answer the question of whether general rules are violating a legal standard, they often seem to limit themselves to answering the question of whether the body could have reasonably established that rule; just as the courts do when an individual decision is at hand. An example can be found in a case about a regulation to compensate for damage as a result of a poultry disease. In this case, there had been an outbreak of a poultry disease in a region of the country. The minister issued an order to restrict the transportation of poultry in that region. The transport restrictions generated new health risks and threats to the welfare of the animals in the region. Furthermore, the minister held the opinion that there were too many poultry farms in the region anyway. Therefore, the minister made an offer to farmers that the state would buy their (healthy) poultry. A farmer was offered a sum of almost €87,000 on the basis of the Compensation Regulation that the minister issued. The farmer brought the decision that he would be paid only €87,000 to the administrative court. One of his arguments was that his poultry had been perfectly healthy, and that it was unreasonable that the regulation had limited the compensation to only 80% of the market value of such poultry.

The court considered that it was competent to determine that such a regulation is an act of 'arbitrariness' (*willekeur*). In this case, the court came to the conclusion that the minister, considering all relevant interests, could not reasonably have chosen this criterion of 80%. The court then considered how the court should deal with this question:

> The court is not assigned to assess the value or societal importance of these interests at its own discretion. Furthermore, the nature of the

68 Although there is no possibility of a *direct* appeal, regulations can be subject to control by the administrative courts in an indirect way whenever the plaintiff who has challenged an individual decision argues that the individual decision is illegal because the regulation on which the decision is based is violating norms of a hierarchical higher order. For examples, see the cases that will be discussed next (*Groningse duivenvoerder* and *Financial Compensation poultry disease*).

69 *Groningse duivenvoerder* ABRvS 16 December 2009, *AB* 2010/178 (note Damen).

regulatory function and the position of the court in the legal system, imply that the control by the court should be restrained.[70]

In this example, the court confines itself to answering the question of whether the criteria for compensation could pass the test of arbitrariness. It does not explicitly answer questions of necessity or suitability, although the case concerned a *general rule*, instead of an individual decision. The reason why the court did not do so may relate to the fact that the plaintiff only complained about the unreasonableness of the compensation, but one could argue that applying a proportionality test is a matter of applying legal standards, and therefore, the court should, *ex officio*, follow the line of reasoning of such a test.

5.8 How is the test on arbitrariness applied?

Since Dutch law shows hardly any cases in which an 'EU-type of proportionality test' is performed, the last questions about proportionality in Dutch administrative law are about the Dutch equivalent of proportionality in the narrow sense: the prohibition of arbitrariness.

5.8.1 Does the intensity of review vary depending on the type of case?

The intensity of review may vary depending on the type of case. For example, a local-government decision based on its authority in the field of public order is considered a type of case where the courts should allow broad margins of discretion. Cases about the closing of a café because soft drugs have been sold there can serve as an example. Sometimes, a café is closed for the duration of twelve months. The purpose of determining such a long period is not to punish the owner, but to prevent further violations of the law. Often, the owner of such a café argues that this is disproportionate, because it will ruin the café. Such arguments will generally not convince the court. The reasoning of the court is that, for the sanction to be effective, such a long period may be necessary.[71]

70 *Financial Compensation poultry disease* ABRvS 22 June 2005, *AB* 2006/4 (note Van Duijvenvoorde & Van Ballegooij). On another occasion, the Council of State used the formulation: 'in such a case the court cannot answer the question of whether it could imagine a more righteous or just arrangement, but should confine itself to answering the question of whether the administrative body, considering all relevant interests, could reasonably have come to the regulation at hand'; *Codfish quota* ABRvS 4 December, 1990, *AB* 1991/597 (note Simon). Another example: in *Terrasboot Delft* ABRvS 18 July 2001, *AB* 2003/340 (note Damen), the Council of State does not mention proportionality, but it calls the control the court should perform in a case like that an 'extremely marginal' control.

71 See *De Danssalon* ABRvS 3 May 2006, *AB* 2006/392 and *Coffeeshop De Zone* ABRvS 5 July 2006, *AB* 2006/394 and see FR Vermeer, *Gedogen door bestuursorganen* (Kluwer 2010) 171ff. However, the court considered the five-year closure of a shop where soft drugs had been sold to be too long in ABRvS 8 September 2010, *AB* 2010/307 (note Tollenaar and Vermeer). The court found that a five-year closure period would convert the restorative measure into a punitive sanction.

A strong reason for the courts to show restraint is that the subject matter is highly politically sensitive or requires special (non-legal) expertise. As already mentioned, some decisions are expressly excluded from the possibility of appeal in the GALA, such as a decision to apply a statute safeguarding the military interests of the Kingdom of the Netherlands or its allies, or a decision that is based on an exam (Art. 8:4 GALA). High political sensitivity may be implied in a statutory criterion. An old but clear example is the case of the refusal of a permit to export four submarines to Taiwan. The criterion that was used in the decision to refuse the permit was 'the interest of the international legal order'. The minister refused the permit because China, which was formally still at war with Taiwan, had threatened to break all relations with the Netherlands and Dutch companies. There were conflicting interests involved: the refusal of the permit caused loss of employment at the shipyard. Deciding on such a permit is a matter that has a high degree of political sensitivity.[72]

5.8.2 What factors make the judicial review more or less intense?

It is exceptional that courts explicitly indicate why the control they exercise is more or less intense. However, it is safe to say that much depends of the regulatory context. Take, for instance, administrative decisions in which Art. 4:6 GALA is applied. That provision holds that administrative bodies can reject applications in a very simple way, in case they constitute a mere repetition of a previous application that was also rejected and the applicant does not provide new facts. The legislator intended this provision to avoid excessive administrative burdens. If the courts were to exercise an intensive control, that objective would not be reached.

The intensity of control may also depend on developments in the case. The history of a conflict may influence the intensity of control by the courts. If the administration has taken a lot of time to make a decision, or if a previous decision had been quashed by the court in the same case, these would be factors that tend to intensify the testing.

5.8.3 The prohibition of arbitrariness in the case-law and the literature

Above, it was argued that Dutch courts hardly ever perform a proportionality test like the ECJ uses. If we limit the scope to proportionality in the narrow sense and look at the Dutch equivalent, the prohibition of arbitrariness, one can say that scholars often criticise the courts for the way they perform their

72 CBb 28 March 1984, *AB* 1984/499 (note Van der Wielen). Damen and others (n 34, 337) mentions the case as one in which the court would read a margin of appreciation in the statutory formula. However, in his doctoral dissertation, Klap (n 59, 255) argues that the court did not show much restraint, but relied on the parliamentary history of the statutory provision and concluded that the minister was right to argue that 'military interests' included 'good relations with foreign countries'.

control. Arnout Klap concludes in his doctoral thesis on vague legal terms, published in 1994, that the Dutch courts hardly ever indicate why they have chosen a marginal or integral way of control. That is not problematic, provided that the courts act in a way that can be expected on the basis of doctrine. This is not always the case and, moreover, the intensity of control by the courts suffers from inconsistencies, Klap concludes.[73] Some twenty years later, Leo Damen published a series of twenty-five case notes in 2012–2013. His findings in many cases are rather harsh: the courts often leave a margin of appreciation in cases where, according to the doctrine, there is no reason to do so.[74] In addition, the courts are very inconsistent in the use of terminology. They often use 'margin of appreciation' where the doctrine would say 'discretionary power' and vice versa.[75]

5.9 Conclusions

The GALA requires that administrative bodies observe proportionality. However, when an administrative decision is brought to court, in general, the court does not perform a proportionality test as German courts, the ECJ or the ECtHR do. A Dutch administrative court will not follow the first three steps of such a test, although it has the power to use criteria that are comparable to those of the first steps of a proportionality test. The court will only perform such a check on these criteria in case there is an explicit complaint that a specific criterion is being violated. For example, the court can find that a decision is illegal because there was a violation of the principle that administrative authorities may not put a burden on people that is heavier than necessary. In Dutch law, this test of necessity is considered as a check on whether the action is according to the law and does not violate principles of good administration. If the decision fails the test, this will be an autonomous ground for quashing the decision, and the court will probably not refer to proportionality.

As for the fourth and last step of an EU-style proportionality test (proportionality in the narrow sense): the court does control the balancing of interests by the administration. However, this control has the character of a marginal control ('prohibition of arbitrariness'). The court does not apply a test of means and ends itself, but restricts its control to the question of whether the administrative body could reasonably have come to the result of the decision that was challenged in court. Only in cases where the administration has

73 Klap (n 59) 253.

74 For instance, in the case of the interpretation of a regulatory criterion, in his note under ABRvS 8 August 2012, *AB* 2012/310, Damen writes that there was no reason for a marginal control of the regulatory criterion concerned, and even if there had been, there was no reason whatsoever for the court to accept the interpretation the administrative body had produced. For a similar case, with similar comments by Damen, see ABRvS 8 December 2010, *AB* 2012/248.

75 ABRvS 25 April 2012, *AB* 2012/300 (comment by Damen).

imposed a punitive sanction, will the judicial control be more intense. In other words, the courts perform a restrictive control whenever it is up to the administration to decide on a discretionary basis. It is not always clear at first sight whether choices made by an administrative body have to be respected by the courts. There are two types of situation in which the courts are obliged to restrict themselves to a marginal control of the views of the administration. In the first, the administration has discretionary power. In that situation, it can decide whether it will use a power in a specific case or not. In the second type of situation, the space to choose does not concern the question of whether to take a positive or a negative decision. Instead, it concerns questions about the conditions in which a power can be used; e.g., of whether a power can be used in case of 'an immediate risk of a financial crisis'. The court does not always perform a full control of the way the administration has valued these conditions. It sometimes finds reasons to leave a margin of appreciation to the administration. In such a case, the courts will exercise a marginal control of the views of the administration only; just like a case where an administrative body has a discretionary power. In para 5.6 above, an analysis is given of the circumstances that give reason for the courts to assume that they should leave a margin of appreciation to the administration. para 5.7 goes into the question of in what circumstances an EU-style proportionality test is used in Dutch administrative law. The conclusion is that such a test is hardly ever used outside the field of the application of EU law by national authorities. Para 5.8 focuses on the application of the 'prohibition of arbitrariness' in Dutch law. The intensity of the control varies. Although the courts distinguish between situations where there is discretionary power and situations where there is a margin of appreciation, the courts are not very consistent in the use of the terminology.

References

Abas P, Giltay Veth NJP, Scholten Y, Wolffensperger GJ (eds), *Non sine causa* (WEJ Tjeenk Willink 1979).

Barak A, *Proportionality. Constitutional rights and their limitations* (CUP 2012).

Boasson JJ, *De rechter tegenover de vrijheid van de administratie* (Wolters 1911).

Brown NL, and Bell JS Commissie wetgeving algemene regels van bestuursrecht, *Voorontwerp Algemene wet bestuursrecht, Eerste deel* (Staatsuitgeverij 1987).

—— *French Administrative Law* (5th edn, Clarendon Press 1998).

Daalder EJ and de Groot GRJ (eds), *De parlementaire geschiedenis van de Algemene wet bestuursrecht, Eerste Tranche* (HD Tjeenk Willink 1993).

Damen LJA, Albers CLGFH, de Graaf KJ, Jans JH, Klap AP, Klingenberg AM, Marseille AT, Nicolaï P, Olivier BK, Tolsma HD, Vermeer FR, *Bestuursrecht. Deel 1* (Boom Juridische uitgevers 2013).

Duk W, 'De zachte kern van het bestuursrecht'(1978) *RMThemis* 564.

—— 'Beoordelingsvrijheid en beleidsvrijheid' (1988) *RMThemis* 156.

Endicott T, *Administrative Law* (2nd edn, OUP 2011).

Gerards J, 'Het evenredigheidsbeginsel van art. 3:4 Awb en het Europees recht', in Barkhuysen, Den Ouden and Steyger (eds), *Europees recht effectueren* (Kluwer 2007) 73.

Harlow C, and Rawlings R, *Law and Administration* (CUP 2009).

Hirsch Ballin EMH & Moor-van Vugt AJC de, 'Doel en middel in het bestuursrecht'(1986) *AA* 783.

Jans JH, S Prechal, R de Lange, RJGM Widdershoven, *Europeanisation of Public Law* (Europa Law Publishing 2007).

Klap AP, *Vage normen in het bestuursrecht* (WEJ Tjeenk Willink 1994).

—— 'Rechter en bestuur: communicerende vaten of concurrerende machten?', in *NTB* (2007) 183.

Koch O, *Der Grundsatz der Verhältnismäßigkeit in der Rechtsprechung des Gerichtshofs der Europäischen Gemeinschaften*, Duncker & Humblot 2003.

Moor-van Vugt AJC de, *Algemene beginselen van behoorlijk bestuur en buitenlandse equivalenten* (WEJ Tjeenk Willink 1987).

—— *Maten en gewichten. Het evenredigheidsbeginsel in Europees perspectief* (WEJ Tjeenk Willink 1995).

—— *VUGA Commentaar, Comments on Art. 3:4* (Reed Business Elsevier 1995).

Nicolaï P, *Beginselen van behoorlijk bestuur* (Kluwer 1990).

Nieuwenhuis AJ, 'Van proportionaliteit en appreciatiemarge: de noodzakelijkheidstoets in de jurisprudentie van het EHRM', in Nieuwenhuis AJ, Schueler BJ and Zoethout CM (eds), *Proportionaliteit in het publiekrecht* (Kluwer 2005) 37.

Rodriquez S, 'Traditional Model vs. Dialogue Model in US Legal System', in Roberto Caranta and Anna Gerbrandy (eds), *Traditions and Change in European Administrative Law* (Europa Law Publishing 2007) 267.

Schlössels RJN, and Zijlstra SE, *Bestuursrecht in de sociale rechtsstaat* (Kluwer 2010).

Struycken AAH, *Administratie of rechter* (1910).

Van Wijk HD, *Voortgaande terugtred* (VU 1959).

——, Konijnenbelt W, Van Male R, *Hoofdstukken van Bestuursrecht*, edited by Willem Konijnenbelt en Ron M. van Male (16th ed, Kluwer 2014).

Waard BWN de, *Beginselen van behoorlijke rechtspleging* (WEJ Tjeenk Willink 1987).

—— 'De matigende rechter', in T Barkhuysen, W den Ouden & JEM Polak (eds), *Bestuursrecht harmoniseren* (BJu 2010) 476.

Wiarda GJ, 'De betekenis van art. 6. lid 1 van het Europese Verdrag tot bescherming van de rechten van de mens voor de Nederlandse administratieve rechtsgangen' in P Abas and others (eds) *Non sine causa* (WEJ Tjeenk Willink 1979) 459.

6 The principle of proportionality in European law

Catherine Haguenau-Moizard, Yoan Sanchez

6.1 Introduction

It is no longer possible to do without a study of European law when analysing control of the administration's discretionary power. The influence of European law is increasing,[1] which is interesting both for the specialists of European law and for those of any other field of law. The Member States are nowadays highly influenced by the case law of the Court of Justice of the European Union (ECJ) and of the European Court of Human Rights (ECtHR). The proportionality test is no exception to this trend. For both courts, it has become an important means of controlling national authorities. However, each court uses a different kind of control. Although the primary purpose is always the limitation of public authorities' powers, the foundations of the proportionality control are substantially different.

The Council of Europe originally aimed – and still does – to 'achieve greater unity between its members for the purpose of safeguarding and realizing ideals and principles which are their common heritage, facilitating their economic and social progress'.[2] The European Convention is thus primarily based on this desire for closer links between its members through the protection of human rights. The EU had initially chosen an economic path before entering a more political integration. In the beginning, the EU aimed to map out the route to a solid economic integration and monetary union.[3] However, the EU quickly transformed into 'more than a mere market' as it became clear that 'the economic advantages of European unification [were] valid arguments for further construction of the EU . . . and the creation of a European way of life'.[4] This transformation meant that European integration

1 Matthias Ruffert, 'Europäisierung des Verwaltungsrechts', in A Bogdandy, S Cassese, M Huber (eds), *Handbuch Ius Publicum Europaeum*, Vol V (CF Müller 2011) 1221.

2 Bernadette Rainey, Elizabeth Vicks, LL Clare Ovey, Robin C A White, *Jacobs, White and Ovey: The European Convention of Human Rights* (OUP 2014) 5.

3 Charles R Bean, 'Economic and Monetary Union in Europe' (1992) 6(4) *Journal of Economic Perspectives* 31.

4 Jurgen Habermas, 'Why Europe Needs a Constitution' in Erik O Eriksen, John Erik Fossum, Agustín Menéndez (ed), *Developing a Constitution for Europe* (Routledge 2004) 19, 20.

would be further strengthened by the protection of fundamental rights. In this chapter, we will deal successively with the case law of these two institutions, striving to maintain a similar pattern to facilitate comparisons. We will begin by studying the proportionality test under the ECtHR (para 6.2), and we will devote more attention to ECJ case law in para 6.3.

6.2 The proportionality test in ECtHR case law

The proportionality test has become the favourite tool for monitoring compliance with the rights enshrined in the text of the European Convention. Unique both in its origin and in its diverse forms of expression, it has become an indispensable method of control, irrigating nearly all the articles of the Convention. Far from exercising a static control, the ECtHR has been able to use it flexibly in order to adapt it to the concrete circumstances and the particular requirements of the cases it has had to deal with.

6.2.1 The origins and diversity of expression of the proportionality test

6.2.1.1 A. The origins

The proportionality test – often described as an original German invention (see chapter 2) – appears to have been fully adopted and reshaped by the ECtHR. The Strasbourg judges appear to have created their own version of the proportionality test and apply it in different ways. In fact, there is ongoing dispute in the literature as to whether the ECtHR has been significantly influenced by the German 'version' of the principle of proportionality, or whether German law was a mere source of inspiration.[5]

Reading the text of the Convention or its additional Protocols, one finds little specific information on the proportionality test.[6] The Convention never uses the words 'proportionate', 'balanced' or 'disproportionate'. However, this does not mean that the idea of proportionality was not already there when the Convention text was drafted. In fact, some articles and subjects are structured in such a way that the idea of proportionality is fairly obvious. Such is the case with articles that establish the principle of the protection of a right or freedom first, and only then the possible restrictions. For example, in its first paragraph, Article 8 protects the right to family life and admits that this right may be limited, especially if it is 'necessary' to deal with certain situations. Article 10 protects the freedom of expression and provides, in

5 See Jonas Christoffersen, *Fair Balance: Proportionality, Subsidiarity and Primarity in the European Convention of Human Rights* (Brill 2009) 33–34.

6 See Jeremy McBride, 'Proportionality and the European Convention on Human Rights' in Evelyn Ellis (ed), *The Principle of Proportionality in the Laws of Europe* (Hart 1999) 23.

paragraph 2, that restrictions can be made – again, if it is 'necessary'. This two-step formulation helps to demonstrate that the *principle* is the protection of the right or freedom in question, and that the restriction must *necessarily* be the exception.

More surprisingly, the Court was able to reach a requirement of proportionality with respect to articles that do not contain such an idea. Thus, Article 14, which prohibits discrimination regarding the application of the Convention, is framed in absolute terms, far from the diptych described above. However, the ECtHR has decided that discrimination is possible when it is not disproportionate. In 1968, in a case against Belgium, concerning the use of languages in education (*Belgian Linguistic Case*), the judges stated that:

> the Court . . . does not consider that the measures adopted in this matter by the Belgian legislature are disproportionate to the requirements of the public interest which are being pursued as to constitute a discrimination contrary to Article 14 of the Convention.[7]

In the context of the *Belgian Linguistic Case*, one could conclude that a difference in treatment could be qualified as discrimination:

a) *unless it had a legitimate aim*, and
b) *unless there was a reasonable relationship of proportionality between the means employed and the aim pursued.*[8]

Speaking more in general terms, the Court added, nonetheless, that the ECHR implies 'a just balance between the protection of the general interest of the Community and the respect due to fundamental human rights.'[9] The term 'just balance' used in 1968 in the *Belgian Linguistic Case* evolved later into 'fair balance'.[10]

Similarly, in Article 1 of the First Protocol, protecting property rights, the ECtHR uses a proportionality test to ensure that the decision of compulsory purchase properly balances the public interest and the respect for fundamental rights. The Court derives this obligation from the text of the Convention, but this result could not have been predicted by simply reading it. The proportionality test is based both on the diptych structure of some articles, and the interpretation of other articles. Since no article clearly defines this test, the Court has been free to use and develop various forms of this test.

7 Case relating to certain aspects of the laws on the use of languages in education in Belgium (*Belgian Linguistic Case*) App no 1474/62 (ECtHR, 23 July 1968) para 7.

8 Yutaka Arai-Takahashi, *The Margin of Appreciation Doctrine and the Principle of Proportionality in the Jurisprudence of the ECtHR* (Intersentia 2001) 164.

9 *Belgian Linguistic Case* (n 7) para 7.

10 Jonas Christoffersen, *Fair Balance: Proportionality, Subsidiarity and Primarity in the European Convention of Human Rights* (Brill 2009) 39.

6.2.1.2 B. The different faces of the proportionality test

The systematisation of the proportionality test used by the ECtHR is not a simple task. While the study of individual cases might reveal a common structure at first sight, there are also many exceptions.

It is indeed remarkable that, in principle, the Court reasons in two stages. First, it ensures that the measures in question have a 'legitimate aim', and second, it ensures that they are proportionate. But in many other cases, the Court's reasoning develops in more stages. First, the Court checks whether there is an 'interference' and whether the interference with the right protected by the Convention is in accordance with the law. Second, the Court verifies whether that interference has a legitimate aim. Third, the Court examines whether the measure under analysis is necessary in a democratic society. This difference in structure is actually more apparent than substantial. In the multi-step method, the last two are actually comprehended in the first method. Why, then, is there an apparent difference?

The three-step test refers more explicitly to the *idea of proportionality*. The judges make an explicit reference to the requirement that the interference is prescribed by law, it is necessary in a democratic society, and meets specific and legitimate goals. However, once an article is explicitly considered by the Court, the latter will not automatically use the three-step method, or make explicit reference to the notion of an interference 'necessary in a democratic society'. The terminology is not clearly fixed and intangible. Two things should be remembered, however.

The first is the importance given to the purpose of the decision, including its legitimacy. Although it cannot be considered a full stage of the proportionality test, the control of the legitimate aim affects it. This appears clearly in 1986 in the *Gillow* judgment.[11]

While analysing whether the measure was 'necessary in a democratic society', the ECtHR stated that 'the notion of necessity implies a pressing social need, in particular, the measure employed must be proportionate to the legitimate aim pursued'.[12]

By referring to the 'pressing social need', the Court makes a direct link between the purpose of the measure and its proportionality. If the need is great, the decision can be strict. This brings us to our second point. The control of proportionality is part of the abovementioned third element: the exclusive acceptance of interferences that are necessary in a democratic society reveals the need to promote democracy in the contracting states. Through the control of proportionality, the Court defends a society based on 'pluralism, tolerance and broadmindedness.' In the absence of such a notion, the Court verifies that the measure is not 'excessive' or 'disproportionate'. The measure is deemed proportionate if it is first necessary and second not disproportionate.

11 *Gillow v UK* App no 9063/80 (ECtHR, 24 November 1986).

12 *Gillow* (n 11) para 55.

A measure is considered 'necessary' if the state did not have other options in order to achieve the same aim with less interference in the individual right. Thus, the Court in Strasbourg could quash the decision of authorities to isolate an AIDS patient because they had not looked for less stringent measures.[13] The Court also ensures that the measure is not disproportionate, i.e., that the drawbacks are balanced by the advantages. The advantages are evaluated in relation to the general interest of the measure, the drawbacks in relation to the 'damage' for individuals. The judge thus ensures that the owner of a property gets adequate compensation when deprived of that property,[14] that a search does not affect Article 8,[15] that the prohibition of a newspaper article does not violate the freedom of expression when the aim is maintenance of the authority and impartiality of the judiciary.[16]

The purpose of the review of proportionality appears clearly in the case of *Young, James and Webster v the UK*, in which the Court stated that:

> pluralism, tolerance and broadmindedness are hallmarks of a 'democratic society'. Although individual interests must on occasion be subordinated to those of a group, democracy does not simply mean that the views of a majority must always prevail: a balance must be achieved which ensures the fair and proper treatment of minorities and avoids any abuse of a dominant position.[17]

This brief overview of the case law already shows that the case law does not employ a precise terminology. This is a sign that the ECtHR has wrought this tool to meet its needs. The same is true about the concrete application of the proportionality test.

6.2.2 The application of the proportionality test

As we have already shown, the text of the Convention does not expressly require the proportionality test. The Court has full control over the shape of the control, but also over its areas of application. The proportionality test has been used first to limit state interference in the conditional rights

13 *Enhorn v Sweden* App no 56529/00 (ECtHR 2005, 25 January 2005), para 44. The same control is used in the *Handyside* case App no 5493/72 (ECtHR 7 December 1976) para 53, but the Court concluded that the seizure of books was lawful.

14 *Scordino v Italy* (n°1) App no 36813/97 (ECtHR 2006, 29 July 2004) para 101.

15 *Niemietz v Germany* (ECtHR 16 December 1992) para 37: the Court declared that 'having regard to the materials that were in fact inspected, the search impinged on professional secrecy to an extent that appears disproportionate in the circumstances'.

16 *Sunday Times v UK* App no 6538/74 (ECtHR 26 April 1979), para 58: the Court said 'being called upon to weigh the interests involved and assess their respective force' (para 66, §4). In this case, the ban on publication of an article on a current trial is disproportionate because it carries a too-strong infringement on the freedom of expression in consideration of the advantages that it gives, in that case, to the good administration of justice.

17 *Young, James and Webster v UK* (Series A no 44) App no 7601/76 (ECtHR 13 August 1981) para 63.

contained in the Convention, and then gradually extended to more original or unexpected situations.

6.2.2.1 A. *The use of the proportionality test to limit state interference with conditional rights*

We have already seen that the Court could easily use the proportionality test to ensure compliance with articles in a diptych. The first part of the article establishes the principle of respect of the right or freedom, and the second part allows restrictions. In short, freedom is the principle, and limitations are the exception. This gives rise to the idea that the exception should be limited to respect the principle. The Court thus ensures that the interference of the state, which limits the right or liberty of an individual, is as limited as possible in terms of what is needed. That is exactly the idea reflected in the *Gillow* case, where an interference with right to property was at stake. Here, the Court declared that 'the [interference] measure employed must be proportionate to the legitimate aim pursued'. In addition, it further declared that proportionality must be assessed with reference to the 'the severity of the restriction' imposed. Here, the judges intend to limit the action of the state. But the Court has extended this control to more original cases. Applying the proportionality test in a case involving a conditional right is not really a surprise. Using it in respect of absolute rights is more surprising.

6.2.2.2 B. *The original cases: proportionality in the control of absolute rights and positive obligations of the state*

An absolute right is a right that is not subject to any derogation, restriction or limitation. Such is the case, for example, with section 3, which provides that 'no one shall be subjected to torture or to inhuman or degrading treatment or punishment', or section 4, which prohibits forced labour. Once a treatment is found 'inhuman' or 'degrading' or a job is found 'forced', the section applies and the measure is censored. No element, no circumstance can validate the measure. In short, the idea of 'necessity' is not present under these articles. But if the state would not limit those rights when necessary, then proportionality would have no role to play in this context. Despite these considerations, the judges in Strasbourg have been able to use it, not to allow exemptions to unwarranted interferences, but to qualify certain forms of treatment as 'degrading' or work as 'forced'.

In the case, *Van Der Mussele v Belgium*, a trainee lawyer refused his *pro bono* appointment for the protection of an individual. He claimed that the compulsory *pro bono* work required of Belgian trainee lawyers (pupil *avocats*) constituted 'forced labour', which was contrary to Article 4 of the ECHR. In addition, the young lawyer claimed that only the pupil *avocats* were forced to accept this type of work, which was not imposed on more experienced professionals. Among other arguments against this claim of a violation of Article 4 of the Convention, the ECtHR noted that 'the applicant did not have a disproportionate burden of work imposed on him', especially as the costs involved were relatively small. From these considerations, in addition to the fact noted by the Court that the individual had chosen knowingly and voluntarily to become a lawyer, the Court declared that it was clear that:

> this being so, a considerable and unreasonable imbalance between the aim pursued – to qualify as a lawyer (avocat) – and the obligations undertaken in order to achieve that aim would alone be capable of warranting the conclusion that the services exacted of Mr. Van der Mussele in relation to legal aid were compulsory despite his consent.[18]

The proportionality test has been used in another atypical area. In principle, the Court uses this control to limit the action of the state. The goal is to limit state interference to what is strictly necessary, that is to say, to ensure that the government respects its negative obligations. But the Court has used this control to set the positive obligations of the State, which are to be found particularly in the interpretation of Article 8. It is indeed recognised that, in some cases, the exercise of rights requires that state authorities not only restrain themselves, but also have to take positive steps in order to make the right effective. The Court has held that the obligations of the state should not be too onerous. They must, therefore, be proportional. The applicable principles are broadly similar:

> whether the present case be analysed in terms of a positive duty on the State to take reasonable and appropriate measures to secure the applicants' rights under paragraph 1 of Article 8 (art. 8–1) or in terms of an 'interference by a public authority' to be justified in accordance with paragraph 2 (art. 8–2). In both contexts regard must be had to the fair balance that has to be struck between the competing interests of the individual and of the community as a whole.[19]

The level of positive obligations is thus determined by a 'fair balance', which is underlined by the idea of proportionality. The requirement is that the measure should not be excessive; it must be proportionate to the interests of individuals.

The Court has been able to extend its control of proportionality in areas that could seem foreign to any idea of conciliation, or where there was no intention to limit the action of the state. In this, as stated by the Court, the search for proportionality in the obligations of the state is 'inherent to the whole of the Convention'.[20] Although the entire Convention is based on this search for 'balance', the control of proportionality varies in order to be adapted to each individual case.

18 *Van der Mussele v Belgium* App no 8919/80 (ECtHR 23 November 1983) para 40.

19 *Powell and Rayner v The UK*, Series A no 172 (ECtHR 21 February 1990) para 41. See also *Dickson v UK* App no 44362/04 (ECtHR 4 December 2007) para 70.

20 Christoffersen (n 5) 33.

6.2.3 The change in the intensity of the proportionality test

The requirements of the proportionality test are not always similar. To preserve state autonomy in assessing the solutions needed to solve problems, the Court created the concept of 'national margin of appreciation'. This concept is correlated with the change in the intensity of the control of the judges, and is determined on certain criteria.

6.2.3.1 A The national margin of appreciation as a means of limiting the control of proportionality

It soon became clear to the ECtHR that it does not automatically need to substitute its judgment for that of the states. The judges state that the states have, in some cases, a 'national margin of appreciation'. This notion has played an important role since 1979, serving a more dynamic interpretation of the rights protection potential of the Convention.[21] It is interesting to note that this was originally restricted to cases decided in the context of Article 15.[22] This article provides that states may derogate from the articles of the Convention in the event of a 'war or other public emergency threatening the life of the nation'. The states can take measures 'to the extent strictly required by the situation'. The Court will grant more discretion to national authorities if required by the circumstances. Bringing forth this notion, the Court thus wishes to allow more flexibility to the state on sensitive issues. This discretion has been extended to other areas, such as discrimination, or respect for the right to privacy. An important question must be asked in this context: what is the basis of the discretion left to the state?

The Court seems to rely on the specific nature of the European Convention, including its subsidiarity. This means that, in principle, the states are required to ensure respect for rights and freedoms. The Court is to act only as an exception, as a corrective. This is clear from the *Handyside* case in which the Court points out that:

> the machinery of protection established by the Convention is subsidiary to the national systems safeguarding human rights . . . The Convention leaves to each Contracting State, in the first place, the task of securing the rights and liberties it enshrines . . . By reason of their direct and continuous contact with the vital forces of their countries, State authorities are in principle in a better position than the international judge to give an opinion on the exact content of these requirements as well as on the 'necessity' of a 'restriction' or 'penalty' intended to meet them.[23]

21 See Howard C Yourow, *The Margin of Appreciation Doctrine in the Dynamics of the European Human Rights Jurisprudence* (Martinus Nijhoff Publishers 1996) 56.

22 See, for example, *Klass and others v Germany*, App no 5029/71 (ECtHR 6 September 1978).

23 *Handyside*, (n 13) para 48.

The control of the Court is not intended to replace the discretion of the states, but only to correct their errors and excesses.

The link between the subsidiary nature of the Convention and 'national discretion' is obvious in Protocol No. 15 of June 24, 2013, Article 1, amending the preamble of the Convention. It provides that 'in accordance with the principle of subsidiarity', the states provide the primary warrants of fundamental rights and that as such they 'enjoy a margin of appreciation'. This textual recognition of national discretion has not, however, contributed to its exacerbation. The Court has explained that the recognition of the principle of subsidiarity reflects its case law and that the authors of the protocol did not intend to change the substance of the limitations on the national margin of appreciation.

'National discretion' however, is not fixed in advance. As noted by the Court, 'the scope of the margin of appreciation will vary according to the circumstances, the subject-matter and the background'. In order to identify the intensity of judicial review, which depends on the extent of the margin, we should study the factors taken into account by the Court.

6.2.3.2 B The reasons explaining variations in the intensity

Several elements are taken into account by the Court to reduce or increase the range of feasible solutions and thus decide on the discretion of the state.

An explanation for the factors the Court uses is the presence or absence of European consensus on this issue. In its judgment in *X, Y, and Z v UK*, the judges noted on the issue of transsexuality that:

> since the issues in the case touch on areas where there is little common ground amongst the member States of the Council of Europe and, generally speaking, the law appears to be in a transitional stage, the respondent State must be afforded a wide margin of appreciation.[24]

On the other hand, if there is such a consensus, the Court accepts a reduction in the discretion of the state. Two elements should be noted, however. The first is that the appreciation of this consensus is made 'in the light of present-day conditions'. The lack of consensus on a question raised in a case does not bind the Court for the following cases if a change in law and state practice occurs.

The second element is that the 'European consensus' on the issue is not critical, it is only a clue. Thus, the Court accepts a reduction in the discretionary power of the state when there is no European consensus and vice versa.

24 *X, Y and Z v UK* App no 21830/93 (ECtHR, 22 April 1997) para 44. See also *Rasmussen v Denmark* App no 8777/79 (ECtHR 28 November 1984) para 40.

Other elements are thus taken into account in determining the discretion of the state. For example, the Court takes into account the importance of the interference with the right in question. As a consequence, the proportionality test of the Court is wider when concerning the dissolution of a political party than if it is about the restriction of the right of public employees to participate in political life. If the right in issue is a personal right, which is part of the intimate sphere of the individual, the margin of appreciation is limited and the control is stricter.[25] This is the case, for example, for the right to have homosexual relationships[26] or the right of data protection.[27] In less personal or more technical cases, such as commercial cases or cases about competition, the margin of appreciation is wider.

Another factor taken into account by the Court is the importance given to local circumstances in the choice of the measure: if the Court decides to give importance to them, then discretion is increased. This fits perfectly with the idea behind the existence of discretion, i.e., the subsidiary character of the Convention.

The last relevant factor to be addressed here is the complexity of the area in question, particularly in the implementation of economic and social policies. The Court finds that the national authorities are better placed to decide how to balance the requirements of this policy, and respect for rights. This does not mean that the Court gives up its control. It means that it is less strict.

In developing the concept of a 'margin of appreciation' that has to be left to national authorities, the ECtHR wished to maintain a certain leeway. The level of this margin – and consequently the level of intensity of the review of proportionality – is determined case by case, depending on the facts and their context. None of the elements listed above is decisive in itself. The Court freely determines the intensity of its control. A pragmatic approach of the Court seems to have dictated this judicial perspective. The concern of the Court is to afford both the rights of the Convention and the requirements of public policy. This allows the Court to legitimise its case law and ensure that its judgments are better accepted by the states.

6.3 The test of proportionality in ECJ case law

6.3.1 Introduction

6.3.1.1 A Origins of the proportionality test

The principle of proportionality was already present in the formative years of the Court of Justice of the European Union (ECJ). This principle, elevated to the category of general principle of EU Law, has been often applied

25 See *S and Marper v UK* App nos 30562/04 and 30566/04 (ECtHR 4 December 2008) para 102.

26 *Dudgeon v UK* App no 7525/76 (ECtHR 22 October 1981).

27 *S and Marper v UK* (n 25) para 102.

by the ECJ as a form of rationalising its decision-making.[28] The German principle of proportionality also seems, here, to be the main source of inspiration for the Luxembourg court. Over the years, the ECJ has, nevertheless, developed its own proportionality doctrine, refusing to apply this principle in the exact same way or with the same intensity as the German administrative courts.[29] According to Sionaidh Douglas-Scott, the divergences can be explained by the different underlying interests that are protected by the principle of proportionality: in the EU context, the principle is not only applied to control the measures adopted by Community institutions but also Member State action in the Community sphere.[30]

The Court of Justice started early on to use a proportionality test of the measures adopted by the Community institutions in light of the objectives of the treaties. In the case of *Fédération charbonnietre de Belgique v High Authority* in 1956, the judge held that according to a 'generally accepted rule of law', the reaction of the High Authority to violations of Community law 'must be in proportion to the scale of that action'.[31]

Since the 1970s, the proportionality test has been turned into a general principle of law, highlighting its importance for the Community Court. The generality of the principle was inspired in particular by the German example. At this time, the control of proportionality had virtually no explicit textual basis.[32]

However, in the early treaties, some articles had a sectorial approach to the idea of proportionality. For example, the Treaty of Rome provided in Article 40, paragraph 3 (on the common agricultural policy governed by Article 39) that 'the Community may take all necessary measures to achieve the objectives set out in Article 39'.[33] Similarly, Article 115 on the implementation of the common commercial policy by the Member States, provided that 'priority should be given to measures which least disturb the functioning of the common market and taking into account the need to hasten the extent possible, the establishment of the Common Customs Tariff'.[34]

The principle of proportionality appears to underlie both dispositions. However, it is only with the Maastricht Treaty of 7 February 1992 that the proportionality test is awarded a general textual status. Former Article 5 (3) of the EC Treaty provided that 'action by the Community shall not

28 Tor-Inge Harbo, 'The Function of the Proportionality Principle in the EU Law' (2010) 16 (2) *European Law Journal* 158, 160.

29 Sionaidh Douglas-Scott, *Constitutional Law of the European Union* (Longman 2002) 184.

30 Ibid 184.

31 Case 8/55 *Fédération charbonnière de Belgique v High Authority* [1956] ECLI:EU:C:1956:11.

32 On the history of the principle of proportionality in EC law and its national origins: Nicholas Emiliou, *The Principle of Proportionality in European Law: A Comparative Study* (Kluwer 1996).

33 Treaty Establishing the European Economic Community, March 25, 1957, art 40, 298 UNTS 31.

34 Treaty Establishing the European Economic Community, March 25, 1957, art 115, 298 UNTS 60–61.

go beyond what is necessary to achieve the objectives of this Treaty.' We see that, if the term 'proportionality' does not appear explicitly, the term 'necessary' is employed in this context to represent its essence. Moreover, the generality of its wording gives a very general scope to the control of proportionality.

The Treaty of Lisbon of December 13, 2007 brought a double innovation in the field of proportionality. First, the term 'proportionality' appears in the texts. Article 5 of the Treaty on European Union (TEU) states that 'under the principle of proportionality, the content and form of Union action shall not exceed what is necessary to achieve the objectives of the Treaties'. Second, the Lisbon Treaty has granted the Charter of Fundamental Rights of the European Union the status of primary law through Article 6 TEU and therefore its ability to be invoked before the Community and national courts. Aimed at protecting the EU level of human rights, the Charter also provides in Article 52, paragraph 1 that 'under the principle of proportionality, limitations may be made only if they are necessary and genuinely meet objectives of general interest recognized by the Union or the need to protect the rights and freedoms of others'.

Nowadays, there are two foundations and two meanings of the proportionality test in EU law.[35] Under article 5 TEU, the action of the EU must be proportionate, but it merely means that the test of necessity applies. Under ECJ case law, proportionality remains a general principle of EU law. In both cases, the principle of proportionality is superior to secondary law.

6.3.1.2 B. The different expressions of the proportionality test

Despite the changes brought by the Lisbon Treaty, the texts have not clearly systematised the test of proportionality. The extent of the control is still determined by the judges. The influence of German law is not so strong nowadays. As Diana Urania Galetta puts it, there is clearly a 'European Union law model' of proportionality.[36] The German judges have developed a subjective approach and take into account the effects of the decision on the individual. Conversely, the Luxemburg judges adopt a more objective approach. They put all the interests at stake in a balance, without insisting on the sacrifice of the individual.

We can identify two methods used by the Courts of the Union: they either highlight three requirements, or two.

In the case law, the control of proportionality is divided into three parts: adequacy, necessity and proportionality in the strict sense. These three criteria

35 Diana Urania Galetta, 'Le principe de proportionnalité', in Jean-Bernard Auby & Jacqueline Dutheil de la Rochère (eds), *Traité de droit administratif européen* (2nd edn, Bruylant 2014) 501–525.

36 Galetta (n 35).

are well summed up in the *Omega Air* case.[37] The Court explains that the principle of proportionality:

> requires that measures adopted by Community institutions should not exceed the limits of what is appropriate and necessary in order to attain the objectives pursued by the legislation in question, and where there is a choice between several appropriate measures, recourse must be had to the least onerous, and the disadvantages caused must not be disproportionate to the aims pursued.[38]

The decision dealt with a preliminary question raised by the British High Court about a regulation that prohibited registering and operating civil subsonic jet aeroplanes. The Court controlled first whether the regulation is 'adequate' in the sense of suitable to achieve a certain goal. The objective was to reduce damage to the environment caused by aeroplanes.[39] The Court checked then whether the European institutions were not able to find a less intrusive measure. This is the control of necessity.[40] In the end, the Court balanced the costs and advantages of the regulation. In the *Omega Air* case, the judges do not seem to make such a control. It is possible to illustrate this third element of the control of proportionality with the *Fedesa* case. The High Court had asked the ECJ a question on the validity of a directive on livestock farming, which prohibited the use of certain substances that have a hormonal action. After having used the first two criteria, the Court stated that 'the importance of the objectives pursued is such as to justify even substantial negative financial consequences for certain traders'.[41]

The *Omega Air* and *Fedesa* cases show that the ECJ controls whether the principle of proportionality has not been violated. This is done by using the mentioned three criteria, in a logical order. However, the three criteria will not all be used if this proves to be unnecessary. This happened in the *Omega Air* case, where the first two criteria might prove sufficient to draw a conclusion on the proportionality of the measures.

6.3.2 The scope of the proportionality test

6.3.2.1 A. The authorities subject to the control of proportionality

The ECJ often uses the control of proportionality because it is one of the founding principles of the Union. The principle of proportionality must be

37 Joined Cases C-27/00 and C-122/00 *Omega Air Ltd* (ECJ 12 March 2002).

38 Para 62.

39 Para 66.

40 Para 72.

41 Case C-331/88 *The Queen v Ministry of Agriculture, Fisheries and Food, ex parte Fedesa* (*Fedesa case*) (ECJ 13 November 1990) para 17.

respected whether the Union has exclusive or shared competences. Even in the area of the common foreign and security policy, Article 26 (2) TEU provides that the institutions 'take the decisions necessary for defining and implementing it'.

Despite the text of Article 5 (3), the principle of proportionality not only applies to EU institutions,[42] it also applies to Member States when they implement EU law or when a decision made under national law derogates from EU law.[43] Hence, the principle of proportionality has become a guiding principle underlying the whole legal order of the EU.[44]

Whenever a Member State derogates from EU law, the ECJ checks whether the derogation is justified and proportionate.[45] The Court insists on the legitimacy of the aim and the impossibility of a less stringent measure.[46] The Court goes into the 'X' side when it looks at the aim of the measure. The case *Commission v Germany* of 1987 is a good example of this line of reasoning.

In the 1987 case *Commission v Germany*, the German authorities had imposed restrictions on the import of beer from other Member States because some additives were supposed to be dangerous.[47] The aim was to protect public health. In order to control proportionality, the Court examined the danger of those additives.[48] The Court was not convinced by the arguments presented by the German Government. It had to look at the facts of the case to be able to reach this conclusion. When the Court of Justice reviews such actions, two options are open. It either controls the national enforcement measure directly, through the test of proportionality, or it refers the matter to the national court. It then provides guiding principles, so that the national court itself can apply the proportionality test.

6.3.2.2 B. The rights protected

The rights protected by the Court of Justice are very different in nature. In the beginning, the EU showed little interest in the protection of fundamental rights. It mainly aimed at the realisation of the internal market. The judges

42 The cases *Buitoni* (Case C-122/78, ECJ 20 February 1979) and *Fedesa* are examples in which the principle of proportionality was applied to EU institutions.

43 Case C-534/06 *Industria Lavorazione Carni Ovine* (ECJ 5 June 2008): the principle of proportionality 'must be observed as such both by the Community legislature and by the national legislatures and courts which apply Community law' (para 25).

44 Jürgen Schwarze, *Europäisches Verwaltungsrecht* (2nd edn, Nomos 2006) 663.

45 Case C-473/98 *Kemikalieinspektionen v Toolex Alpha AB (Toolex case)* (ECJ 11 July 2000) para 40.

46 *Toolex*, para 40: 'national rules or practices having, or likely to have, a restrictive effect on the importation of products are compatible with the Treaty only to the extent that they are necessary for the effective protection of the health and life of humans. A national rule or practice cannot therefore benefit from the derogation provided for in Article 36 of the Treaty if the health and life of humans may be protected just as effectively by measures which are less restrictive of intra-Community trade'.

47 Case C-178/84 *Commission v Germany* (*Reinheitsgebot* case) (ECJ 12 March 1987).

48 Paras 48–54.

of Luxembourg ensured that the free movement of goods was respected by Member States. In *Commission v Germany*, the Court stated that:

> it follows from Article 36 that national rules or practices having, or likely to have, a restrictive effect on the importation of pharmaceutical products is compatible with the Treaty only to the extent that they are necessary for the effective protection of health and life of humans.[49]

Under pressure, notably from Germany, the Court of Justice gradually developed a stronger protection of fundamental rights. The ECJ was inspired at this level by the European Convention on Human Rights and by the traditions common to Member States, and has decided that 'the interests involved must be weighed having regard to all the circumstances of the case in order to determine whether a fair balance was struck between those interests'.[50]

In its case law, the ECJ has also examined whether freedom of expression and freedom of assembly could justify a limitation to the free movement of goods,[51] or whether public order could justify a limitation to the freedom to provide services.[52] The Court has also relied on the Charter of fundamental rights in order to acknowledge rights and to balance them with the provisions of the treaties through the control of proportionality.[53] In future, the ECJ might do even more since the Charter has been given the same legal value as the treaties by the Treaty of Lisbon.[54]

6.3.3 The change in the intensity of the supervision of the Court

The ECJ has not always developed a three-step control. It concentrates on the necessity and the appropriateness of the measure, without controlling its reasonableness.[55] This does not mean that the control of proportionality is not taken seriously by the Court.

Taking into account all the circumstances of the case, the Court of Justice was able to develop a control with variable intensity. In some cases, it states that 'the legality of a measure adopted in that sphere can be affected

49 *Commission v Germany (Reinheitsgebot)* (n 47) para 11.

50 Case C-112/00 *Schmidberger v Austria* (ECJ 12 June 2003) paras 71 and 81.

51 Same case, para 82.

52 Case C-36/02 *Omega Spielhallen- und Automatenaufstellungs-GmbH* (*Omega Spielhallen* case) (ECJ 14 October 2004), para 36–41: the Court granted permission to forbid a 'laserdrome' activity because it contravened human dignity. The decision of the state is not disproportionate.

53 Case C-438/05 *International Transport Workers' Federation and Finnish Seamen's Union v Viking Line ABP and OÜ Viking Line Eesti* (*International Transport Workers' Federation* case) (ECJ 11 December 2007) para 44–47.

54 For an example about the protection of the privacy contained in Article 8 (1) of the Charter, see joined Cases C-92/09 and C-93/09 *Volker und Markus Schecke and Eifert* (ECJ 9 November 2010) para 50.

55 Verica Trstenjank & Erwin Beysen, 'Das Prinzip der Verhältnismässigkeit in der Unionrechtsordnung' (2012) *Europarecht* 265–284.

only if the measure is manifestly inappropriate having regard to the objective which the competent institution is seeking to pursue'.[56] Several factors can justify this restricted proportionality test.

It is important to underline that the ECJ changes the intensity of the control of proportionality according to the decision-maker and to the subject matter. As noted earlier, the ECJ does not insist on the effects on the individual, unlike the German judges. The control is not the same when the decision has been made by a national authority or by a European authority. When an EU authority is involved, the control is more flexible than the control over a national authority.[57] This can be explained by the aims of the ECJ's judicial review. When controlling proportionality, the Court wants to reinforce European integration. Therefore, the ECJ will limit the derogations from EU law.

However, the ECJ does not always control the proportionality of national decisions that limit the effective application of EU law very strictly. The Court allows a wide margin of appreciation to the Member States when the matter is complex or sensitive, as for instance when a Member State has refused entry to a national of another Member State because of a threat to public order.[58] This is also the case when it comes to restrictions of imports justified on the grounds of public morality.[59] On the other hand, when a Member State invokes public health to derogate from EU law, its decision is subject to a full control of proportionality. This is true only when there is a consensus on the threat to public health. On the other hand, if there is no such consensus, the Court's control might be 'weaker', comprehending the possibility to tolerate absolute prohibitions.

It may be noted that when the Court of Justice leaves the control of proportionality to the national courts, a sign of flexibility is given to national authorities. This is justified by the fact that national courts are more likely, in some cases, to judge the relevance of the objectives of the national measure, or values that the state intends to defend, especially when they are not common to the other Member States. However, these elements must be reconciled with the need for the Court to standardise the test of proportionality. The reference to national courts, if justified in some situations, should not lead to too great a diversity of solutions. The Court of Justice has to find the right balance between respect for state-specific values and uniformity of rights, a corollary of the rule of law in the European Union.

Similarly, the deference to European institutions should not be exaggerated. On one hand, even if the ECJ does lower its control, it does not mean that it does not operate a detailed study of the elements underlying the case. On the other hand, even though the Court of Justice limits its control over

56 *Fedesa* case (n 41) para 14.

57 Case C-84/94 *Council v UK*, ECJ 12 November 1996) para 58; case C-135/08 *Janko Rottmann* (ECJ 2 March 2010) para 56.

58 Case C-41/74 *Van Duyn* (ECJ 4 December 1974) paras 19–24.

59 Case C-34/79 *R v Henn and Darby* (ECJ 14 December 1979) para 16.

the actions of European institutions, it does not do so without justification. In the *British American Tobacco* case, the ECJ stated first that the proportionality test 'requires that measures implemented through Community provisions should be appropriate for attaining the objective pursued and must not go beyond what is necessary to achieve it' before noting that the authority:

> must be allowed a broad discretion in an area such as that involved in the present case, which entails political, economic and social choices on its part, and in which it is called upon to undertake complex assessments. Consequently, the legality of a measure adopted in that sphere can be affected only if the measure is manifestly inappropriate having regard to the objective which the competent institution is seeking to pursue.[60]

Discretionary power is reduced when fundamental rights are involved and if 'restrictions may be imposed on their exercise, provided that the restrictions correspond to objectives of general interest and do not constitute in relation to the aim pursued a disproportionate and intolerable interference, impairing the very substance of the rights guaranteed'.[61]

The ECJ is pragmatic. When the derogation invades the core of national sovereignty, such as maintaining public order in the territory of the State, the latter is granted a wider margin of appreciation. When the derogation from core EU law dispositions is at stake, the control of proportionality is stricter. Here again, this shows the integrative purpose of the ECJ.

The ECJ has also been challenged to deal with the control of proportionality when rights were in conflict. The cases are not numerous so far. The ECJ has always attempted to conciliate the rights by granting them the same value and then by evaluating the necessity and the appropriateness of the measure.[62] In the *Lindqvist* case, for example, the ECJ conciliated the protection of private life with the freedom of expression. It ordered the national courts to interpret Directive 95/46 on the processing of personal data in a way that would enable the protection of fundamental rights and respect the principle of proportionality.[63] Since the Lisbon Treaty, the Charter of fundamental rights has been conferred legal value. The conciliation of conflicting rights is therefore likely to knock at the door of the ECJ more frequently in the future.

6.4 Conclusion

Although the system of the European Convention and the system of the European Union have different purposes, many similarities in the control

60 Case C-491/01 *British American Tobacco* (ECJ 10 December 2002) para 122–123.

61 Joined Cases C-184/02 and C-223/02 *Spain and Finland v European Parliament and Council* (ECJ 9 September 2004) para 52.

62 Verica Trstenjank & Erwin Beysen (n 55).

63 Case C-101/01 *Bodil Lindqvist* (ECJ 6 November 2003).

of proportionality can be noticed. The ECtHR and the ECJ both operate a strong control over the actions of states while leaving them some leeway. Both Courts seek to reconcile the respect for human rights, the texts, and the freedom of the state, on a case-by-case basis, depending on the species and circumstances. The proportionality test reflects the pragmatism shown by the judges. While ensuring the best possible compliance with the law, they refuse to replace the states and to judge the appropriateness of states' measures.

This conclusion is not surprising. Influenced by the legal traditions of the Member States, the courts have been able to be inspired by an old technique of control, which had been perfected by the national judge. By using the proportionality test at European level in a pragmatic way, they show its utility.

References

Arai-Takahashi Y, *The Margin of Appreciation Doctrine and the Principle of Proportionality in the Jurisprudence of the ECtHR* (Intersentia 2001).

Bean CR, 'Economic and Monetary Union in Europe' (1992) 6(4) *Journal of Economic Perspectives* 31.

Christoffersen J, *Fair Balance: Proportionality, Subsidiarity and Primarity in the European Convention of Human Rights* (Brill 2009).

Douglas-Scott S, *Constitutional Law of the European Union* (Longman 2002) 184.

Emiliou N, *The principle of proportionality in European Law: a comparative study* (Kluwer 1996).

Galetta DU, 'Le principe de proportionnalité', in Jean-Bernard Auby & Jacqueline Dutheil de la Rochère (eds), *Traité de droit administratif européen* (2nd edn, Bruylant 2014).

Habermas J, 'Why Europe Needs a Constitution' in Erik O Eriksen, John Erik Fossum, Agustín Menéndez (ed), *Developing a Constitution for Europe* (Routledge 2004) 19.

Harbo TI, 'The Function of the Proportionality Principle in the EU Law' (2010) 16 (2) *European Law Journal* 158.

McBride J, 'Proportionality and the European Convention on Human Rights' in Ellis E (ed), *The Principle of Proportionality in the Laws of Europe* (Hart 1999) 23.

Rainey B, Vicks E, Ovey L, White RCA, *Jacobs, White and Ovey: The European Convention of Human Rights* (OUP 2014).

Ruffert M, 'Europäisierung des Verwaltungsrechts', in Bogdandy, A, Cassese, S, Huber, B (eds), *Handbuch Ius Publicum Europaeum*, band IV (CF Müller 2011) 1221.

Schwarze J, *Europäisches Verwaltungsrecht* (2nd edn, Nomos 2006).

Scott SD, *Constitutional Law of the European Union* (Longman 2002).

Takahashi YA, *The Margin of Appreciation Doctrine and the Principle of Proportionality in the Jurisprudence of the ECHR* (Intersentia 2001).

Trstenjank V, Beysen E 'Das Prinzip der Verhältnismässigkeit in der Unionrechtsordnung' (2012) *Europarecht* 265.

Yourow HC, *The Margin of Appreciation Doctrine in the Dynamics of the European Human Rights Jurisprudence* (Martinus Nijhoff Publishers 1996).

7 Agency discretion, judicial review and 'proportionality' in US administrative law

Jud Mathews[1]

7.1 Introduction

Officially, there is no such thing as 'proportionality review' in American administrative law. The Administrative Procedure Act (APA) of 1946, the framework statute governing administrative law, does not recognise proportionality as a general head of review. Nor have American courts ever developed a judge-made doctrine of proportionality as such, either prior to or following the APA's enactment. While the immense scholarly literature on proportionality continues to grow by leaps and bounds, virtually nothing has been written about proportionality in American administrative law, no doubt, in part, because it is assumed there is nothing to write.[2]

Why, then, include a chapter about the United States in a book about proportionality review in administrative law? In lieu of proportionality, American administrative law features a congeries of doctrines that courts deploy to evaluate agency exercises of discretion under different circumstances, in ways described in detail below. In some respects, these frameworks for review resemble proportionality in operation, but there are also notable differences. For these reasons, the contrast between proportionality review and American approaches to the review of discretion is potentially illuminating, highlighting what may be distinctive features of both.[3]

1 Assistant Professor of Law, Penn State Law. Thanks to Jamison Colburn, Paul Craig, William Fox, Arden Rowell, Jamelle Sharpe, Takis Tridimas, and Chris Walker for helpful comments and conversations, and to Rebecca Buckley-Stein for excellent research assistance.

2 Perhaps the closest thing is historical scholarship on nineteenth-century understandings of the states' police power. William Novak's important book has shown how state police powers could curb private property rights and other private interests, under conditions of 'necessity.' *See* William J Novak, *The People's Welfare: Law and Regulation in Nineteenth-Century America* (University of North Carolina Press 1996).

3 In some respects, the closest analogue to proportionality analysis in American administrative law is in the regulatory review process, which is carried out not by courts, but within the executive branch. Early in his first term, President Ronald Reagan issued an executive order instructing agencies, to the extent permitted by law, to undertake regulatory action only when 'the potential benefits to society for the regulation outweigh the potential costs;' to choose objectives 'to maximize the net benefits to society;' and when considering alternative approaches to an objective, to choose the one 'involving the least net cost to society.' Executive Order No 12291, 46 Fed Reg 13193. For major rules, the order further

Looking at the doctrines governing judicial review of administrative discretion in the United States, three features stand out. First, American judicial review is characterised by a high degree of unpredictability. Of course, law is rarely perfectly predictable, but I would contend that judicial review of discretion is in a special class. Not only is it often difficult to predict the outcome of judicial review in particular cases, but the uncertainty runs deeper. In a considerable number of cases, there is substantial uncertainty even as to what framework of review the court will apply. Even when it is nominally clear which standard governs, there often remains substantial uncertainty over what kind of analysis the court will perform, and how intensively it will scrutinise the challenged agency action.

The second point speaks directly to a contrast with proportionality. Classical proportionality review is designed to detect and correct a particular kind of administrative failure: an overreach, in which the government uses measures that are excessive in relation to the ends they are designed to achieve. Judicial control of discretion in American administrative law is more symmetrical, in that the agency is required to explain its actions – whether the claim is that they go too far, or that they do not go far enough. However, as further described below, there are countervailing doctrines in American administrative law that make judicial redress more likely for agency failures of commission than for failures of omission.

Third, reviewing courts in American administrative law tend to 'proceduralise' substantive review, focusing more on the agency's failures to thoroughly ventilate the relevant issues than the merits of the agency's conclusions.[4] The end result may often be the same, in terms of what agency actions are blocked. But proceduralising substantive review may have other consequences, both for the burdens that agencies face before reviewing courts (which may be more substantial), and for the ultimate ability of agencies to realise favoured policy options (which may be greater).

This chapter develops these points in the course of a discussion of the judicial review of agency exercises of discretion under American administrative law. The next section sets the stage for that discussion by sketching the doctrinal lay of the land. The APA looms large here, as this statute defines the basic categories of agency action and the standards of judicial review. The APA makes review broadly available, but a number of exceptions, both

requires agencies to submit to the Office of Information and Regulatory Affairs (OIRA), which is located within the Executive Office of the President, a regulatory impact analysis that demonstrates the rule's cost-benefit justification and its superiority to alternatives. President Reagan's successors have continued regulatory review but tweaked it, broadening the set of values that agencies should consider in their analysis to include equity, human dignity, fairness, and distributive impacts. Thus, at the behest of the White House, agencies themselves now are expected to conduct a sort of proportionality review in-house. But executive branch regulatory review is beyond the scope of this chapter.

4 Jerry L Mashaw and David L Harfst, 'Regulation and Legal Culture: the Case of Motor Vehicle Safety' (1986) 4 *Yale Journal on Regulation* 257.

statutory and judge-made, shield much of what agencies do from the scrutiny of courts. When review is available, the scope of review under the APA may turn on a series of distinctions: whether the agency acts through adjudication or rule-making; whether it uses formal or informal procedures; and whether the challenge addresses a determination of fact, law, or policy.

The following section focuses sustained attention on the review standard most closely associated with agency discretion: arbitrary and capricious review. I work in detail through the reasoning employed in three important arbitrary and capricious review cases, decided over a span of almost forty years: *National Tire Dealers and Retreaders v. Brinegar*; *Motor Vehicle Manufacturers Association v. State Farm Mutual Automobile Insurance Co.*; and *FCC v. Fox Television Stations, Inc.* The detailed analyses of these cases build a platform for considering both how arbitrary and capricious review may be changing, and for ways in which it is similar to and different from proportionality review.

Agencies also exercise significant discretion in the course of interpreting the statutes they administer, and the penultimate section of the chapter considers how courts review agency interpretations of statutes. In spite of judicial and scholarly engagement with this topic, this section shows that it is not entirely clear how the standards of review employed in this context relate to arbitrary and capricious review. A brief final section concludes.

7.2 Judicial review in American administrative law: an overview

Although all American states have their own agencies, which are also subject to judicial review, this chapter concerns federal administrative law exclusively.[5] The focus here is squarely on the federal APA, which lays out the default rules of administrative law, although Congress can dictate agency-specific alternatives by statute.[6] The APA lays out both the procedures that agencies must follow in carrying out their mandates under the statutes that they administer, and the standards that courts apply in reviewing agency action. The courts that review administrative actions in the United States are ordinary federal courts, as opposed to specialised administrative tribunals.

7.2.1 The availability of review

The APA contains generous provisions for judicial review, accompanied by generous exceptions. First, the APA defines 'agency' broadly to include 'each

5 The majority of states have adopted or been influenced by model administrative procedure acts that resemble the APA in important respects. Arthur Earl Bonfield, 'The Federal APA and State Administrative Law' (1986) 72 *Virginia Law Review* 297; Ronald M Levin, 'Rulemaking under the 2010 Model State Administrative Procedure Act' (2010) 20 *Widener Law Journal* 855.

6 See, for instance, Occupational Safety and Health Act, 29 USC § 655(f) (providing that substantial evidence review, rather than the APA default of arbitrary and capricious review, will apply to health and safety rules promulgated by the Occupational Safety and Health Commission).

authority of the Government of the United States, whether or not it is within or subject to review by another agency,' except for Congress, the courts, territorial governments, and a few other exceptions.[7] The APA further provides that '[a]gency action made reviewable by statute and final agency action for which there is no other adequate remedy in a court are subject to judicial review.'[8] Courts have read this provision to establish a general presumption that final agency action is subject to judicial review.[9]

'Agency action,' in turn, is defined in expansive terms, to include 'the whole or a part of an agency rule, order, license, sanction, relief, or the equivalent or denial thereof, or failure to act.'[10] Notably, this provision extends judicial review to include agency rules, which are the chief instruments of agency policy-making. In principle, then, the APA empowers courts to sit in judgment over agency policy choices and the design of regulatory programmes, to a degree that administrative lawyers in other legal systems might find surprising.[11]

The APA is also generous in granting rights to initiate judicial review. A different provision of the APA permits any person 'adversely affected or aggrieved by agency action within the meaning of a relevant statute' to initiate judicial review.[12]

However, judicial review is not as widely available as a quick read of the APA might suggest. First, as already noted, the APA is only a default statute, and it recognises that an agency's organic statute may preclude judicial review entirely (although few do).[13]

Second, the APA expressly precludes review to the extent that 'agency action is committed to agency discretion by law.'[14] The question inevitably follows: what does it mean for agency action to be 'committed to agency discretion by law'? In *Citizens to Preserve Overton Park*, the Supreme Court approvingly quoted the legislative history of the APA for the proposition that the exception covers 'those rare instances where "statutes are drawn in such broad terms that in a given case there is no law to apply."'[15] For instance, the National Security Act provided that the Director of the CIA 'may, in his discretion, terminate employment of any officer or employee of the Agency whenever he shall deem such termination necessary or advisable

7 5 USC §§ 551(1) (defining agencies for purposes of the APA's requirements), 701(b) (defining agencies for purposes of judicial review). The Supreme Court has also held that the president does not qualify as an agency for purposes of the APA. *Franklin v Massachusetts*, 505 US 788, 801 (1992).

8 5 USC § 704.

9 *Citizens to Preserve Overton Park v Volpe*, 401 US 402 (1971). See also Nicholas Bagley 'The Puzzling Presumption of Reviewability' (2014) 127 *Harvard Law Review* 1285 (challenging the presumption).

10 5 USC § 551(13).

11 Susan Rose-Ackerman *Controlling Environmental Policy: the Limits of Public Law in Germany and the United States* (Yale University Press 1995).

12 5 USC § 702.

13 5 USC § 701(a)(1).

14 5 USC § 701(a)(2).

15 *Overton Park* (n 8) 410 (quoting S Rep No 752, 79th Cong, 1st Sess, 26) (1945).

in the interest of the United States.'[16] Finding that the language 'fairly exudes deference to the Director,' the Supreme Court in 1988 held that the decision to fire a covert electronics technician on account of his sexual orientation was committed to the agency's discretion, and hence unreviewable, except insofar as it was the basis for constitutional claims.[17]

Although the 'committed to agency discretion' exception permits relatively few agency actions to evade judicial review, its greater impact may be blocking review of agency *inaction*. The Supreme Court has analogised agency discretion over bringing enforcement actions to prosecutorial discretion, and found 'a general presumption of unreviewability of decisions not to enforce.'[18] For instance, executions by lethal injection in the United States are carried out using drugs that are regulated by the Food and Drug Administration (FDA). Death-row inmates petitioned the FDA to investigate the use of these drugs in executions as the 'unapproved use of an approved drug' in violation of the Federal Food, Drug, and Cosmetics Act, which the FDA administered. The agency declined to do so, and the inmates sued. The Supreme Court found for the agency, holding that 'an agency's decision not to prosecute or enforce, whether through civil or criminal process, is a decision generally committed to an agency's absolute discretion.'[19]

An agency, with finite resources for enforcement, must make choices about how to deploy them, and these choices 'often involve a complicated balancing of a number of factors which are peculiarly within its expertise.'[20] The matter is different when a statute mandates certain enforcement actions.

Moreover, the requirement that agency action be 'final' means that even consequential agency actions can be shielded from review altogether where agency choices are given legal effect by other governmental actors. For instance, in *Dalton v. Specter*,[21] the Supreme Court found the Secretary of Defense's order to close the Philadelphia Naval Shipyard unreviewable. Under the governing statute, a commission with input from military leaders makes recommendations to the president on which military bases should be closed or realigned, and the president must either accept or reject the commission's recommendations in their entirety. Petitioners alleged procedural and substantive problems with the commission's work, as well as with the actions of the Secretaries of the Navy and Defense. The Supreme Court, however, found the decision to close the base unreviewable. The commission's recommendations did not constitute a final agency action, since they lacked legal

16 50 USC § 403(c) (1988).

17 *Webster v Doe*, 486 US 592 (1988). Justice Scalia, in dissent, proposed a broader reading of the exception, which would encompass the pre-APA 'common law' of unreviewable executive discretion. Ibid 608–10 (Scalia, J, dissenting).

18 *Heckler v Chaney*, 470 US 821 (1985).

19 Ibid 831.

20 Ibid.

21 511 US 462 (1994).

effect before the president acted on them, and the president's endorsement of the recommendations was not subject to review, because the president is not an agency within the meaning of the APA.

In addition, notwithstanding the APA's statement that a 'failure to act' is reviewable, judicial restrictions on what kinds of failures to act are reviewable have come close to rendering this provision a dead letter. In *Norton v. Southern Utah Wilderness Alliance*, an environmental group sought to challenge the Environmental Protection Agency's (EPA) failure to take steps to protect a Wilderness Study Area against environmental degradation, as required by federal law.[22] The Supreme Court turned back the challenge without reaching its merits, holding that the only failures to act made reviewable by the APA are failures to take a *discrete* agency action that is *mandated* by law.

Furthermore, broad exceptions from the notice-and-comment rule-making procedures for military and foreign affairs functions, interpretative rules, general statements of policy, and other matters where the agency finds 'good cause' decreases the potency of judicial review where they apply by exempting agency activity from the procedural standards that agencies would otherwise have to observe.[23] Moreover, agencies may be able to delay review or evade it entirely by using interpretative rules, guidance documents, and policy statements to make consequential policy choices. So-called non-legislative rules are generally subject only to collateral challenge incidental to agency enforcement actions against regulated parties. To the extent that non-legislative rules *favour* regulated parties, or their *in terrorem* effect induces compliance, they will not face judicial review at all.[24] Finally, as further discussed below, restrictive judicial rulings on who has standing to bring suit in federal court as a constitutional matter have undercut somewhat the APA's broad provisions for access to judicial review.

7.2.2 The scope of review

If the rules governing the availability of judicial review in American administrative law are somewhat difficult to navigate, the same can be said of the scope of review. According to the *Attorney General's Manual to the Administrative Procedure Act*, long considered the most reliable contemporaneous guide to the intentions of the statute's drafters, the APA was meant to restate and codify existing practices with respect to the scope of judicial review.[25] Prior to the enactment of the APA, judges had developed a variety of standards for reviewing administrative actions, including abuse of discretion, arbitrary and capricious, and not supported by substantial evidence. Given that these standards of review had been developed piecemeal by different courts over a period of

22 542 US 54 (2002).

23 5 USC § 553(a)(1), (b)(3)–(4).

24 David L Franklin, 'Legislative Rules, Nonlegislative Rules, and the Perils of the Short Cut,' (2010) 120 *Yale Law Journal* 276.

25 *Attorney General's Manual on the Administrative Procedure Act* (1947) 108.

years, it is no surprise that, in the words of some leading scholars, '§ 706 [the scope of review section] is not a model of linguistic clarity or coherence.'[26]

Which framework for review applies may depend on the form of agency action at issue, the level of procedural formality involved, and also the nature of the agency determination that is being contested. With respect to the form of agency action, the APA generally requires agencies to act through one of two processes: adjudication and rule-making. The APA also establishes two levels of procedural formality: formal – on-the-record; and informal – referring to the statutes that agencies are required to observe.

On-the-record adjudications resemble trials, complete with an impartial decision-maker presiding, the presentation of evidence, and opportunities for direct- and cross-examination of witnesses. On-the-record adjudications are typically employed to decide individual claims within a statutory framework administered by an agency. So, for instance, individuals' applications for disability benefits and foreign nationals' petitions for asylum are both handled through formal adjudications, conducted by the Social Security Administration and the Executive Office of Immigration Review, respectively. Agencies also tend to use formal adjudications when they put individuals or entities 'on trial' for statutory violations, as when the Federal Trade Commission brings charges against a business for using unfair or deceptive acts or practices.

Rule-making paradigmatically involves the formation of agency policy, rather than the resolution of individual claims or charges. The APA contemplates that rules will have prospective effect and 'implement, interpret, or prescribe law or policy.'[27] When the EPA promulgates national ambient air quality standards under the Clean Air Act, for instance, it does so by making a rule. In contrast to adjudications, rule-making is more often conducted using informal procedures, which dispense with the trappings of a trial, but afford public notice of the agency's plans and an opportunity for interested individuals to comment – hence, 'notice-and-comment rulemaking.'[28]

A further set of distinctions can be drawn between agency actions that involve determinations on matters of fact, matters of law, and matters of policy or discretion. The fact that the compartments dividing issues of fact, law, and policy are by no means watertight has not stopped Congress and the courts from outlining and elaborating judicial review doctrines that rely on these distinctions.[29] Although adjudication is modelled on judicial trials and rule-making is modelled on the legislative process, as a practical matter, either process can involve all these types of determinations.

26 Ronald A Cass and others, *Administrative Law: Cases and Materials* (6th edn, Aspen 2011) 113.

27 5 USC § 551(4).

28 While these generalisations about the uses of adjudication and rule-making generally hold, they are not ironclad. The Supreme Court has ruled that agencies with authority to conduct both rule-making and adjudications can use either to make policy, and the National Labour Relations Board in particular has historically favoured the use of adjudication as a policy-making tool. See *NLRB v Wyman-Gordon Co*, 394 US 759 (1969).

29 Christopher Edley, *Administrative Law: Rethinking Judicial Control of Bureaucracy* (Yale University Press 1992).

Putting the pieces together now, what framework courts use to review an administrative action may depend on (1) the process used (rule-making or adjudication), (2) the level of formality (formal or informal), and (3) the kind of agency determination at issue (fact, law, or policy). For instance, the APA specifies that factual findings made in on-the-record proceedings are subject to 'substantial evidence' review. In other words, they will be upheld unless the reviewing court finds them to be 'unsupported by substantial evidence' in the record as a whole.[30] As a practical matter, these on-the-record proceedings are almost always adjudications.[31]

With respect to legal questions, the APA provides that 'the reviewing court shall decide all relevant questions of law, [and] interpret constitutional and statutory provisions.'[32] In fact, when reviewing agency actions, courts have never decided all questions of law *de novo*, but have instead devised a number of deference formulas, some of which are further discussed below. The APA also seems to contemplate some *de novo* judicial fact-finding: it commands the reviewing court to set aside agency action 'unwarranted by the facts to the extent that the facts are subject to trial de novo by the reviewing court.'[33] Commentators have differed on whether courts should resort to *de novo* review of facts when the agency has compiled no record,[34] but in any event, the Supreme Court has given a narrow construction to the *de novo* review provision.[35]

Most relevant for present purposes is the provision of the APA that permits courts to hold unlawful and set aside agency action, findings, and conclusions found to be 'arbitrary, capricious, an abuse of discretion, or otherwise not in accordance with law.'[36] This provision governs agency determinations that are neither questions of law nor questions of fact decided in on-the-record proceedings, and so sweep in the bulk of agency discretionary decisions, including 'informal adjudications': the countless, run-of-the-mill agency decisions that are neither rule-makings nor formal

30 5 USC 70(2) (E). See also *Universal Camera Corp v NLRB*, 340 US 474 (1951) (making clear, in the context of the similarly worded scope of review provision of the National Labour Relations Act, that the substantiality of evidence must be determined on the basis of the record as a whole).

31 On-the-record rule-makings are notoriously inefficient policy-making tools. An egregious and oft-cited example is the FDA rule-making to determine the minimum peanut content of peanut butter, which lasted nine years and produced a transcript 7,736 pages long. Robert W Hamilton, 'Rulemaking on a Record by the Food and Drug Administration' (1972) 50 *Texas Law Review* 1132, 1143–45.

32 5 USC § 704.

33 5 USC § 706(2)(D).

34 Compare Nathaniel L Nathanson, 'Probing the Mind of the Administrator: Hearing Variations and Standards of Judicial Review Under the Administrative Procedure Act and Other Federal Statutes,' (1975) 75 *Columbia Law Review* 721 (supporting *de novo* review in this circumstance), with Stephanie Hoffer and Christopher J Walker, 'The Death of Tax Court Exceptionalism,' (2015) 99 *Minnesota Law Review* (forthcoming) (urging remand to the agency to produce a record).

35 *Overton Park* (n 8) 415.

36 5 USC § 706(2)(A).

adjudications.[37] The next section is devoted to an examination of arbitrary and capricious review.[38]

7.3 Arbitrary and capricious review

Drawing on the language of older judicial opinions, the APA permits courts to set aside actions that are 'arbitrary, capricious, an abuse of discretion, or otherwise not in accordance with law,' but courts have never taken pains to distinguish between the various grounds for reversal listed in 5 USC § 706(2)(A). Instead, courts characteristically refer to 'arbitrary and capricious' review as a single standard. In three respects, arbitrary and capricious review probably occupies the position in American administrative law closest to the position occupied by proportionality review in some other administrative law systems.[39]

First, while arbitrary and capricious review is not exactly a general head of review in American administrative law, it is something very close.[40] Although certain kinds of agency decisions are subject to different standards of review – as noted above, for instance, on-the-record factual determinations are reviewed under the substantial evidence standard – in the words of then-Judge Scalia, arbitrary and capricious review 'is a catchall, picking up administrative misconduct not covered by the other more specific paragraphs.'[41] In addition, because '[t]he 'scope of review' provisions of the APA . . . are cumulative,' every agency action subject to judicial review must satisfy the arbitrary and capricious standard, whatever other tests it might have to survive.

Second, arbitrary and capricious review applies to much of the discretionary decision-making of agencies. Other scope-of-review provisions in the APA govern questions of fact (in on-the-record proceedings) and questions of law. Arbitrary and capricious review covers what is left over. While acknowledging again the imprecision of the fact-law-policy distinction, a good part of the agency decisions that raise neither issues of fact nor issues of law could plausibly be described as policy choices, or as exercises of agency discretion.

Third and finally, unlike the other bases of review recognised in § 706, arbitrary and capricious review authorises courts to evaluate and overturn

37 *Overton Park* (n 8) 410.

38 The APA also establishes other heads of review that are of great importance to administrative law, but of limited relevance to judicial control of agency discretion. Specifically, reviewing courts have the power to set aside agency actions that are unconstitutional (5 USC § 706(2)(B)), *ultra vires* (§ 706(2)(C)), or procedurally defective (§ 706(2)(D).

39 See chapters 2 to 6 and, in particular, chapter 2 on the principle of proportionality in Germany.

40 Proportionality is a general criterion of review in EU law, see Takis Tridimas, *The General Principles of EU Law* (2nd edn, OUP 2006) 132, and in German *Polizei- und Ordungsrecht*, a body of law dealing not only with the police, but the regulation of threats to public welfare more generally, see Volkmar Götz, *Allgemeines Polizei- Und Ordnungsrecht: Ein Studienbuch* (15th edn, CH Beck 2012) 129–30. A debate continues in England over whether proportionality should be treated as a general head of review in administrative law. See Paul Craig, *Administrative Law* (7th edn, Sweet & Maxwell 2012) 668–75.

41 *Association of Data Processing Serv. Orgs, Inc v Bd of Governors of the Fed Reserve Systems*, 745 F 2d 677, 683 (DC Cir 1984).

agency actions on the basis of their substance, as opposed to procedural shortcomings,[42] jurisdictional overreaching,[43] or lack of conformity with the Constitution.[44] Arbitrary and capricious review is a form of merits review, in which the policy choice made by the agency is evaluated on its merits.[45] However, as discussed below, there is a strong tendency in American administrative law, even in arbitrary and capricious review, to describe problems with agency policy choices in terms of procedural failings.

7.3.1 The advent of 'hard look' review

Exactly what is 'arbitrary and capricious' review? Its meaning has evolved over time, and even now, it remains something of a moving target. This section recounts its origins, and then explores in some depth its use in three cases: *National Tire Dealers and Retreaders v. Brinegar*, *Motor Vehicle Manufacturers Association v. State Farm Mutual Automobile Insurance Co.*; and *FCC v. Fox Television Stations, Inc.* to illustrate the varied modes of analysis that modern arbitrary and capricious review can entail.

At the time the APA was enacted, arbitrary and capricious review was understood to be highly deferential to agency exercises of discretion. Arbitrary and capricious review was animated by the same spirit of deference to the policy choices of non-judicial actors as the 'rational basis' review of legislation.[46] *National Broadcasting Co. v. United States*,[47] an important pre-APA Supreme Court case, illustrates the point. In that case, the NBC broadcasting network brought a number of challenges to radio regulations promulgated by the Federal Communications Commission. After dispensing with the petitioners' claims that the agency had exceeded its authority under the governing statute, the Court turned to their argument that the regulations were nonetheless unlawful with the following words:

> The Regulations are assailed as 'arbitrary and capricious'. If this contention means that the Regulations are unwise, that they are not likely to succeed in accomplishing what the Commission intended, we can say only that the appellants have selected the wrong forum for such a plea. What was said in Board of Trade v. United States is relevant here: 'We certainly have neither technical competence nor legal authority to pronounce upon the wisdom of the course taken by the Commission.' Our

42 5 USC § 706(2)(B).

43 5 USC § 706(2)(C).

44 5 USC § 706(2)(D).

45 On merits review, which is a central organising category of Australian administrative law in particular, see Peter Cane, 'Judicial Review and Merits Review: Comparing Administrative Adjudication By Courts and Tribunals' in Susan Rose-Ackerman and Peter L Lindseth (eds), *Comparative Administrative Law* (Edward Elgar 2010) 426.

46 *See Wickard v Fillburn*, 317 US 111, 129–30 (turning back a challenge to the Agricultural Adjustment Act of 1938 as arbitrary and capricious).

47 319 US 190 (1943).

> duty is at an end when we find that the action of the Commission was based upon findings supported by evidence, and was made pursuant to authority granted by Congress. It is not for us to say that the 'public interest' will be furthered or retarded by the Chain Broadcasting Regulations. The responsibility belongs to the Congress for the grant of valid legislative authority and to the Commission for its exercise . . . If time and changing circumstances reveal that the 'public interest' is not served by application of the Regulations, it must be assumed that the Commission will act in accordance with its statutory obligations.[48]

Things began to change in the 1960s, thanks largely to the DC Circuit Court of Appeals, the influential appellate court that handles the lion's share of administrative law litigation. At a time when agencies were increasingly turning to notice-and-comment rule-making as a policy-making tool,[49] the judges of the DC Circuit began ratcheting up the scrutiny paid to agency choices through increasingly stringent application of arbitrary and capricious review. This more aggressive form of arbitrary and capricious review became known as 'hard look' review.

The name 'hard look' review is itself instructive, if often misunderstood. Many assume that it refers to the court's vigorous scrutiny of the agency, but the phrase originated to describe the kind of close attention *an agency* must give to the issues at hand.[50] To quote from the seminal opinion, authored by Judge Harold Leventhal:

> Its supervisory function calls on the court to intervene not merely in case of procedural inadequacies, or bypassing of the mandate in the legislative charter, but more broadly if the court becomes aware, especially from a combination of danger signals, that the agency has not really taken a 'hard look' at the salient problems, and has not genuinely engaged in reasoned decision-making.[51]

For much of the 1970s, some judges on the DC Circuit took the view that reviewing courts should prescribe additional procedures, such as hearings, to remedy agencies' failures to consider issues thoroughly.[52] The Supreme Court put an end to this practice in the 1978 *Vermont Yankee* case,[53] which held that courts may not impose procedural requirements not contained in the APA. But even when courts do not mandate specific procedures for agencies to follow, hard look review often casts substantive review in procedural terms. It

48 Ibid 224–25.

49 Reuel E Schiller, 'Rulemaking's Promise: Administrative Law and Legal Culture in the 1960s and 1970s,' (2001) 53 *Administrative Law Review* 1139.

50 *Natural Lime Association v EPA*, 627 F 2d 416, 451 n 126 (DC Cir 1980).

51 *Greater Boston Television Corp v FCC*, 444 F 2d 841 (DC Cir 1970).

52 For a detailed discussion of the debates over hard look review within the DC Circuit, see Schiller (n 48).

53 *Vermont Yankee Nuclear Power Corp. v. NRDC*, 435 US 519 (1978).

is not the agency's policy choices that are themselves inherently arbitrary and capricious. Rather, what is arbitrary and capricious is the agency's failure to justify its choices adequately in the face of the totality of the arguments and evidence before it. The agency is faulted not so much for its decision as for how it came to its decision. For a better sense of classical hard look review in action, we begin with a closer look at one of the DC Circuit's cases, *National Tire Dealers and Retreaders Association, Inc. v. Brinegar.*[54]

7.3.2 Hard look review in action: National Tire Dealers

The National Traffic and Motor Vehicle Act of 1966 grants the Secretary of Transportation the authority to 'establish by order appropriate Federal motor vehicle safety standards.'[55] The statute requires that each standard 'shall be practicable, shall meet the need for motor vehicle safety, and shall be stated in objective terms.'[56] In addition, the Act imposes the duty to establish standards on some specific matters. It specifies, among other things, that all safety standards for tyres 'shall require that tires . . . be permanently and conspicuously labelled with such safety information as [the Secretary] determines to be necessary to carry out the purposes of this Act.'[57] The statute further requires that tyre labels shall include, at a minimum, the number of plies in a tyre, the maximum permissible load, and certain other information.

The agency promulgated by regulation a tyre safety standard in 1972. The regulation required that all retreaded passenger tyres be permanently moulded with the ply and load information specifically required by the statute, as well as the tyre size, maximum inflation, and the words 'tubeless' or 'tube-type' and 'belted' or 'radial,' as applicable. The standard was challenged by a trade association of tyre dealers and retreaders. Specifically, the challengers denied that the agency had demonstrated that the needs of motor vehicle safety could only be met through a *permanent* label containing the specified information.[58]

The court noted that a permanent label was plainly not necessary to protect the original purchaser of retreaded tyres, who could equally well be informed by a non-permanent, affixed label at the point of sale. But, as the court acknowledged, the agency justified the requirement of a permanent label with reference to used retreaded tyres. The preamble to the standard stated:

> Tires . . . may be subject to many applications during their useful life. They are transferred from wheel to wheel and from vehicle to vehicle, and each time this takes place the information on the tire sidewall becomes important. Permanent labelling is therefore required if the information

54 491 F 2d 31 (DC Cir 1974).
55 Public Law 89–563, Sept 9, 1966, 80 Stat 718, 719 §103(a).
56 Ibid.
57 Ibid § 201.
58 491 F 2d 36.

is to perform its function, as it can be readily assumed that affixed labels will last little longer than the first time the tire is mounted.[59]

Still, the court argued, this did not go far enough to justify requiring permanent labels: 'The Secretary has supplied no illustrations or references to the record to amplify these observations.'[60] The court itself imagined two scenarios in which the lack of a permanent label could impair safety: when an original purchaser of retreaded tyres needed to replace one or more with matching tyres, and when a driver wishes to purchase used retreaded tyres for a vehicle. Still, according to the court, the agency had not provided sufficient information to justify the conclusion that the permanent labelling requirement was appropriate:

There is no suggestion in the record or briefs of how frequently these hypothetical situations arise. They might occur so rarely that a costly and burdensome permanent labelling requirement geared to ensure safety in such situations is unreasonable. Furthermore, it is not clear that a second-hand purchaser of retreads or an original owner who seeks replacements is dependent on the tyres' labelling for information necessary for proper match-ups, inflation, and loading. The Secretary's brief observes that an expert can determine many of the critical characteristics of a tyre by mere inspection.[61]

The court went on to note that the 'apparently remote relationship between the permanent labelling requirement . . . and the goal of motor vehicle safety might be tolerable if those standards imposed no significant burden on the tire retreading industry.'[62] In fact, however, evidence in the record suggests that permanent labelling would place a heavy burden on retreaders, and the agency met this evidence with 'mere assertions, unsupported by any citations to the record, that the requirements are practicable.' To develop the point, the court proceeded to undertake a deep-dive into the mechanics of tyre labelling.

For approximately two-thirds of the tyre casings used by retreaders, the information required by the standard is not already printed in a location that would be visible after retreading. The retreading process involves removing the old tyre tread, buffing the surface, affixing a new rubber tread with adhesive, and then vulcanizing it to the casing. According to the court, to permanently label tyres during this process:

> it would be necessary for an employee to work with hand-tools on a mould that would have a temperature somewhere between 250 and 300 degrees F. exposing him to the danger of burns in an effort to change the varied plates with this information on it as each tire is changed in the

58 491 F 2d 36.

60 Ibid.

61 Ibid 37.

62 Ibid.

> mould.' Altering the mould plates in this fashion would be necessary for almost every tire run through the production lines, since the size, number of plies, construction, maximum pressure, and other characteristics vary from tire to tire. Thus, permanent labelling of retreads with the various items specified in Standard No. 117 might be loosely analogised to personalizing a set of wedding invitations by engraving each one with the name of the individual invitee: the engraving plate would have to be changed for each invitation printed.[63]

Although the comments 'raise serious doubts' about the regulation, the court found the agency's response inadequate. The agency noted that manufacturers are already required to imprint information on each tyre they retread under a different regulation, but the court found that the existing regulation is substantially less onerous, because the information it requires does not change from tyre to tyre.

As practised in *National Tire Dealers*, hard look review shares substantial similarities with proportionality review. At the heart of the court's analysis is what amounts to a necessity test: to serve the legitimate purpose of promoting motor vehicle safety, is it really necessary that tyres be labelled *permanently* with this information? In application here, the test is quite demanding, because the court places the burden of establishing the necessity of its measure squarely on the shoulders of the agency. In the preamble to the rule, the agency articulated a plausible reason why the information needed to be permanently affixed to the tyre – to make the information available after the point of sale to those who might need it to select or match tyres – but this is not enough for the court. The court further requires the agency to establish that 'these hypothetical situations' arise frequently enough to justify the requirement.

The opinion suggests, however, that the intensity of its necessity analysis is not a constant but a variable, to be adjusted based on the magnitude of the burden the challenged measure imposes. As the court notes, the looseness of fit between the permanent labelling requirement and the goal of vehicle safety might not be fatal were the challenged measure less burdensome on tyre retreaders. The court seems to be endorsing variable intensity review, along lines similar to those suggested by some scholars of proportionality.[64] This kind of analysis, which pegs the intensity of necessity review to the burden that a challenged measure imposes, permits the court to roughly balance benefits and harms from the measure: the greater the burden, the more intensive the review, and therefore, the lower the measure's chances of surviving. This approach gives the court a way to consider the weights of competing interests without engaging in an explicit balancing analysis. This kind of 'stealth balancing' may hold particular

63 Ibid 39 (quoting a comment from a tyre retreader to NHTSA).

64 Julian Rivers, 'Proportionality and Variable Intensity of Review' (2006) 65 *Cambridge Law Journal* 174.

appeal for judges in the United States, where judicial balancing of values can be controversial.

7.3.3 A hard look from the Supreme Court: State Farm

The United States Supreme Court hears only a handful of administrative law cases each term,[65] and for more than a decade, it was not clear how the high court would receive the DC Circuit's experiment with hard look arbitrary and capricious review. The *Vermont Yankee* decision of 1978,[66] which took appeals courts to task for imposing on agencies procedural requirements not contained in the APA, suggested to many scholars that the Court would look with disfavour on the DC Circuit's upgrade to the historically deferential arbitrary and capricious review. In fact, however, the Supreme Court surprised many in 1983 with its decision in *Motor Vehicle Manufacturers Association v. State Farm Mutual Automobile Insurance Co.*,[67] while giving a full-throated endorsement to the hard look version of arbitrary and capricious review.

Like *National Tire Dealers*, *State Farm* concerned a protracted rule-making process conducted by the hapless National Highway Traffic Safety Administration, this one involving passenger restraint safety standards. The Department of Transportation first issued a rule requiring seatbelts in passenger vehicles in 1967, but seatbelts could only work if worn, and the majority of motorists in the late 1960s declined to buckle up. In 1969, the agency responded by proposing a standard requiring passive restraints, which as a practical matter meant either automatic seatbelts or airbags. After much wrangling, the agency adopted a final rule in 1977, which required manufacturers to equip all new cars with passive restraints by model year 1984. Then in 1981, the agency reopened the rule-making process, and after a comment period, rescinded the passive restraint requirement altogether. An insurance company and trade association for insurers sued to challenge the rescission as arbitrary and capricious. They won in the appeals court, and the Motor Vehicle Manufacturers Association, an intervener in the case, petitioned for review in the Supreme Court.

Writing for the Court, Justice Byron White laid out the arbitrary and capricious standard as follows:

> The scope of review under the 'arbitrary and capricious' standard is narrow and a court is not to substitute its judgment for that of the agency. Nevertheless, the agency must examine the relevant data and articulate a satisfactory explanation for its action including a 'rational connection between the facts found and the choice made.' In reviewing that

65 Peter L Strauss, 'One Hundred Fifty Cases Per Year: Some Implications of the Supreme Court's Limited Resources for Judicial Review of Agency Action' (1987) 87 *Columbia Law Review* 1093.

66 *Vermont Yankee* (n 52).

67 463 US 29 (1983).

> explanation, we must 'consider whether the decision was based on a consideration of the relevant factors and whether there has been a clear error of judgment.' Normally, an agency rule would be arbitrary and capricious if the agency has relied on factors which Congress has not intended it to consider, entirely failed to consider an important aspect of the problem, offered an explanation for its decision that runs counter to the evidence before the agency, or is so implausible that it could not be ascribed to a difference in view or the product of agency expertise.[68]

The Supreme Court's decision put the agency's explanation for changing course squarely at the centre of its analysis. In a statement accompanying the rescission, the agency explained that new information undermined its earlier projections about the safety benefits of the passive restraint requirement. Initially, the agency had anticipated that roughly 60% of vehicles would meet the new requirements with airbags, but as the vehicle industry began finalising its compliance plans, it became clear that around 99% of new cars would feature automatic seatbelts instead. Moreover, the vast majority of automatic seatbelts would be detachable belts, which, once detached, would remain disabled until rebuckled by the motorist. Because detachable belts require 'the same kind of affirmative action that is the stumbling block to obtaining high usage levels of manual belts,' according to the agency, it was no longer clear that the standard would significantly increase motor vehicle safety.[69]

Justice White subjected the agency's reasoning to a demanding examination. The Court took issue, not only with how the agency considered the issues, but also with its failure to consider all the alternatives. 'The first and most obvious reason for finding the rescission arbitrary and capricious,' according to the Court, 'is that NHTSA apparently gave no consideration whatever to modifying the Standard to require that airbag technology be utilized.'[70] The Court noted that the agency's original rule proposal would have required installing airbags in all new cars, and that when an automatic seatbelt option was later proposed, the use of detachable seatbelts was approved only with manufacturers' assurances that they would not compromise the standard's safety goals. The Court stops short of insisting that the agency should have returned to an all-airbag standard. Rather, if the agency believed an all-airbag standard was unworkable, it had a duty to explain why.

Given the effectiveness ascribed to airbag technology by the agency, the mandate of the Act to achieve traffic safety would suggest that the logical response to the faults of detachable seatbelts would be to require the installation of airbags. At the very least, this alternative way of achieving the objectives of the Act should have been addressed, and adequate reasons

68 Ibid n 43.
69 Ibid 39.
70 Ibid 46.

given for its abandonment. But the agency not only did not require compliance through airbags, it also did not even consider the possibility in its 1981 rule-making. Not one sentence of its rule-making statement discusses the airbags-only option.[71]

Although concerns about an airbag-only standard emerged in the briefs and oral arguments before the Supreme Court, the Court disregarded them, noting that 'the courts may not accept appellate counsel's *post hoc* rationalizations for agency action.'[72]

The Court also concluded that the agency was 'too quick to dismiss the safety benefits of automatic seatbelts.'[73] The agency dismissed the results of a study showing a substantial increase in seatbelt use in vehicles with passive belts, on the grounds that participants in the study were not typical: they had purchased vehicles with extra safety features not required by law. The Court accepted that 'it is within the agency's discretion to pass upon the generalizability of these field studies.'[74] However, the Court rejected the train of reasoning that led the agency to conclude that the use of detachable belts would not necessarily lead to even a five percentage point increase in seatbelt usage, because the agency 'apparently take no account of the critical difference between detachable automatic belts and current manual belts.'[75] The Court elaborated:

> A detached passive belt does require an affirmative act to reconnect it, but – unlike a manual seatbelt – the passive belt, once reattached, will continue to function automatically unless again disconnected. Thus, inertia – a factor which the agency's own studies have found significant in explaining the current low usage rates for seatbelts – works in favour of, not against, use of the protective device. Since 20% to 50% of motorists currently wear seatbelts on some occasions, there would seem to be grounds to believe that seatbelt use by occasional users will be substantially increased by the detachable passive belts. Whether this is in fact the case is a matter for the agency to decide, but it must bring its expertise to bear on the question.[76]

In other words, the Court has a different theory from the agency about how occasional seatbelt users might respond to detachable belts. While the Court does not assert that its own theory is superior to the agency's, it does demand that the agency at least consider the alternative theory and reject it explicitly.

Finally, the Court found fault with the agency for failing to explain why it had not required *non-detachable* automatic belts in the safety standard. Specifically, the Court was not satisfied with the agency's reasons for not requiring

71 Ibid 48.
72 Ibid 50.
73 Ibid 51.
74 Ibid 53.
75 Ibid 54.
76 Ibid.

a continuous passive seatbelt, which the user can spool out to create the slack necessary to enter and exit the car seat. In its rule, the agency explained that requiring passive belts with use-compelling features, such as continuous belts and ignition interlocks (which prevent ignition if the driver's belt is not fastened), would be 'counterproductive.' The agency noted 'a widespread, latent and irrational fear in many members of the public that they could be trapped by the seat belt after a crash,' and concluded that 'it would be highly inappropriate to impose a technology which by its very nature could heighten or trigger that concern.'[77] Moreover, the agency added, it 'would be unable to find the cause of safety served by imposing any requirement which would further complicate the extrication of any occupant from his or her car, as some use-compelling features would.'[78]

The Court was not satisfied. The agency gave no reasons to justify its conclusion that the continuous belt option would not be popular with the public, as the ignition interlock was. Nor had the agency cited any grounds for departing from its earlier conclusion that non-detachable belts with spool releases were no less safe than detachable belts. 'While the agency is entitled to change its view on the acceptability of continuous passive belts,' the Court concluded, 'it is obligated to explain its reasons for doing so'.[79]

To those familiar with proportionality review, the *State Farm* decision is notable in several respects. First, the case does not concern administrative overreaching, as in the paradigm proportionality case, in which the administration has taken measures that are excessive in context. Rather, the claim is that the agency has *underreached*: its regulation does not go far enough to promote car safety. This is not so much a matter of the authorities shooting at sparrows with cannons, in Fritz Fleiner's memorable phrase, as of shooting at condors with a peashooter.[80] In general, arbitrary and capricious review is symmetrical in a way that classic proportionality review is not: administrative action is subject to challenge, and the agency's reasons for its choices must stand up to the same scrutiny, whether the claim is that the agency has done too much or that it has not done enough.[81]

That said, there are doctrines in American administrative law that, as a practical matter, mean that arbitrary and capricious review is more often available to challenge agency overreach than agency underreach. First, although American standing doctrines are fairly liberal by international standards, they are generally more favourable to the targets of regulation than to the beneficiaries of regulation. The requirement that plaintiffs suffer an injury that

77 46 Fed Reg 53419.

78 Ibid.

79 *State Farm* (n 67) 56.

80 Fritz Fleiner, *Institutionen Des Deutschen Verwaltungsrechts* (Mohr Siebeck 1928) 404.

81 See *Riverkeeper Inc v EPA*, 475 F 3d 83 (2d Cir 2007) (sustaining an arbitrary and capricious challenge to environmental regulations for power plant cooling towers brought by an environmental advocacy group), *overturned by Entergy Corp v Riverkeeper*, 556 US 208 (2009).

is 'concrete and particularised' and 'actual or imminent' can pose obstacles for the advocates of more vigorous regulation in areas where the benefits of agency action are diffuse.[82] Second, notwithstanding the APA's instance that the 'failure to act' qualifies as agency action, courts are generally very reluctant to review agencies' exercise of discretion not to take action, as noted above.[83] *State Farm* is something of a special case, because the agency had first passed, and then rescinded, a passive restraint requirement. Had the agency never itself raised the possibility of passive restraints, it seems unlikely that the courts would have required the agency to mandate them. All that being said, reviewability doctrines are sufficiently malleable that courts may permit would-be beneficiaries of regulation to challenge agency inaction as arbitrary and capricious when they wish to. Notably, in 2007 a narrow majority of the Supreme Court chose to entertain, and ultimately upheld, the state of Massachusetts' claim that it was arbitrary and capricious for the EPA to fail to determine whether greenhouse gas emissions contribute to global warming.[84]

As in proportionality analysis, the agency's consideration of alternative measures is relevant to hard look review, but in hard look review, the obligation to consider alternatives extends farther, because it is not tethered to the question of whether the chosen measure is excessive. An actor subject to proportionality is required to consider whether the government's objective could be equally well pursued using alternative measures that infringed less on the interests of others. The failure to consider less restrictive alternatives would be grounds for finding agency action arbitrary and capricious under hard look review, but so might the failure to consider *more effective* alternatives.

Even if the Supreme Court accepted NHTSA's conclusion that its passive restraint standard would not significantly improve car safety, that would not justify the agency's rescission under hard look review. Rather, the agency had an obligation to consider an airbag-only alternative that might be more effective in meeting the statute's goals. Significantly, hard look review does not merely impose an obligation to consider alternatives generated through the notice-and-comment process, although agencies have an obligation to address these as well.[85] Instead, in its contemporaneous explanation of its policy choices, the agency is responsible for anticipating and responding to alternative possibilities that a reviewing court might later dream up. In *State Farm*, it appears that the possibility of an airbags-only rule was first raised by the Court of Appeals,[86] not by commenters on the agency's proposal.[87]

Furthermore, under hard look review as practiced in *State Farm*, the agency is on the hook not only for considering alternative policy choices, but

82 *Lujan v Defenders of Wildlife*, 504 US 555, 561 (1992).

83 See text to notes 17 to 23.

84 *Massachusetts v EPA*, 549 US 497 (2007).

85 *See Nova Scotia Food Prods Corp v United States*, 568 F2d 240 (2d Cir 1977).

86 680 F 2d 206 at 236–38.

87 46 Fed Reg 53419, 53427–29.

alternative empirical predictions. As described above, NHTSA's projection that the use of detachable belts would not significantly enhance car safety was based on a prediction about motorist behaviour. The agency assumed that motorists who do not usually use manual belts would disconnect detachable belts and then leave them disconnected. The Court countered that even motorists who do not usually use manual belts habitually do buckle up some of the time, and suggested that such motorists might well end up leaving their automatic buckles attached. The Court expected the agency to explain why its theory of seatbelt use is more plausible.

Another factor to mention here is the open-endedness of hard look review. While proportionality challenges predictably feature some version of the claim that the agency has used disproportionate measures, under hard look review, an agency's action is vulnerable if there is *any* respect in which it is not rationally justifiable. And given the plasticity of the arbitrary and capricious challenge, judicial review does not reliably proceed according to a pre-defined series of tests, as proportionality does. It may be very difficult for an agency to anticipate all of the faults that an aggrieved person may find with its actions, not to mention the ways in which the reviewing court may probe its reasoning.

In these respects, hard look review might appear to be even more demanding than proportionality review. Indeed, starting in the 1980s, many administrative law scholars claimed that unduly intensive judicial review was 'ossifying' rule-making, and pointed to hard look review as chief culprit.[88] Writing about NHTSA, Jerry Mashaw and David Harfst conclude that '[t]he result of judicial requirements for comprehensive rationality has been a general suppression of the use of rules'.[89] Still, concerns over ossification seem to have faded over recent decades, perhaps in part because it is by no means clear that hard look review is still the dominant approach to arbitrary and capricious review, as further discussed below.[90]

In another respect, though, hard look review is more forgiving than proportionality analysis, precisely because of its emphasis on the agency's reasoning process. It is difficult, if not impossible, to redeem a measure that has been reviewed on its merits and deemed disproportionate. By contrast, because hard look review focuses on the agency's reasoning, rather than the substance of its action itself, it leaves agencies that fail the test more latitude to achieve their desired results,

88 See Mashaw and Harfst (n 3); Richard J Pierce, 'Unruly Judicial Review of Rulemaking' (1990) 5 *Natural Resources & Environment* 23. Writing in 1990, Pierce wrote that '[i]ncreasingly, agencies are abandoning rulemaking because of the extraordinary burdens courts have imposed on the rulemaking process.' Ibid at 23.

89 Jerry L Mashaw and David L Harfst, *The Struggle for Auto Safety* (Harvard University Press 1990).

90 It is also clear that, notwithstanding Professor Pierce's concerns, agencies have not given up on rule-making. See Anne Joseph O'Connell, 'Political Cycles of Rulemaking: an Empirical Portrait of the Modern Administrative State' (2008) 94 *Virginia Law Review* 889, 964–65 (noting extensive use of rule-making from the 1980s through to the early 2000s).

if they can only give a better account of their choices. While some observers are sceptical that the focus on agency reasoning is little more than window dressing for judicial judgments about the content of agency choices, one empirical study suggests that agencies generally do eventually win judicial approval of policies first announced in rules found to be arbitrary and capricious.[91]

7.3.4 The twilight of hard look? Fox Television

How widely is the 'hard look' version of arbitrary and capricious review actually practiced by American courts? A firm answer is not easy to come by, but there are reasons to expect that *State Farm* may be an outlier in terms of its intensity of review. Although the Supreme Court has never repudiated *State Farm*, Michael Herz noted in 2004 that 'the Supreme Court has cited *State Farm* only twenty-five times since Rehnquist became Chief Justice [in 1986] and then almost always in a dissent, or only to be distinguished, or for a pabulum proposition, or in a mild and revisionist manner.'[92] This stands in stark contrast to the *Chevron v. Natural Resources Defense Council* decision, handed down the year after *State Farm*, which the Supreme Court has cited favourably scores of times. *Chevron*, which applies to agency interpretations of statutes, embodies a more deferential form of scrutiny than the hard look variant of arbitrary and capricious review, as discussed below.[93]

The *FCC v. Fox Television Stations, Inc.* case from 2009 illustrates a more recent, and far more forgiving, application of arbitrary and capricious review.[94] The case played out against a backdrop of prodigiously profane celebrity appearances on award shows broadcast on American network television. Cher dropped a choice four-letter word into her acceptance speech at the 2002 Billboard Music Awards, and Nicole Ritchie used a few more at the following year's ceremony. Although federal law prohibits the broadcast of 'obscene, indecent, or profane language,' the broadcasters were not initially subject to penalties, because staff rulings of the Federal Communications Commission (FCC) had established a safe harbour for 'fleeting expletives' – nonliteral and non-repetitive utterances of offensive words. But when Bono used a vulgar intensifier to underline his excitement over winning an award at the 2003 Golden Globes, the FCC changed course. Reversing a staff ruling that the Golden Globes broadcast was not indecent, the FCC in 2004 issued an order declaring that fleeting expletives could violate broadcasting laws and be a basis for penalties. Relying on its Golden Globes order, in 2006 the agency declared that the 2002 and 2003 Billboard broadcasts were also

91 William S Jordan III, 'Ossification Revisited: Does Arbitrary and Capricious Review Significantly Interfere With Agency Ability to Achieve Regulatory Goals Through Informal Rulemaking' (1999) 94 *Northwestern Law Review* 393.

92 Michael Herz 'Rehnquist Court and Administrative Law' (2004) 99 *Northwestern Law Review* 314.

93 See text at 100 to 104.

94 556 US 502.

indecent, but declined to impose fines. Fox challenged the indecency findings as arbitrary and capricious.

A central issue for the Supreme Court was whether, and how, it was relevant to arbitrary and capricious analysis that the agency was changing its policy. Writing for a 5–4 majority on this point, Justice Scalia concluded that the agency's past position had limited relevance:

> [The agency] need not demonstrate to a court's satisfaction that the reasons for the new policy are better than the reasons for the old one; it suffices that the new policy is permissible under the statute, that there are good reasons for it, and that the agency believes it to be better, which the conscious change of course adequately indicates.[95]

Writing for the four dissenters, Justice Breyer denied that the agency's switch dictated a heightened level of scrutiny, but insisted that it was, nonetheless, relevant to the analysis. The action that the agency must justify is a change in policy, and so the agency must give an adequate account of that change. That requires 'the agency here to focus upon the reasons that led the agency to adopt the initial policy, and to explain why it now comes to a new judgment.'[96]

The majority wasted little time in concluding that the agency's new approach to fleeting expletives was not arbitrary or capricious. According to the Court:

> it was certainly reasonable to determine that it made no sense to distinguish between literal and nonliteral uses of offensive words, requiring repetitive use to render only the latter indecent. As the Commission said with regard to the expletive use of the F-Word, 'the word's power to insult and offend derives from its sexual meaning'.[97]

Moreover, the agency's conclusion that a safe harbour for fleeting uses of words would lead to more widespread use of offensive language was 'surely rational (if not inescapable).'[98] The majority's application of the arbitrary and capricious standard to the facts of this case consumed all of two pages in the case report.

In a portion of the opinion that commanded only four votes, Justice Scalia dismissed arguments made in dissent that the FCC, like the Department of Transportation in *State Farm*, had failed to address important aspects of the problem before it. Justice Breyer's dissent noted that the FCC had initially justified its policy on fleeting expletives to avoid running afoul of First

95 Ibid 516.
96 Ibid 550 (Breyer J, dissenting).
97 Ibid 512.
98 Ibid 518.

Amendment protections for free expression. Against that backdrop, according to Justice Breyer, the agency had not explained why the constitutional calculus had changed. Justice Scalia, for his part, denied that the agency had any obligation to perform a constitutional analysis, but pointed out that the agency's order did justify the regulation of indecency in general (if not this policy in particular) as constitutional.

Justice Breyer also faulted the agency for failing to consider the policy's chilling impact on small broadcasters, who would likely be unable to afford the pricey equipment needed to 'bleep' bad language. The FCC had said nothing about this issue, but Justice Scalia stepped into the breach with some arguments of his own. Justice Scalia first posited that the 'down-home local guests [on locally produced programming] probably employ vulgarity less than big-city folks; and small-town stations generally cannot afford or cannot attract foul-mouthed "glitteratae" from Hollywood.'[99] Moreover, small broadcasters had little to fear, since the FCC's order stated that it might be inequitable to penalise expletives that surface during the live broadcast of a public event, and in any case, the agency had the discretion to craft appropriate remedies that took account of relevant circumstances.

Plainly, *Fox Television* presents a brand of arbitrary and capricious review that is substantially less searching than the hard look review of *National Tire Dealers* and *State Farm*. The core of the Court's analysis resembles a fairly casual reasonableness review, in which the agency's action is sustained because it is 'reasonable' and 'rational.' And the fact that the agency once rejected the policy it now embraces out of concerns that it could unduly chill constitutionally protected expression hardly enters the picture. The agency is not required to explain why these concerns now hold no sway, and indeed, the Court itself supplies arguments on the agency's behalf to fend off the First Amendment objections. To the extent that *Fox Television Stations* is the shape of things to come, it signals a departure from the aggressive scrutiny of hard look review.

The Court's review in *Fox Television* is also notably less stringent than proportionality review. From a proportionality perspective, the central question is whether, in pursuing its goal of keeping the airwaves free from indecency, the FCC chose a policy that went too far, and unduly burdened free expression. Framed in this way, the agency's justification must focus on explaining why the policy's adverse impact on free expression would be limited, and acceptable in light of the gains made in pursuing the statute's objective of keeping indecency off the air. The Court's analysis, by contrast, does not require the FCC to justify its policy in these terms, or to explain why its choice strikes the balance between these competing considerations better than alternative approaches. Indeed, the agency has almost nothing to say on its policy's impact on expression. Because the Court stops after evaluating the agency's policy on its own terms and pronouncing it reasonable, it never squarely engages with the other interests at stake.

99 Ibid 527.

7.4 Agency discretion and statutory interpretation

As a practical matter, many of the important discretionary choices that agencies make are reflected in their interpretations of the statutes that they administer. A formidable body of law has grown up to address the sort of deference that courts owe to agency interpretations of statutes under different circumstances. This is not the place for a comprehensive analysis of these doctrines, but a discussion of judicial control of agency discretion would be incomplete without some reference to them.

The centrepiece of the Supreme Court's deference jurisprudence is the famous *Chevron* decision from 1984.[100] In *Chevron*, the Court devised a two-step analysis for evaluating agency interpretations of statutes:

> When a court reviews an agency's construction of the statute which it administers, it is confronted with two questions. First, always, is the question whether Congress has directly spoken to the precise question at issue. If the intent of Congress is clear, that is the end of the matter; for the court, as well as the agency, must give effect to the unambiguously expressed intent of Congress. If, however, the court determines Congress has not directly addressed the precise question at issue, the court does not simply impose its own construction on the statute, as would be necessary in the absence of an administrative interpretation. Rather, if the statute is silent or ambiguous with respect to the specific issue, the question for the court is whether the agency's answer is based on a permissible construction of the statute.[101]

Chevron is important conceptually, not least because it explicitly recognises agency statutory interpretation as a means by which agencies exercise discretionary decision-making power delegated by Congress. The Court draws a connection between the actions that agencies take pursuant to express grants of discretion, which are subject to arbitrary and capricious review, and the policy choices that agencies make pursuant to implicit delegations in the form of statutory ambiguities, which are subject to *Chevron* reasonableness review:

> If Congress has explicitly left a gap for the agency to fill, there is an express delegation of authority to the agency to elucidate a specific provision of the statute by regulation. Such legislative regulations are given controlling weight unless they are arbitrary, capricious, or manifestly contrary to the statute. Sometimes the legislative delegation to an agency on a particular question is implicit, rather than explicit. In such a case, a court may not substitute its own construction of a statutory provision for a reasonable interpretation made by the administrator of an agency.[102]

100 *Chevron USA, Inc v Nat'l Res Def Council*, 467 US 837, 842–43 (1984).
101 Ibid.
102 Ibid 843–44 (emphasis added).

In the *Chevron* case itself, the key interpretive question concerned the 'bubble concept': whether the EPA would be permitted to treat an entire industrial facility as a 'stationary source' of pollution for purposes of the pollution-permitting regime of the Clean Air Act. The EPA's interpretation would allow polluters to modify their facilities without obtaining new permits so long as total emissions did not rise. Environmental groups protested that the interpretation would undercut the statute's goal of pollution reduction, while the agency maintained that its interpretation would encourage facilities to favour technologies that polluted less. The Court concluded that 'Congress did not have a specific intention on the applicability of the bubble concept in these cases,' and that 'the EPA's use of that concept here is a reasonable policy choice for the agency to make.'[103] The Court concluded the agency's choice was reasonable, largely because it represented a 'reasonable accommodation' of the competing economic and environmental goals animating the Clean Air Act.[104]

As prominent as it is, *Chevron* does not occupy the whole field of statutory interpretation. *Chevron* does not apply to all agency interpretations of statutes, and exactly when it applies remains a source of some confusion and controversy even now.

In a 2001 case, *United States v. Mead Corporation*,[105] the Supreme Court explained that *Chevron* applied whenever 'Congress would expect the agency to be able to speak with the force of law when it addresses ambiguity in the statute or fills a space in the enacted law.'[106] A congressional grant of rule-making or formal adjudication power is 'a very good indicator of delegation meriting *Chevron* treatment,' but it is not dispositive.[107] In the event that an agency interpretation does not merit *Chevron* review, it will be afforded the 'sliding-scale' deference mandated by *Skidmore v. Swift & Co.*[108] Under *Skidmore*, the weight that a reviewing court will give to an agency's interpretation 'will depend upon the thoroughness evident in its consideration, the validity of its reasoning, its consistency with earlier and later pronouncements, and all those factors which give it power to persuade, if lacking power to control.'[109]

The mixed deference regime inaugurated by *Mead* has drawn criticism from some prominent scholars for providing poor guidance to agencies and lower courts.[110] In particular, it is not obvious how courts are to determine whether Congress would expect agencies to speak to a given issue with the force of law. The presumption that notice-and-comment rule-makings and formal adjudications are *Chevron*-eligible turns out not to hold up in practice,

103 Ibid 844.
104 Ibid 865.
105 533 US 218 (2001).
106 Ibid at 229.
107 Ibid.
108 323 US 132 (1944).
109 Ibid 140.
110 Thomas W Merrill, 'The Mead Doctrine: of Rules and Standards, Meta-Rules and Meta-Standards,' (2002) 54 *Administrative Law Review* 807.

at least as far as the Supreme Court is concerned: an empirical study by William Eskridge and Lauren Baer finds that, through 2006, the Supreme Court evaluated only a minority of these statutory interpretations under *Chevron* or a more deferential standard.[111]

7.4.1 A convergence of standards?

How does judicial review of agency statutory interpretations compare to arbitrary and capricious review? There are really two questions here. First, what is the difference between an agency interpreting a statute and an agency exercising discretion under a statute? Second, what are the substantive differences, if any, between the standards of review that courts apply in these two situations? The answer to neither question is completely clear.

In some cases, an agency is clearly either interpreting a statute or exercising discretion, and of course the parties' pleading can help to clarify the questions before the court. In other cases, however, the distinction will not be so obvious, with the result that it is also not obvious how the court should review the agency's action. Jack Beermann, for instance, makes a convincing argument that the Supreme Court could have approached *Fox Television* as a statutory interpretation case, the central question being whether the agency permissibly interpreted the statutes' prohibition on 'obscene, indecent, or profane language.'[112] This would counsel reviewing the agency under the *Chevron* framework. In actuality, *Chevron* is mentioned nowhere in *Fox Television*'s five opinions.

The Court faced a choice between these two frameworks directly in *Judalung v. Holder*, from 2011.[113] This case concerned a Bureau of Immigration Appeals policy restricting relief from deportation for non-citizen criminals to those who would have had comparable grounds for relief under a provision of immigration law that had since been repealed. Arguing on the agency's behalf, the Solicitor General maintained that the agency's 'comparable grounds' doctrine was entitled to deference under *Chevron* step two, as a reasonable interpretation of an ambiguous provision of federal law. The Court rejected this contention, and instead reviewed the agency under the arbitrary and capricious standard. In a footnote, the Court suggested that the choice was immaterial, since the standards are equivalent: 'Were we to apply *Chevron*, our analysis would be the same, because under *Chevron* step two, we ask whether an agency interpretation is "arbitrary or capricious in substance."'[114]

111 William N Eskridge and Lauren E Baer, 'The Continuum of Deference: Supreme Court Treatment of Agency Statutory Interpretations from *Chevron* to *Hamdan*' (2008) 96 Geo LJ 1083.

112 Jack Beermann, '*Chevron* At the Roberts Court: Still Failing After All These Years,' (2014) 83 *Fordham Law Review* 114.

113 132 S Ct 476 (2011).

114 Judulang, 132 S Ct at 483 (n 7). The Court went on to conclude that the case did not present a question of statutory interpretation, so its comment on the equivalence of *Chevron* and arbitrary and capricious review was dicta.

Judalung was not the only time the Supreme Court has suggested that *Chevron* step two reasonableness review is the same as arbitrary and capricious review,[115] and a number of appeals courts have made this claim for years.[116] They are joined by some legal scholars who have also argued that *Chevron* step two either is, or should be, identical to arbitrary and capricious review.[117] One argument in favour of harmonising *Chevron* step two and arbitrary and capricious review is that it would seem anomalous to subject agencies to more intensive review for discretionary policy choices than for statutory interpretations – that is, an intensive hard look review for the former, and a more relaxed reasonableness review for the latter.[118] If substantial deference to the agency is warranted in *Chevron* step two because Congress has implicitly left a matter up to the agency to decide, should not at least as much deference be given when the agency is exercising discretionary authority that Congress has plainly granted it?

But apart from the question of what courts *should be* doing, there is the question of what they *are* doing. Are arbitrary and capricious review and *Chevron* step two, as applied by courts, actually the same thing?

A definitive answer is not in reach, but some empirical data provide tentative grounds for concluding that they are not. At least as practised by the Supreme Court, *Chevron* step two appears to be a more deferential form of review. According to the data collected by Eskridge and Baer, of the fifty-four cases decided between 1984 and 2006 in which the Supreme Court applied *Chevron* step two, the Court concluded that the agency's interpretation was reasonable in fifty-three cases.[119] By way of contrast, in a study of all cases in which actions of the EPA or National Labour Relations Board are subjected to arbitrariness review in the appeals courts between 1995 and 2006, Thomas Miles and Cass Sunstein find that the agencies won 64% of the time.[120] Although these studies involve different courts, different years, and (in the case of the latter) only a small sample of agencies, they provide some reason to think that, as actually practised

115 See *Household Credit Services, Inc v Pfennig*, 541 US 232, 242 (2004); *Astrue v Capato ex rel BNC*, 132 S Ct 2021, 2034 (2012).

116 See *Nat'l Assn of Reg Utility Comm'rs v ICC*, 41 F3d 721 (DC Cir 1994); Nat'l Org of Veterans Advocates, Inc v Sec'y of Veterans' Affairs, 669 F3d 1340 (Fed Cir 2012).

117 Mark Seidenfeld, 'A Syncopated *Chevron*: Emphasizing Reasoned Decisionmaking in Reviewing Agency Interpretations of Statutes' (1994) 73 *Texas Law Review* 83; Ronald M Levin, 'The Anatomy of *Chevron*: Step Two Reconsidered, *72 Chicago-Kent Law Review* (1997) 1253; see also *Verizon Commc'ns, Inc v FCC*, 535 US 467 (2002) (adopting a similar approach).

118 Then-Judge (now Justice) Stephen Breyer flagged the anomaly in a law review article almost thirty years ago. Stephen Breyer, 'Judicial Review of Questions of Law and Policy' (1986) 38 *Administrative Law Review* 363.

119 Eskridge and Baer (n 110).

120 Thomas J Miles and Cass R Sunstein, 'The Real World of Arbitrariness Review' (2008) 75 *University of Chicago Law Review* 761. The Miles and Sunstein data includes both arbitrary and capricious review and substantial evidence review.

by courts, *Chevron* step-two review is substantially less intensive than arbitrary and capricious review.

To the extent that we expect courts to continue to favour the hard look variant of arbitrary and capricious review, these findings should not come as a surprise. *Chevron* step two does not require the agency to demonstrate the superiority of its policy choice to the alternatives, but courts applying hard look review may well expect such a showing from agencies. However, to the extent that the Supreme Court has signalled a pullback from the intensity of hard look review in *Fox Television*, we may witness something like a convergence between *Chevron* step two and arbitrary and capricious review in years to come.[121]

7.5 Conclusion

The intricacies and vagaries of American administrative law doctrine, coupled with the difficulty of reliably assessing empirically what courts are doing in practice, make it hazardous to generalise about judicial review. Still, as I suggested at the outset, a few points stand out.

One of these is closely related to the intricacies and vagaries of doctrine: namely, that judicial review is unpredictable. As this chapter demonstrates, the unpredictability operates on more than one level. For instance, it is not always clear whether a court will treat an agency's exercise of discretion as a policy choice, to be evaluated under the arbitrary and capricious standard, or as a construction of an ambiguous statute, to be evaluated within the *Mead/Chevron/Skidmore* framework. But even assuming that the court applies the arbitrary and capricious standard, how intensively will it scrutinise the agency action? Will the court apply hard look review, à la *State Farm*, or reasonableness review, à la *Fox Television*? If, on the other hand, the court treats the agency action as a statutory interpretation, will it apply the *Chevron* two-step approach or *Skidmore*'s sliding scale of deference? More fundamentally, how do the method and intensity of review under the different approaches compare? I have argued elsewhere that some forms of

121 Another topic of ongoing debate concerns how the intensity of arbitrary and capricious review compares to substantial evidence review. The various courts of appeals have staked out different positions on the issue. The DC Circuit has concluded that the 'quantum of factual support . . . demanded by the substantial evidence provision of the APA . . . [is] no different from that demanded by the arbitrary or capricious standard.' *Data Processing* (n 40) 686. The Eleventh Circuit, by contrast, decided that substantial evidence review requires a 'harder look' than 'the more deferential arbitrary and capricious standard.' AFL-CIO v OSHA, 965 F 2d 962 (11th Cir 1992). Nor is the confusion confined to the lower federal courts. In the words of the current edition of the venerable Gellhorn and Byse casebook, 'If one looks for it, one can find Supreme Court statements that seem to suggest that the "arbitrary and capricious" standard is less demanding than the "substantial evidence" test; that the two standards are the same; and even perhaps that the "arbitrary and capricious" standard is more demanding.' Peter Strauss and others, *Gellhorn and Byse's Administrative Law, Cases and Comments* (11th edn, Foundation Press 2011) 960.

uncertainty in administrative law can have value as levers for shaping agency behaviour under some circumstances.[122] But no one, I think, would argue that the level of unpredictability that pervades American judicial review doctrine is optimally calibrated to serve any end.

One consequence of the confusions in judicial review doctrine may be that they create more space for the play of politics in the judicial review of discretionary decisions by agencies. To take one example, the Miles and Sunstein study of arbitrariness review cases notes a statistically significant relationship between the political party of the president who appoints a judge and how that judge votes. Miles and Sunstein find that Democratic panels of judges approve liberal agency decisions at higher rates than they approve conservative agency decisions, and they find the opposite pattern for Republican panels.[123] Doctrinal uncertainty may abet politically motivated judging, by creating decision environments in which judges can, in fact, be guided by policy considerations, and still credibly claim to find support for their approaches in one or another strand of doctrine. It may also be the case, of course, that the causal arrow also points the other way: that the politics of judging may themselves generate some of the puzzles and inconsistencies we find in the doctrine.

A second key point is that judicial review in American administrative law is symmetrical in a way that traditional proportionality review in most jurisdictions – notably in Germany – is not. Whether proceeding under the arbitrary and capricious rubric, *Chevron*, *Skidmore*, or a different standard, American courts can hear claims not only that the agency has adopted measures that infringe too much on private interests, but also that the agency's chosen means are not sufficiently potent to achieve policy objectives.[124] This was the nature of the challenge in *State Farm*, as well as in several of the DC Circuit's influential hard look precedents.[125] This equal opportunity scrutiny presents a significant contrast with traditional proportionality review, the subtests of which are all squarely trained on detecting government overreach. The symmetry of review may also be among the factors that often make it difficult for agencies to anticipate what will transpire in court. Relative to the traditional German proportionality (see chapter 2), the American approach opens new angles of attack from which parties can challenge agency choices, and – especially when coupled with the hard look insistence that an agency's record comprehensively justifies its choice – can make judicial review a harrowing and unpredictable experience.

In principle, it makes sense for a judicial review regime to hold agencies to account for doing too little with their discretionary powers as well as

122 See Jud Mathews, 'Deference Lotteries,' (2013) 91 *Texas Law Review* 1349.

123 Miles and Sunstein (n 119).

124 A similar symmetry can be found in the French proportionality test (see chapter 3).

125 See Industrial Union Dep't, AFL-CIO v. Hodgson, 409 F 2d 467 (1974) (remanding portions of an asbestos regulation deemed insufficiently protective of workers' health).

too much. One-sided scrutiny runs the risk of creating a systematic anti-regulatory bias in judicial review. In practice, however, it is not entirely clear that the American approach successfully avoids this result. Ironically, it is possible that penalizing agencies for doing too little gives them an incentive to do nothing at all. As noted already, it is very difficult in the American system to obtain judicial review of agency inaction. Shielding agencies from judicial review when they do nothing, but subjecting them to aggressive scrutiny reversal when they take discretionary actions that do not go far enough, gives agencies interested in avoiding judicial reversal an added reason simply not to act at all. This observation feeds into the broader critique, discussed above, that aggressive judicial review can lead to the ossification of the rule-making process. In this context, however, relaxing the scrutiny of judicial review is not the only option for reducing perverse incentives for agencies not to act: lowering the barriers to judicial review of agency inaction could also have an effect.

I close with the observation that there is a tendency in American administrative law to proceduralise substantive review. Even though the Supreme Court in *Vermont Yankee*[126] stopped courts from imposing on agencies additional procedural requirements, such as hearings, reviewing courts still have a tendency to describe the faults they find with agency choices in terms of the agency's decision-making process. So, the Supreme Court in *State Farm* does not hold that NHTSA's failure to impose an airbag-only requirement was inherently irrational, but instead faults the agency for failing to adequately consider an airbag-only option.

The proceduralisation of review may serve as a judicial defence mechanism of sorts. Required to sit in judgment over agencies' sensitive policy choices, judges would understandably seek to conduct their review in a way that anticipates and diffuses the charge that they are simply substituting their own judgment for agencies'. Shifting the analytical focus from the policy's merits to the agency's justification is one way to do this. One consequence may be to hamper agency action by requiring agencies to shoulder burdens of justification that may sometimes verge on the unreasonable. But as noted, another may be to create more space for second attempts in administrative law. A judicial remand of agency policy is not necessarily a dead end if agencies can come back to court with justifications for their policies that pass judicial muster.

References

Bagley N, 'The Puzzling Presumption' (2014) 127 *Harvard Law Review* 1285.

Beermann, J, '*Chevron* at the Roberts Court: Still Failing After All These Years' (2014) 83 *Fordham Law Review* 114.

Bonfield AE, 'The Federal APA and State Administrative Law' (1986) 72 *Virginia Law Review* 297.

126 *Vermont Yankee* (n 52).

Craig P, *Administrative Law* (7th edn, Sweet & Maxwell 2012).
Edley C, *Administrative Law: Rethinking Judicial Control of Bureaucracy* (Yale UP 1992).
Eskridge WN, Baer LE, 'The Continuum of Deference: Supreme Court Treatment of Agency Statutory Interpretations from *Chevron* to *Hamdan*' (2008) 96 *Geo LJ* 1083.
Fleiner F, *Institutionen Des Deutschen Verwaltungsrechts* (Mohr Siebeck 1928).
Franklin DL, 'Legislative Rules, Nonlegislative Rules, and the Perils of the Short Cut' (2010) 120 *Yale Law Journal* 276.
Götz V, *Allgemeines Polizei- Und Ordnungsrecht: Ein Studienbuch* (15th edn, CH Beck 2012).
Hamilton RW, 'Rulemaking on a Record By the Food and Drug Administration' (1972) 50 *Texas Law Review 1132.*
Herz M, 'Rehnquist Court and Administrative Law' (2004) 99 *Northwestern Law Review* 314.
Hoffer S; Walker CJ, 'The Death of Tax Court Exceptionalism' (forthcoming 2015) 99 *Minnesota Law Review* (forthcoming).
Jordan WS, 'Ossification Revisited: Does Arbitrary and Capricious Review Significantly Interfere with Agency Ability to Achieve Regulatory Goals Through Informal Rulemaking' (1999) 94 *Northwestern Law Review* 393.
Levin RM, 'Rulemaking Under the 2010 Model State Administrative Procedure Act' (2010) 20 *Widener Law Journal.*
—— 'The Anatomy of *Chevron*: Step Two Reconsidered' (1997) 72 *Chicago-Kent Law Review* 1253.
Mashaw JL, Harfst DL, 'Regulation and Legal Culture: the Case of Motor Vehicle Safety' (1986) 4 *Yale Journal on Regulation* 257.
—— *The Struggle for Auto Safety* (Harvard UP 1990).
Mathews J, 'Deference Lotteries' (2013) 91 *Texas Law Review* 1349.
Merrill TW, 'The Mead Doctrine: of Rules and Standards, Meta-Rules and Meta-Standards' (2002) 54 *Administrative Law Review* 807.
Miles TJ; Sunstein CR, 'The Real World of Arbitrariness Review' (2008) 75 *University of Chicago Law Review* 761.
Nathanson NL, 'Probing the Mind of the Administrator: Hearing Variations and Standards of Judicial Review under the Administrative Procedure Act and Other Federal Statutes' (1975) 75 *Columbia Law Review* 721.
Novak WJ, *The People's Welfare: Law and Regulation in Nineteenth-Century America* (University of North Carolina Press, 1996).
O'Connell AJ, 'Political Cycles of Rulemaking: an Empirical Portrait of the Modern Administrative State' (2008) 94 *Virginia Law Review* 889.
Pierce RJ, 'Unruly Judicial Review of Rulemaking' (1990) 5 *Natural Resources & Environment* 23.
Rivers J, 'Proportionality and Variable Intensity of Review' (2006) 65 *Cambridge Law Journal* 174.
Rose-Ackerman S, *Controlling Environmental Policy: the Limits of Public Law in Germany and the United States* (Yale University Press, 1995).
—— Lindseth P (eds), *Comparative Administrative Law* (Edward Elgar 2010).
Schiller RE, 'Rulemaking's Promise: Administrative Law and Legal Culture in the 1960s and 1970s' (2001) 53 *Administrative Law Review* 1139.
Seidenfeld M, 'A Syncopated *Chevron*: Emphasizing Reasoned Decisionmaking in Reviewing Agency Interpretations of Statutes' (1994) 73 *Texas Law Review* 83.
Strauss PL, 'One Hundred Fifty Cases Per Year: Some Implications of the Supreme Court's Limited Resources for Judicial Review of Agency Action' (1987) 87 *Columbia Law Review* 1093.
—— *Gellhorn and Byse's Administrative Law, Cases and Comments* (11th edn, Foundation Press 2011).
Tridimas T, *The General Principles of EU Law* (2nd edn, OUP 2006).

8 Concluding remarks

Sofia Ranchordás and Boudewijn de Waard

8.1 Proportionality: indispensable criterion in administrative law

This book offered comparative law reflections upon the meaning of the principle of proportionality (and its equivalents) in administrative law. The different chapters aimed to answer one crucial question: *what role does proportionality play in judicial control of administrative decisions?*

At the end of this book, we are inclined to give a straightforward and almost obvious answer: the principle of proportionality plays a very important role. It forms and frames judicial control of administrative decisions, it strengthens or weakens the intensity of this control, and it enhances or limits the margin of appreciation of public bodies.

A second – and perhaps less important – question was also brought up at the beginning of this book (see chapter 1): *is it still necessary and adequate to discuss and carry out research on proportionality in the context of comparative administrative law?*

Another evident answer lurks in the hearts of most public law lawyers: this research is justified by the aim of clarifying the origins of this principle, its evolution, its use, its present – and more importantly – its future employment.

It is well established that proportionality is an essential element in the field of civil and political rights and that this principle has won its position in the field of constitutional law.[1] However, the administrative law approach should not be overlooked either since it offers a slightly broader and more concrete perspective on questions about proportionality. The analysis of the principle of proportionality invites us to reflect upon varied forms of administrative action or situations where this action is contested: a municipal body that prohibits a demonstration or a show to safeguard public order (see chapters 2 and 3), a company contesting an administrative exemption granted to its competitor (chapter 5), a trainee lawyer that considers himself a victim of forced labour because his local Bar compels him to work *pro bono* in order to conclude his 'apprenticeship' (chapter 6) or even the case of civil servants

1 Aharon Barak, *Proportionality: Constitutional Rights and their Limitations* (CUP 2012) 131.

that should not or should have been dismissed by public bodies as a result of faults committed (chapters 7 and 3, respectively). In all these cases, courts were asked to decide on the adequacy, necessity and proportionality *stricto sensu* of these administrative actions. The courts from the different jurisdictions did not always employ these terms, but a similar frame of mind was often present.

8.1.1 A European proportionality?

This book is, however, not only about traditional administrative law. Rather, it also devotes attention to another field of application of the principle of proportionality: administrative decisions with an impact on human rights. Strasbourg was, in this case, our main destination. In fact, there are at least two good reasons to delve into the case law of the European Court on Human Rights (ECtHR). The first is that the court has been using a proportionality test for a long time, applying it to an increasing number of fields, narrowing and broadening its application depending on the concrete circumstances of the case or infringed rights. The second reason has to do with the intriguing question of whether the proportionality control in cases involving human rights is different from other administrative law cases.

The reference to the case law of the ECHR was, in this book, also complemented by the case law of another European institution that makes ample use of the proportionality test as a criterion for control of legality. In this case, we travelled to Luxembourg, where the European Court of Justice of the European Union (ECJ) has employed the principle of proportionality to assess the administrative action of its institutions and of those of Member States, when EU law was at stake. For countries that are part of the EU and/or the European Convention on Human Rights, the case law of both European courts is not just an interesting object for a comparative study, it is much more than that. First, the study of these courts allows us to explore how those 'European' courts deal with questions that also arise in national legal systems. Second, the case law of these courts sends a vivid signal to the different national orders as to how the principle of proportionality should be understood and implemented in practice. In addition, the legal orders of most countries studied in this book are deeply linked to – or even interwoven with – EU law and the ECHR.

The chapter on proportionality in European law by Catherine Haguenau-Moizard and Yoan Sanchez (chapter 6) shows that the intensity with which the test is applied may differ in different cases, but the structure of the proportionality test is, generally speaking, the same. The analysis of the case law of these courts allowed us to see, not only the influence of EU law in the national approaches to proportionality, but also the historical role of German law in the consolidation of this principle. In fact, and despite a number of methodological differences, there is still a high degree of similarity between the approach of the European courts and the way that German courts apply the proportionality test. That is not surprising, because of the common background, as described in chapter 2 on Germany, by Nikolaus Marsch and Vanessa Tünsmeyer.

However, despite the obvious influence of the aforementioned 'German export hit' in different countries (see chapter 2), there does not seem to be a single 'European proportionality test' in the old continent. In the other European countries analysed in this book, courts seem reluctant to adopt *explicitly* a proportionality test like the German one. Chapter 3 on French Law by Yoan Sanchez, indicates that, in recent case law from the highest French administrative court, the *Conseil d'Etat*, a proportionality test has been used. However, the *Conseil d'État* seems reluctant to admit that it is also being seduced by German proportionality. In France, the proportionality test remains fairly implicit and non-systematic.

When English courts decide on cases other than human rights cases, they still hold on to the good old *Wednesbury* reasonableness test instead of adopting the likewise old – but more dynamic – proportionality test. This was well illustrated in the chapter 4 by A.C.L. Davies and J.R. Williams.

The Dutch courts do not seem more generous in their use of proportionality tests. In the Netherlands, examples of the application of a three- or four-step proportionality test exist, but they are rare. As far as proportionality in the narrow sense is concerned, Dutch administrative courts generally use a criterion of 'arbitrariness' that is more similar to the English 'unreasonableness'.

Since there is apparently no 'European-style proportionality', we turned to the US. Here, we found out that American courts are also concerned with the 'reasonableness' of administrative or agency action, and courts verify whether this action was 'arbitrary and capricious' and whether the original legislative intent of the legislator was respected by the executive. However, we realised here that the 'German export hit' had not managed to get a 'green card' in this jurisdiction. Instead, judicial control of agency discretion in the New World does not appear to be more any more intense than the control of the reasonableness of administrative action in England.

In conclusion, the courts in all the countries that are included in this book, except Germany, seem hesitant to use a proportionality test. Presumably, they have different reasons for this, but some of the hesitance may have a similar background. That is the main topic in these concluding remarks: *why and how are administrative courts avoiding the use of some form of proportionality test?*

8.2 A 'kind of proportionality' is needed

A state that claims it is governed by the rule of law must have a court that has the power to assess whether the state´s institutions have violated legal requirements. At the same time, the idea of separation of powers – an essential element of the rule of law – demands that courts do not interfere with the powers of the legislator or the public administration. This creates a universal problem for the courts in such states: in developing regulations and individual decisions, administrative bodies have to weigh interests and arguments that can be of quite diverse natures. On the one hand, courts have to offer protection against violations of legal requirements by the state. On the other, courts also have to take care not to take over the role of the administration. In this context, courts are faced with a scenario where they have to use instruments to control administrative decision-making, without interfering with administrative powers. *Proportionality control seems to be the perfect candidate (or at least one of the most qualified ones) for this job.*

8.2.1 Courts avoid taking over the role of the administration

The case law delving into proportionality (or one of its national equivalents) shows the difficulties involved with development of a more solid or systematic proportionality test. Some of the obstacles encountered by courts are quite similar.[2] An illustration comes from the English chapter (paragraph 4.2), it reads: 'The court does not ask itself the question, "Is this decision right or wrong?" Far less does the judge ask himself whether he would himself have arrived at the decision in question. The only question for the judge is whether the decision taken by the body under review was one that it was legally permitted to take in the way that it did'.[3]

In the US case law on the 'arbitrary and capricious' standard, a similar consideration can be found: 'a court is not to substitute its judgment for that of the agency'.[4] Case law of the ECtHR appears to hold the same kind of approach.[5] It would not be surprising if a Dutch court were to use the same argument. In fact, this leads us to the main question of this chapter: *how do courts avoid, in practice, taking over the role of the administration?*

A *first* 'technique' consists in turning to standards that are provided by the legislator. If the court can refer to statutory limits, it cannot be accused of using its own standards. Therefore, the courts can look at the wording of statutes, the explicit or implicit intent of parliament, the compatibility of administrative action with the statutory requirements. In addition, parliament can ask whether the administrative action is based on an adequate legal basis (e.g., whether there is a legitimate aim, etc.) and whether the public

2 In some legal cultures, courts do not seem to have the 'habit' of fully disclosing the method of reasoning that they have employed. Among the legal systems that are discussed in this book, France seems to be the best example of the opacity of judicial reasoning.

3 *R v Somerset CC, ex p Fewings* (1995) 1 All ER 513 (QB), 515, see Davies/Williams.

4 Justice Byron White, writing for the court, in *State Farm*, as quoted by Jud Mathews in chapter 7.

5 E.g., the *Case of Christian Democratic People's Party v Moldova (No 2)*, App no 25196/04, ECtHR 2 February 2010, para 22: 'When the Court carries out its scrutiny, its task is not to substitute its own view for that of the relevant national authorities but rather to review under Article 11 the decisions they have delivered in the exercise of their discretion'.

body went beyond the scope of the statutory requirements. Courts can ensure that the bodies of public administration do not act against legislation. Moreover, they can also make sure that whenever it is clear that the legislator wanted the administration to act, the administrative body does take up the task and responsibility, conferred to it by the legislator. There must be 'no fettering of discretion', as the English courts say. Based on the previous chapters, we can only say that at least German[6] and Dutch[7] courts would agree with this. In addition, courts refer to the interests underlying statutory provisions since any weighing of interests performed by a public body would be defective if it did not include certain interests that the legislator meant to protect.

A *second* method for the court to avoid taking over the role of the administration is to 'proceduralise', that is, to look at the way in which the administration has prepared its decision (e.g., did the public body take a 'hard look' at the issue?) and at the reasons it has given. Jud Mathews argues that US courts tend to do so.[8] Hard look review and its equivalents have the obvious advantage that the court does not interfere with the substance. Mathews also shows a major disadvantage that such review might have, if this standard is applied too impetuously. Mathews writes:

> It may be very difficult for an agency to anticipate all of the faults that an aggrieved person may find with its actions, not to mention the ways in which the reviewing court may probe its reasoning.

In the control of reasoning, a court may touch upon the substance, but it can also choose to avoid taking a substantive position on the matter. This appears to have been the case in *State Farm*. Jud Mathews quotes the court. It stated 'While the agency is entitled to change its view . . . it is obligated to explain its reasons for doing so'.[9]

This attempt to hide behind procedural arguments is also present in Europe. In Dutch administrative law, the obligation for administrative bodies to carefully investigate relevant factors prior to taking a decision and to give reasons for decisions have been prominent in case law. The intensity of control can be so high that the courts could be criticised for interfering with the tasks of the administration, although the courts keep away from judging substantive matters.[10]

6 Marsch & Tünsmeyer (on *Ermessensausfall* or *Ermessensnichtgebrauch*).

7 Further examples in BWN de Waard, 'Rechtsbescherming in bescherming' (1997) *NTB* 6, 6–12.

8 See chapter 7, referring to Mashaw and Harfst (n 3). See also Mathews, quoting Judge Harold Leventhal: 'that the agency has not really taken a "hard look" at the salient problems, and has not genuinely engaged in reasoned decision-making'.

9 See text and references in chapter 7 to *Motor Vehicle Manufacturers Association v State Farm Mutual Automobile Insurance Co. (State Farm)*. Another element from the same case: if the agency believed an all-airbag standard was unworkable, it had a duty to explain why (see chapter 7).

In fact, it is interesting to see that the conclusion of courts *on proportionality* sometimes takes a 'proceduralised' form. Davies and Williams put forward that the outcome of an administrative decision must not be considered in isolation from the reasoning process. If the court concludes that a proportionate outcome was reached, the court will pass bypass flaws in the reasoning process. However, flaws in the reasoning, or in the process of preparation of the decision, may lead to the conclusion that a decision is disproportionate.[11]

A third tool used by courts to avoid usurping the role of the administration is to *split the proportionality control in separate steps or stages*. This is done, for example, in the German legal system. This division helps to prevent courts from entering the domain of the administration if it is clear where the 'danger of trespassing' is located. In the German four-step proportionality test, the 'danger zone' is confined to the last stage: only the last step involves 'balancing' of the interests involved.

In order to assess whether a measure is proportionate in the strict sense, one has to attribute weight to the interests involved and predict the effect that the measure will have on these interests. That is a complex operation, which might be dependent on preferences. Courts avoid attributing weight to rights or to relevant interests themselves. The first three steps of the four-step test consist in checking on legitimate aim, suitability and necessity. The requirement that the measure is necessary means that the administration should choose the instrument that is least burdensome, which implies considering alternative options. The hypothesis in such a case is: the goal set by the administration can be reached in different ways, and some are more intrusive than others. In such a case, the least burdensome instrument has to be used. If a legitimate goal is at stake, the court will not question whether the goal should be reached. It is therefore not necessary to weigh the interests of reaching that goal against the interests that are served if the administration refrains from taking the measure. The court can confine itself to assessing whether an alternative measure is less burdensome than the measure that was originally chosen by the administration. This may be a decision that is a little more complex than just assessing the impact of burdens, because some alternatives may not serve the goal as adequately as the original decision.

8.3 Proportionality in the narrow sense

In the context of civil rights, courts often have to verify whether an administrative decision violates a right. That is the typical role of a court. In answering

10 De Waard has argued that the work of administrative bodies in the Netherlands some fifteen years ago was not hampered by judicial control of substance, but that procedural judicial control could also have a hampering effect, because it can lead to control of high intensity. De Waard 'Rechtsbescherming in bescherming' (1997) NTB 6, 6–12.

11 Chapter 4, referring to Kavanagh and to the decision in the *Quila* case.

questions of law, a court generally does not need to hold back. This is different when a civil right is considered as a relative right. When the limitation of rights by state authorities is warranted, the next question to be answered is whether the limitation is justified. Answering such a question involves the weighing of public and private interests.

The ECHR contains provisions that explicitly allow limitations of rights (see Articles 8–11). Such limitations must be 'in accordance with the law', and 'necessary in a democratic society'. Case law holds, in respect to the latter, that a fair balance must be struck. This means that the limitation 'must be proportionate to the legitimate aim pursued'.[12] In answering the question of whether such proportionality is achieved in the case before the court, the courts leaves national authorities a 'margin of appreciation'. As the ECHR explains:

> the breadth of this margin varies and depends on a number of factors including the nature of the Convention right in issue, its importance for the individual, the nature of the interference and the object pursued by the interference.[13]

Another category of rights in the Convention hold rights that are absolute or almost absolute. With regard to such rights, there is hardly any room for proportionality.[14] But there is also a third category of Convention rights that does not face the standard limitation clauses in the same way as the ones applicable to Articles 8–11. Among the rights that can be limited is the right to a fair trial, laid down in Article 6 ECHR. According to the ECtHR, a restriction of that right:

> will not be incompatible with Article 6 where the limitation did not impair the very essence of the right and where it pursued a legitimate aim, and there was a reasonable relationship of proportionality between the means employed and the aim sought to be achieved.[15]

The ECtHR uses the same type of consideration in a case about Article 1 of Protocol No. 1, the *Broniowski* case.[16] Just as with cases where the standard

12 As Haguenau & Sanchez advance, this formula has already been used by the Court in *Handyside* (ECtHR 7 December 1976), para 49.

13 *Nada v Switzerland* App no 10593/08 (ECtHR 12 September 2012), para 184.

14 Sometimes the words of the proportionality test also emerge in a case about an almost absolute right. For example, in *Case Van der Mussele v Belgium* App no 8919/80 (ECtHR 23 November 1983), para 38. However, in that case, the expression 'a burden which was so excessive or disproportionate' did not feature as a criterion for the acceptability of a measure by national authorities, but in the role of finding the answer to the question of whether the facts of the case did qualify as 'slavery or forced labour' in the sense of Article 4 ECHR. FMC Vlemminx, *Het moderne EVRM* (Boom Juridische Uitgevers 2013), 128.

15 *Laskowska v Poland* App no 77765/01 (ECtHR 13 March 2007), para 52.

16 *Broniowski v Poland* App no 31443/96 (ECtHR 28 September 2005), para 150. The paragraph contains the same wording about proportionality as *Laskowska* (n 15): 'there must be a reasonable relationship of proportionality between the means employed and the aim sought to be realised'.

limitations formula applies (Articles 8–11), a fair balance has to be achieved.[17] It is interesting to note that the court specifies at times what this 'reasonable relationship of proportionality' means, in the context of Article 1 of Protocol No. 1; the court explains the need to investigate 'whether . . . the person concerned had to bear a disproportionate and excessive burden'.

In answering the question whether an interference with Convention rights is 'necessary in a democratic society', the ECtHR declares, not only that the interference must be proportionate to the legitimate aim pursued, but also – as the Court considers in *Nada* – whether 'the reasons adduced by the national authorities to justify it are "relevant and sufficient"'.[18] In *Nada*, the Court further specifies the questions that need to be answered:

> the Court must examine whether the Swiss authorities took sufficient account of the particular nature of his case and whether they adopted, in the context of their margin of appreciation, the measures that were called for in order to adapt the sanctions regime to the applicant's individual situation.

In other words, the Court turns to criteria about proper and adequate preparation of administrative decisions (including taking a good – and sometimes hard – look at the available facts), and to the fact that the national authorities considered the merits of the individual case.[19]

The conclusion, so far, can be that the ECtHR, while applying a proportionality test, does not always exercise an intense control. The Court often explicitly leaves a margin of appreciation to national authorities, and uses different methods to avoid taking over the role of those authorities.

An unclear aspect of the proportionality test remains: how do we assess proportionality in the narrow sense, or, the lack of such a form of proportionality? In this book, we have not been able to find satisfactory answers to the problem of incommensurability. A recent case, *Murat Vural v Turkey*,[20] illustrates and sheds some light on this problem.

Murat Vural had poured paint over several statutes of Kemal Atatürk, the founder and first President of the Republic of Turkey. This behaviour was qualified as showing disrespect to the memory of Atatürk, which constitutes a criminal offence, according to a statute on 'Offences Committed Against Atatürk'. Vural was convicted to serve a prison sentence of over thirteen years. This case reached the ECtHR. In his partly concurring

17 Concerning limitation techniques, see Vlemminx (n 14) 130 and G van der Schyff, *Limitation of rights. A study of the European Convention and the South African Bill of Rights* (Wolf Legal Publishers 2005).

18 Quotation from *Nada v Switzerland* (n 13), para 181.

19 Here, we refer to what we said about the methods that courts use to avoid taking over the role of the administration.

20 *Case of Murat Vural v Turkey* App No 9540/07 (ECtHR 21 October 2014).

and partly dissenting opinion, Judge Sajó expressed reservations as to the methodology used by the court. Judge Sajó had also reservations about the 'standard' proportionality approach. He argued that this approach is inappropriate in all cases where a freedom is unconditionally restricted by legislation.

The opinion of Judge Sajó offers much food for thought about proportionality and the role of the ECtHR. One could argue that the Court should look beyond the individual case and raise the question of whether the statute that criminalises acts that are offensive to the memory of Atatürk is compatible with the ECHR. The statute holds a mandatory minimum sanction of one year in prison. According to Judge Sajó: 'A law which enables, and even mandates, such interference is incompatible with the necessities of a democratic society'.

If a proportionality test is applied, one could posit that the aim of the statute is not legitimate, and, apart from that, 'the means chosen are certainly not the least restrictive possible', as Judge Sajó argued.[21] However, we do not want to focus on the question of whether the Court should have passed a judgment on this piece of legislation, *in abstracto*. Our main point here is the way the Court deals with proportionality in the narrow sense in judging the application of the legislation, *in concreto*.

In the case of Murat Vural, the ECtHR held that the prison sentence was disproportional. Judge Sajó agreed that it was, but criticised the Court for not clarifying why the punishment was disproportionate: disproportionate with regard to what and in which sense? Perhaps the Court did not elaborate on this point because it is not easy to agree on specific reasons. Or, perhaps the Court did not want to specify reasons because this would imply that the Court would take a more substantive position than the Court considers to be desirable.

In our opinion, Judge Sajó shows that it is possible to avoid compelling the Court to take a stand about 'which sentence is proportionate' for a specific offence. Instead, the Court could have offered more specific reasons by comparing (hypothetical) cases. A reference to the fact that thirteen years is a sentence that is ordinarily imposed on murderers would have sufficed as a term of comparison. Judge Sajó refers to the case of Buitoni, in which the ECJ made this type of comparison. The ECJ found a penalty for failing *to report* the use of a licence disproportionate because the penalty was the same as for *the actual use* of the licence.[22] In other words: if courts try to be more specific about why a decision (or another point of view by State authorities) is disproportionate, they do not automatically lose an objective method of reasoning; they can use techniques such as the comparing method.

21 Ibid, 26.
22 *Buitoni v Fonds d'Orientation* (1979) ECR 677.

8.4 Proportionality, reasonableness and intensity of judicial control

Applying a proportionality test does not automatically imply a more intense control than a control on 'reasonableness', or an 'arbitrary and capricious review'. That is, of course, *unless* the qualification of something as 'unreasonable' is limited to cases where 'no reasonable person could have reached the decision'. Proportionality control can be performed in diverse forms and with diverse levels of intensity.[23] It can show signs of 'marginal testing'. This is not only the case if a court explicitly considers that there should be a margin of appreciation left to the authorities, but also if a court uses double negatives, such as 'not disproportionate', or adds adjectives like 'manifest' or 'excessive'.[24]

Case law from the ECtHR holds that, if a court applies the proportionality control, it should check whether the administrative body has struck a right balance. It is called 'a' right balance, not 'the' right balance since there may be a range of acceptable outcomes. In other words, the court does not have to do the balancing itself. It can confine itself to taking the balancing – performed by the administrative body – as a starting point, as long as the court has 'full jurisdiction'. There is no full jurisdiction if a court can only use very limited criteria of control, or if the court has no authority to consider whether the facts of the case justify the measures that were taken.[25]

Does proportionality control only relate to the question of whether measures taken by the administration interfere too deeply in somebody's rights or interests, or can a measure also be disproportional if the administrative body did not interfere severely enough? Both overreaching and underreaching can violate the principle of proportionality. This aspect is discussed in chapter 7 by Jud Mathews. The author compares the hard look control with proportionality, and notes that the case of *State Farm* does not concern administrative overreaching but underreaching.

Mathews assumes that proportionality control is directed only to the question of whether an administrative measure is excessive. It is, in fact, true that the 'European proportionality control' – if one were to exist – generally focuses on overreaching. Furthermore, the question of whether administrative measures are 'necessary' also goes in that direction: if there is a choice of means to reach an end, the least burdensome measure should be chosen. However, this is a comparison with the typical use of proportionality in the context of basic rights, or civil and political human rights. In the greater variety of administrative acts, situations may occur where administrative acts qualify as disproportional because the administration is 'not doing enough'.

23 See Haguenau & Sanchez, p 6, referring to the *Handyside* case. As for the ECJ, see JH Jans, R de Lange, S Prechal and RJGM Widdershoven, *Inleiding tot het Europese Bestuursrecht* (2nd ed, Ars Aequi 2002) 200

24 See Haguenau & Sanchez.

25 See, e.g. *Zumtobel v Austria* App No 12235/86 (ECtHR 21 September 1993) and *Ortenberg v Austria* App No 12884/87 (ECtHR 25 November 1994).

Underreaching is also a dimension of the French proportionality control. As Yoan Sanchez mentions in chapter 3, in French case law, an example can be found in the case of Miss L., a childcare assistant who was responsible for the death of a child but was only sanctioned with a two-month suspension. The *Conseil d'État* ruled that the administrative authority should have chosen the heaviest sanction: dismissal.[26] Of course, this is an extraordinary case. The ordinary case in most jurisdictions would be that a person who has been struck by a severe sanction lodges an appeal against that decision. In such a case, an administrative court (at least a Dutch administrative court) would not decide that the sanction was disproportional because it was not severe enough. The reason why it would not decide that a heavier sanction would be appropriate has to do with the idea that, as a rule, an appeal should not lead to a decision that puts the person who lodged the appeal in a worse position. However, we would say that it is not contrary to the concept of proportionality for a court to conclude that an administrative body should have acted in a more vigorous way than it did.[27] Proportionality exists in favour of – or sometimes against – individuals to ensure that there is a just correspondence between the administrative decision and the aim to be achieved.

8.5 Margin of appreciation and deference

This book is not only about proportionality in abstract, but more generally about 'the judge and the proportionate use of discretion'. When should courts only exercise a limited control? The German legal system holds that this is the case whenever the legislator leaves discretion to the administration, by stating that the administration 'can' decide to grant or prohibit something.[28] In that case, the administration has discretion (*Ermessen*). However, German doctrine avoids the word discretion (*Ermessen*) in relation to the statutory conditions that have to be fulfilled in order to use an administrative power. In dealing with these conditions, the main rule is that the courts exercise full control. By way of exception, courts find that they should leave a margin of appreciation to the administration to determine whether the statutory conditions are met (*Beurteilungsspielraum*). Comparable distinctions are made in the Dutch legal system, although the Dutch literature appears to have less difficulty in accepting that it will never succeed in making a sharp distinction.

In France, the level of intensity of control depends on the type of case. A distinction is made between levels of intensity (minimal, normal or maximum). The difference between those levels of intensity refers both to the point of proportionality control and the qualification of facts.[29] Conversely, if

26 See chapter 3, where Sanchez discusses the case *Assistant publique – Hôpitaux de Paris*.

27 Dutch law offers examples in the field of compliance (see chapter 5).

28 See chapter 2 on Germany.

29 See the diagram in the Appendix to the chapter on France.

a court exercises limited control on the qualification of facts in Germany or the Netherlands, that would be considered as leaving a margin of appreciation.

For analytical reasons, the distinction between 'real' discretion and a margin of appreciation remains interesting. If the legislator explicitly makes clear that it is up to the administration to decide how it will decide, then there is no doubt that the courts should lean back. There might still be some uncertainty about the intensity of control, but there is not much more to it. The more interesting category to study is the category of cases in which there is debate about the margin of appreciation. If the debate in court concerns the conditions that have to be met, there is not only more uncertainty about the intensity of control, but also about the more fundamental question of *why* the court should leave a margin of appreciation. The answers may be interesting from a comparative law point of view. The reasons for leaving a margin of appreciation can be reasons of a rather practical nature, such as the example of complex forecasts in the field of environmental law.[30]

It is important to ask a final question: how do the previous considerations relate to the debate on 'deference' in the UK and in the US? Deference seems to relate to matters that, in Germany or the Netherlands, would raise the question of whether a court should leave a margin of appreciation. However, at least in the US, the starting point seems quite opposite to that in Germany or the Netherlands. Whereas, in Germany or the Netherlands, for instance, the interpretation of a statute would be a matter that can be fully controlled by the court, in the US, the courts would consider this a situation that calls for deference.[31] This means, in practice, that the administrative action is practically 'unreviewable' by the court, except insofar as it was the basis for constitutional claims, as Mathews writes. After having discussed *Chevron* and later cases, especially *Judalung v. Holder*, Mathews suggests that there is a possible convergence of deference and 'hard look review'.

Davies and Williams write that in the UK, 'deference' is not to be understood as a situation where there is a kind of 'no-go zone' for judges. Deference is not a concept of non-justiciability. However, Davies and Williams also refer to Allan, a scholar who is critical towards a doctrine of deference. Allan seems to take the position that deference comes rather close to non-justiciability, when he says that deference still 'turns out, on close inspection, to be non-justiciability dressed in pastel colours'.[32] When deference can be characterised as a situation in which 'the court ascribes significant weight to the decision-makers view'[33] that would be in line with how a German or Dutch court would reason in cases where the court leaves a margin of appreciation.

Davies and Williams argue that deference is not the same thing as the ECtHR's margin of appreciation doctrine. We agree that the ECtHR seems

30 See chapter 2.

31 See chapter 7, where Mathews discusses *Chevron*.

32 See chapter 4.

33 See chapter 4, discussing the decision of the Supreme Court in the case of *Carlisle*.

to use the words 'margin of appreciation' in a broader sense than, for example, the German literature does. The ECtHR also refers to situations where national authorities have 'discretion'. But we see similarities where leaving a margin of appreciation would mean that the court accepts that an administrative decision should stand because, if the court were to decide the matter itself, it might not be able to achieve better results compared to the initial decision-maker.[34]

8.6 Closing remarks

In the opinion of the authors of this book, courts in the jurisdictions referred to herein often show too much hesitation in exercising a proportionality control. Furthermore, courts that do use a proportionality test could be more explicit in the way that they apply it.

This does not mean that the authors are advocating an increase in the intensity of judicial control. There may be very good reasons for courts to leave administrative authorities with a margin of appreciation and these reasons may have a very different character. Sometimes, a decision may stand for the simple reason that the procedures that are followed are correct and the law simply does not offer a basis to conclude that another result would have been better. But even then, the last word is to proportionality, as it may explain why one of the parties deserves to win that particular case.

References

Barak A, *Proportionality: Constitutional Rights and their Limitations* (CUP 2012).

Jans JH, de Lange R, Prechal S and Widdershoven RJGM, *Inleiding tot het Europese Bestuursrecht* (2nd edn, Ars Aequi 2002).

van der Schyff G, *Limitation of rights. A study of the European Convention and the South African Bill of Rights* (Wolf Legal Publishers 2005).

Vlemminx FMC, *Het moderne EVRM* (Boom Juridische Uitgevers 2013).

Waard BWN de, 'Rechtsbescherming in bescherming' (1997) *NTB* 6, 6–12.

34 See chapters 4 and 5.

Index

For Product Safety Concerns and Information please contact our EU representative GPSR@taylorandfrancis.com Taylor & Francis Verlag GmbH, Kaufingerstraße 24, 80331 München, Germany